# Kentucky Genealogical Records & Abstracts

## Volume 2

### 1796-1839

## Sherida K. Eddlemon

HERITAGE BOOKS
2006

# HERITAGE BOOKS

*AN IMPRINT OF HERITAGE BOOKS, INC.*

## Books, CDs, and more—Worldwide

For our listing of thousands of titles see our website
at
www.HeritageBooks.com

Published 2006 by
HERITAGE BOOKS, INC.
Publishing Division
65 East Main Street
Westminster, Maryland 21157-5026

International Standard Book Number: 978-0-7884-1024-5

# DEDICATION

This book is dedicated in loving memory to my great grandfather, Eugene "Gene" Martin Pike who had deep family roots in the early Catholic settlement of middle Kentucky. His ancestor, William Pike, a Revolutionary War veteran, was among the exodus of Catholic families who left Maryland in 1789 - 1791 for the "new Holy Land" in Kentucky. There in 1791, William married Susannah Mills. It was their great grandson John F. Pike who ventured forth from western Kentucky after the Civil War to the rich farm and timberlands in Arkansas County, Arkansas.

John F. Pike and his family settled in the Forks LaGrue community of southern Arkansas County where he farmed and had a cotton gin. His wife died and then he married a second young widow, Josephine Roach Kemp Richey. They had one child, my great grandfather, "Gene" Pike.

I was so lucky to have known my great grandfather for so many years. Despite a difficult childhood due to the death of his mother when he was only a toddler, he was a kind and gentle man. He loved history and children. He told me many stories of the olden days in southern Arkansas County. Cut off as it was by rivers and the many lakes, it was a wild area.

It was listening to these stories that first ignited my interest in genealogy by knowing this wonderful man. In so far as it has been documented, I am an eleventh generation member of this Pike family who produced so many farmers and members of the clergy. Despite the diversity of occupations of later generations, most of us still have that innate love for the land and growing things.

I am very proud of my PIKE heritage. I am blessed by having known my great grand father, Eugene Martin Pike, (1891 - 1976) my PaPa.

## PREFACE

Explorers scouted across Kentucky as early as 1634 to the Mississippi River. French fur traders established a small settlement in Kentucky opposite the site of Portsmouth, OH in 1736. Thomas Walker's exploring expedition through the Cumberland Gap in 1750 established the migration trail that thousands of settlers followed into the rich and fertile land. Daniel Boone first came to Kentucky in 1767. The lure of the beckoning wilderness was strong. In this wilderness the white man and Native American Indians fought many battles. These fierce battles helped Kentucky earn its nickname, "the dark and bloody ground." James Harrod and other Pennsylvania colonists established Harrodsburg in 1774. This was the first permanent white settlement in Kentucky. Daniel Boone a year later brought a group of colonists from North Carolina in 1775 to found Boonesboro.

After the Revolutionary War, hundreds of veterans migrated to Kentucky. In 1776 Kentucky became a county of Virginia. The Indian wars raged in Kentucky in 1777 and continued for years. When you read through the earliest issues of the *Kentucky Gazette*, there are constant articles about settlers being killed, wounded or kidnapped by Indians. Many of these early settlers came from Maryland, North Carolina, Pennsylvania, Tennessee and Virginia and their backgrounds were diverse coming from German, English, Irish and Scottish extractions. Unfortunately, the names of these individuals were rarely used. By 1780 Virginia divided Kentucky County into three smaller counties. The Kentuckian settlers wanted more. They demanded statehood. It was not until June 1, 1792, that Kentucky became the 15th state in the Union.

This tremendous struggle to tame the wilderness has molded many great men in America's early history. Not only did many early Kentucky settlers fight in the Revolutionary War, but also in the War of 1812. In the Civil War Kentucky was a state divided and many sons fought as soldiers for both the Confederacy and the Union. Abraham Lincoln and Jefferson Davis the opposing presidents in the Civil War. Other Kentuckians include, Henry Clay, Kit Carson and President Zachary Taylor grew up in Kentucky.

Kentucky is famous for horse racing, coal mining and tobacco. Coal mining began as early as 1827 in the southeastern mountains. Kentucky bluegrass provided excellent pasture for Thoroughbred racing horses which also began in the early 1800's. The first Kentucky Derby was run in 1875 and still continues today. By 1825, Lexington, Kentucky became known as the "Athens of the West," and rivaled New Orleans as a center for portrait painters. The most nationally known of these painters was Frank Duveneck.

Your Kentucky ancestor has a rich heritage in America history. Kentucky has handed down a strong legacy for courage and endurance. So as you search for your ancestor try to remember the events in Kentucky's early beginning that may have influenced them to move, buy land, to fight and even to marry. Good Luck and hopefully you will find your ancestor within these pages.

# ABBREVIATIONS

| | | |
|---|---|---|
| E | ............................................ | Executor |
| S | ............................................ | Security |
| D | ............................................ | Date |
| SG | ............................................ | Surety |
| MD | ............................................ | Marriage Date |
| P | ............................................ | Page Number |
| EN | ............................................ | Entry Name |
| AP | ............................................ | Appraiser |
| CH | ............................................ | Children |
| W | ............................................ | Witness |
| WF | ............................................ | Wife |
| B | ............................................ | Born |
| D | ............................................ | Died or Date |
| Fb | ............................................ | Father Born |
| Mb | ............................................ | Mother Born |
| RES | ............................................ | Residence |
| OC | ............................................ | Occupation |
| PRTS | ............................................ | Parents |
| Dis | ............................................ | Dismissed |
| Exp | ............................................ | Expelled |
| Rec | ............................................ | Received |

| | | |
|---|---|---|
| AR VD | ................................................ | Arrival Date |
| CO | ................................................ | County |
| BP | ................................................ | Birth Place |
| BDMN | ................................................ | Bondsman |
| BOND | ................................................ | Bond Date |
| A | ................................................ | Age |
| Y | ................................................ | Year |
| M | ................................................ | Month |

# TABLE OF CONTENTS

## Fayette County
*(Founded 1780 from Kentucky Co., Virginia)*

## Floyd County
*(Founded 1800 from Fleming, Mason and Montgomery Counties)*

## Fulton County
*(Founded 1845 from Hickman County)*

## Grant County
*(Founded 1820 from Pendleton County)*

## Grayson County
*(Founde1810 from Hardin and Ohio Counties)*

## Greenup County
*(Founde1804 from Mason County)*

## Hardin County
*(Founded 1793 from Nelson County)*

## Lawrence County
*(Founded 1822 from Floyd and Greenup Counties)*

# Oldham County, Kentucky, 1830 Census Index

1

2

4

5

6

7

8

9

14

17

19

|---|---|
| William Wells | 292 |
| Thomas Welman | 273 |
| John Welsh | 265 |
| Williams Welts | 283 |
| Thomas Wertteg | 301 |
| Daniel West | 301 |
| Deborah Wheeler | 281 |
| John Wheeler | 280 |
| John Whelor | 297 |
| John Whelor, Jr. | 288 |
| John S. White | 293 |
| Robert H. White | 275 |
| Truman White | 259 |
| Nimrod Whiteler | 296 |
| Henry Whitesides | 277 |
| John Whitesides | 278 |
| Joseph Whitesides | 279 |
| Martin Whitesides | 290 |
| Phebe Whitesides | 279 |
| Isaac Whitson | 264 |
| Esther Whittaker | 286 |
| Matthew Whittson | 298 |
| John Wigal | 272 |
| Thomas Wilhite | 259 |
| Joshua Wilhoite | 260 |
| Merida Wilkinson | 288 |
| John Willett | 260 |
| William Willett | 267 |
| Aaron Willhoite | 275 |
| Allen Willhoite | 280 |
| Benjamin Willhoite | 270 |
| Elijah Willhoite | 271 |
| Humphrey Willhoite | 274 |
| Ishum Willhoite | 275 |
| Joseph Willhoite | 274 |
| Lamach Willhoite | 261 |
| Larkin Willhoite | 266 |
| Lewis Willhoite | 272 |
| Noah Willhoite | 264 |
| Russel Willhoite | 281 |
| Susannah Willhoite | 269 |
| William Willhoite | 281 |

| Name | Page |
|------|------|
| Henry Young | 300 |
| Isaac Young | 280 |
| James Young | 285 |
| Tavener B. Young | 294 |
| Benjamin Zaring | 270 |
| Gibson Zaring | 272 |
| John Zaring | 269 |
| Elizabeth Zenor | 276 |
| Isaac Zwathmey | 266 |

Capt. Sowel Woolfolk's Company, Nov. 20, 1786, Draper Manuscripts, State Historical Society of Wisconsin.
Lieut. John Whitaker; Ensign John Vaughan; Segeant James Hiter; Jonathan Grey; Samuel Scott; Richard Dawson; John Jones, Jr.; Thomas Jones; Merryman Humphries; Thomas Taylor; Aaron Indicutt; Jacob Sipps; Jacob Devings; Benjamin Taylor, Sr.; John McClain; John Fennell; William Granville; Henry Thorp; William Stevenson; Thomas Morton; Joseph Indicutt; Jeremiah Morton; George Adams; Benjamin Taylor, Jr.; James Lee; Mark Whitaker, Sr.; John Watts; James H. Howard; Thomas Whitaker; Costator Dawson; William Powell; James Rentfro; Henry Walker; Michael Clifford; John Jones, Sr.; Charles Westerman; Richard Haymnes; James Jones; James Valentine; William Conway; Warren Cash; Francis W. Lea; Joseph Patterson; Nathan Neille; Samuel Richey; John Rucker; George Corn; Rawley Stott; John Williams.

Bath County, Kentucky, Bradshaw Cemetery, Old Bascom Farm, East of Sharpsburg, Flat Creek Road.

| Name | Birth | Death |
|------|-------|-------|
| James Bradshaw | Jan., 1787 | 1812 |
| Mary Bradshaw | Mar., 1796 | Apr., 1844 |

Fayette County, Kentucky, 1788 Tax List.
Alexander Adams, James Adkins, George Admire, George Admire, Jr., Joseph Akers, Thomas Akers, James Alexander, John Alexander, Randall Alexander, Robert Alexander, Rowland Alexander, Thomas Alexander, William Alexander, John Alison, John Allen, Elisha Allin, Joseph Allin, Richard Allin, Sylvanus Allin, John Allison, John Allison, Jr., Robert Allison, William Allison, Thomas Ammons, Henry Anderson, Joseph Anderson, Nicholas Anderson, Presley Anderson, Theophilus Anderson, Robert Armstrong, James Arnett, James Arnold, John Arnold, Nicholas Arnold, Samuel Aryes, Robert Ashhurst, James Bacon, James Bacor, Andrew Bags, Ephraim Baites, Ann Baker, John

Baker, Moses Baker, John Baldin, James Ball, William Barker, John Barnett, M. Andrew Barrett, Anthony Bartlet, James Bartlet, John Bartlet, Nathaniel Bartlet, Matthew Bartley, James Barton, John Basket, German Baxter, Samuel Baxter, John Beak, John Bell, Robert Bell, Thomas Bell, Matthew Bennit, Thomas Bennit, Benjamin Berry, Edward Berry, Reuben Berry, Samuel Berry, William Berry, John Bishon, John Bishop, Alexander Black, James Black, James Black, Jr., John Black, Jr., John Black, Joseph Black, Robert Black, George Blackburn, Joseph Blackburn, Samuel Blair, Thomas Blanton, John Bledsoe, William Bledsoe, James Boggs, John Boggs, Robert Boggs, Samuel Boon, Benjamin Boston, Francis Bourne, William Primas Bourne, Abraham Bowman, Hugh Boyd, John Boyd, John Boyd, Jr., Samuel Boyd, John Boyles, John Bradford, Edward Bradley, Edward Bradley, Jr., James Bradley, Lennard Ceoland Bradley, Benjamin Bradshaw, William Bradshaw, William Brady, Samuel Brink, James Bristow, Henry Brock, Ebinezer Brooke, John Brookey, Charles Brown, John Brown, Benjamin Bruce, Bartlett Brundege, Solomon Brundege, James Bryan, Daniel Bryant, Edmund Bryant, Edward Bryant, Jr., John Bryant, William Buchnunry, Nathaniel Bullock, Thomas Burbridge, Elihu Burk, Thomas Burrus, John Burton, Ambrose Bush, Charles Bush, Francis Bush, John Bush, Philip Bush, Sarah Bush, William Bush, William Jun. Bush, Percival Butler, James Bybee, Joseph Byres, Charles Cade, Edmond Calloway, Flanders Calloway, William Calloway, George Campbell, Charles Campbell, Hugh Campbell, James Campbell, John Campbell, Robert Campbell, William Campbell, Benjamin Carathers, James Carathers, Thomas Carathers, John Card, Thomas Carlane, George Carlyle, Thomas Carneal, Joseph Carr, Walter Carr, William Carrington, John Carter, John Casey, Warrin Cash, Lewis Castleman, Edward Cathers, Richard Cave, Thomas Cavin, Robert Cavins, Joseph Chance, David Chancellor, Moses Cherry, William Christian, Thomas Church, Frances Clark, James Clark, John Clark, Thomas Clark, Mastin Clay, Elijah Cleavland, Roger Clements, Michel Clifford, Robert Cloyd, John Cobourn, Ambros Coffee, Jesse Coffer, Michael Coger, Richard Cole, Page Coleman, John Collier, Elisha Collins, Joel Collins, John Collins, Joseph Collins, William Colson, Benjamin Combs, Philip Compton, George Coms, John Congleton, William Congleton, Arthur Connelly, John Connelly, William Connelly, John Conner, William Conner, Hosea Cook, Jesse Cook, Dewett Cooper, Samuel Cooper, Hugh Cothron, Fredrick Couchman, Benjamin Cox, James Coyle, Joseph Coyle, John Craig, Joseph Craig, Lewis Craig, M. John Craig, William Craig, Elisha Craven, Harmin Cravin, William Crawford, Elijah Creed, Charles Creel, John Crittendon, Joseph Crocket, James Crofferd, Harculus Cronkright, Jacob Crosswait, Samuel Crosswait, Jacob Crosthwait, Samuel Crosthwait, John Crow, Starlin Crowder, Anthony Cumings, John

Cummins, William Cummins, Hugh Cunningham, James Curd, Nicholas Curry, James Curd, Nicholas Curry, Christopher Curtner, Abram Dale, George Dale, George Dale, Jr., Isaac Dale, Rawley Dale, Robert Dale, William Dale, William Dale, Jr., Vivion Daniel, Jeremiah Dann, Bacor David, Leonard David, Augustin Davis, Hannaniah Davis, John Davis, Joseph Davis, Partrick Davis, Richard Davis, Robert Davis, William Davis, Mary Davison, Thomas Davison, Christilon Dawson, James Dean, John Dearengar, William Decouse, Samuel Dedman, Richmond Dedmond, Joseph Delaney, Frances Delham, Peter Denhit, Daniel Denison, James Denison, Thomas Denison, Aron Denney, James Devenport, Samuel Dickey, Archey Dickinson, Martin Dickinson, Valentine Dickinson, Samuel Dillen, Thomas Dillon, James Dinwidie, George Dohorty, James Dohorty, Joseph Dohorty, Nathaniel Dondon, Thomas Donnell, Jacob Dooly, Patrick Dornan, Nathaniel Douglas, John Downey, Martin Doyle, Ephram Drake, John Drake, Samuel Drake, Samuel Drake, Jr., David Dryden, Nathaniel Dryden, Samuel Duglas, James Dulin, Daniel Dumford, James Dun, Zephaniah Dun, Charles Duncan, Alex Dunlap, James Dunlap, Bartholomew Dupey, James Dupey, John Dupey, David Durst, John Dyer, Joseph East, Philip Eastin, George Eaton, Joseph Eaton, Robert Ebroad, Peter Eddleman, John Edgar, Joseph Edwards, David Egbird, Josiah Elam, Andrew Elder, Robert Elkin, William Ellett, Robert Elliott, William Elliott, Peter Ellison, Robert Ellison, Thomas Ellison, Jospeh Embree, Stephen Esley, John Ethington, Kellis Eubank, William Eubank, David Evans, Nathaniel Evans, William Evans, Edmond Fair, Abner Farmer, Larkin Fergason, John Ficklin, Henry Fields, James Finch, John Finch, William Finia, John Finley, John Finnea, James Finnee, Robert Finny, Jacob Fishback, Daniel Fisher, James Fisher, Daniel Fitch, Bartlet Fitzgarald, Daniel Fitzgerald, John Flemmen, Thomas Floyd, Peter Foley, Gressum Forester, Bryant Forguson, Robert Forker, John Forkner, Joseph Forkner, James Foster, Samuel Foster, Richard Fox, Jeremiah Frame, John Frame, William Frame, Evan Francis, James Franklin, John Franklin, Joseph Martin Franks, David Frazer, George Frazer, James Frazer, Joseph Frazer, William Frazer, John Frund, Robert Fryer, Henry Fuller, Hugh Fulton, James Fulton, Joseph Gale, Samuel Galey, Samuel Gamilton, John Garnet, Thomas Garnet, William Garrett, Uriah Garton, Andrew Gatewood, Augustus Gatewood, John Gatewood, Peter Gatewood, James Gay, John Gay, Nicholas George, Whitson George, John Gibbens, Mary Gibson, John Gilmoor, John Givens, Thomas Glass, John Glover, William Golding, Bivin Goodlow, Mathew Goore, John Goron, William Gourdin, Arthur Graham, Ferguson Graham, David Graves, Edmond Graves, Robert Graves, David Gray, George Gray, John Gray, Johnathan Gray, Patrick Gray, Richard Gray, Francis Grayum, James Grayum, William Grayum, John Greathouse, William Grayum, John

Greathouse, John Greathouse, Jr., William Greathouse, Stephen Greer, Samuel Gregory, Ebenezer Griffen, Gordon Griffen, Jasper Griffen, John Griffen, Ralph Griffen, William Griffin, Philip Grimes, James Grimsley, William Grinstead, Patrick Gullian, Benjamin Guttrey, William Hadden, Samuel Haden, Nathan Hadway, Paul Haff, Bartholomew Hagard, James Haggard, Isaac Halbert, Aron Hall, Edward Hall, John Hall, Moses Hall, Moses Hall, Jr., Thomas Hall, William Hall, James Halloway, William Halsett, George Hambleton, John Hammond, Andrew Hampton, Thomas Hampton, George Hanks, Elisha Harbert, Thomas Hargester, Peter Harget, Robert Harmon, Thomas Harmon, William Harmon, Mary Harper, John Harris, Thomas Harris, Daniel Harrison, Hezekiah Harrison, Daniel Hathway, Jonathan Hathway, James Hawkins, John Hawkins, Abner Haydon, Benjamin Haydon, Ezekiel Haydon, James Haydon, John Haydon, William Haydon, William Haydon, Jr., William Hays, John Hazelrigg, Charles Hazlerigg, Joseph Hazlerigg, William Hazlerigg, John Hazzard, Martin Hazzard, Richard Headen, Samuel Headen, Benjamin Heat, Abram Hedden, Jacob Hedden, Alexander Henderson, John Henderson, Joseph Henderson, Samuel Henderson, George Hensley, Richerson Hensley, James Herons, William Hestings, Simon Hickey, James Hickman, Joe Hickman, Richard Hickman, John Higgins, James Hiler, John Hill, William Hill, Robert Hillis, Elisha His, James Hogan, John Holder, Daniel Holeman, Edward Holeman, Edward Holeman, Jr., George Holeman, Henry Holeman, Joseph Holeman, Nicholas Holeman, Frances Hollingshead, Honis Hon, Abraham Hornbeck, Andrew House, Peter Houston, Allen Howard, James Howard, Leroy Howeard, John Huckstep, Joshua Hudson, Peter Huffman, Joseph Hughs, William Hughs, Merry Humphrey, Mathew Hunsinger, Wilson Hunt, Jacob Hunter, Jacob Hunter, Jr., John Hunter, Peter Hunter, Jane Huson, Tanley Hutson, Hendrick Hutton, James Hutton, Richard Hynes, Aron Indecut, Barzella Indecut, Joseph Indecut, Moses Indecut, John Ireland, Frances Jack, John Jack, Congraves Jackson, David Jackson, Hezekiah Jackson, J. Chandly Jackson, Philip Jackson, William Jackson, William Jamason, Daniel James, George Jameson, James Jameson, John Jameson, Thomas Jameson, John Jamison, Jr., Samuel Jamison, Ephraim January, James January, John January, Thomas January, Matthew Jenkins, William Jenkins, John Johns, Andrew Johnson, Cave Johnson, Joseph Johnson, William Johnson, James Johnston, Martin Johnston, Sielass Johnston, Eaton Jonathan, David Jones, Ellett Jones, Grace Jones, James Jones, John Jones, John Jones, Jr., Thomas Jones, William Jones, James Jonse, Samuel Jonston, John Kay, Frances Keen, Frederick Keiffer, Jacob Keithley, John Keithley, John Keldar, James Kell, Isaac Kellam, Beluse Kelly, Samuel Kelly, Isaiah Kenny, Casper Kersner, Jacob Kethley, Paulser Killinincreek, Andrew Kincade, Archibald Kincade, David Kincade, Hapson Kincade, John

Kincade, William Kincade, Peter Kinder, William Kindred, Abram King, John King, John Kinkade, Robert Kirkham, Samuel Kirkham, Alexander Kirkpatrick, Christopher Kizer, James Knight, Nathan Lacky, Rene Laforce, John Lail, Samuel Lamb, William Lamb, W. Frances Lea, William Ledgerwood, William Ledgerwood, Jr., James Lee, William Lee, William Lesenby, John Lewis, Nicholas Lewis, Thomas Lewis, William Lewis, James Ligget, John Linsey, Theodones Linsey, Jacob Lips, James Little, James Locket, James Lockheart, Hugh Logan, John Long, William Lot, Frederick Lowen, John Lowry, Stephen Lowry, John Lucas, Samuel Lush, Hugh Lusk, Vincent Lutin, Moses Macingtire, George Madison, Jacob March, Humphrey Marshal, H. Marshall, John Marshall, Thomas Marshall, Thomas Marshall, Jr., Henry Marten, John Marten, William Marten, Alexander Martin, Benjamin Martin, James Martin, Jerimiah Martin, John Martin, Samuel Martin, Thomas Martin, William Martin, Earnest Martiny, John Masten, James Masterson, George Maxwell, John Maxwell, Thomas Maxwell, William Maxwell, John Mayfield, James McBride, Samuel McBride, Andrew McCanley, John McClary, Samuel McClary, Andrew McClure, John McClure, Moses McClure, Nathaniel McClure, Samuel McClure, Thomas McClure, Matt McCommon, Alexander McConnel, John McConnel, James McConnell, Mary McConnell, William McConnell, William McConnell, Jr.,Elizabeth McCorkle, Joseph McCorkle, Robert McCorkle, Cyrus McCrackin, John McCracklin, John McCumsey, Andrew McCune, William McDaniel, John McDonnol, John McDowell, Alexander McGill, James McGill, James McGuire, John McGuire, Samuel McHuron, Silas McHuron, James McIlvain, John McIlvain, Moses McIlvain, Samuel McIlvain, John McKenny, John McLanane, James McLane, Alexander McLoney, John Mc Loucklin, James McMahon, James McMillin, Robert McMillin, James McMullen, Jr., William McMurtry, Hugh McNary, John McNary, William McNary, Jonathan McNeal, Thomas McNeal, John McQuady, William McQuady, Hugh McWilliams, James Meek, John Meek, William Meek, Daniel Megee, Willima Megee, Mark Mickin, H. John Middleton, Dudley Milburn, Eve Miles, Samuel Miles, Henry Miller, John Miller, Robert Mitchel, Samuel Mitchel, John Mitchell, Rosanna Mitchell, Moses Mitchiel, William Moffet, Thomas Montague, Robert Montgomery, Samuel Montgomery, John Mooney, Patrick Mooney, James Moor, Robert Moor, Samuel Moor, William Moor, Benjamin Moore, H. Moore, John Moore, Joseph Moore, Quinten Moore, Robert Morfet, Charles Morgan, John Morgan, Shadrack Morre, Evans Morris, John Morrison, James Morrow, Orson Morton, Frederick Moss, William Moss, Thomas Moston, Jonathan Moulton, George Muir, Hugh Muldery, Isaac Munson, Samuel Munson, Samuel Munson, Jr., Chrisly Musselman, George Mutre, John Napper, Artheur Nash, Charles Neal, George Neal, John Neal, Allen

Neale, Benjamin Nelson, Edward Nelson, Thomas Nelson, William Nevell, John Nevens, John Niblick, Thomas Nicholson, Joseph Nickell, Thomas Nickell, Henry Nixon, John Norton, Enoch Nox, James Nox, R and ol Nox, Elijah Nuttle, John Old, Joseph Older, John Oliver, Robert O'Neal, William O'Neal, Patrick Owens, John Pabtean, Richard Pabtean, Jonathan Paddock, Alexander Pariland, Moses Paris, Robert Parish, Alex Parker, James Parker, John Parker, Ezekal Parkhurst, Thomas Pasley, Joseph Paterson, Mathew Patterson, Moses Patterson, Robert Patterson, John Pattie, James Patton, Edward Payne, Edward Payne, Jr., Henry Payne, Sanford Payne, William Payne, James Payton, Charles Pelham, Robert Peoples, Benjamin Perry, Lewis Perry, William Philip, Joel Philips, Robert Philips, Benjamin Piercen, James Piercen, Conradus Piles, John Pluke, Elizah Poage, Benjamin Poe, John Poe, Peter Polly, Elijah Poston, William Powel, Amborse Powell, Edward Power, Joseph Prait, Andrew Price, John Price, John Price, Jr., P. Price, William Price, Isaac Pritcher, Hezekiah Proctor, John Proctor, Thomas Proctor, William Proctor, Elisha Pruit, Joseph Pruit, William Puckitt, James Quesenberry, John Quesenberry, James Quisenberry, Edmund Ragland, James Ragland, David Rankins, David Rankins, Jr., Thomas Rankins, Dan Rayburn, H. Rayburn, Robert Rayburn, William Rayburn, Jr., Dan Rayney, William Rebelin, Isaac Reding, John Reed, Samuel Reed, James Rentfro, Benjamin Rice, Richard Rice, William Rice, Robert Richards, Mary Richardson, William Richerson, James Richie, Samuel Richie, Joseph Right, William Right, William Roberts, Absalom Robertson, William Robertson, Jr., William Robertson, Sr., Jeremiah Robinson, John Robinson, Joseph Rogers, William Rogers, David Rolston, John Rolston, John Roose, James Rucker, Richard Rue, James Rush, John Russard, Samuel Rutledge, William Said, Samuel Sanduskey, Joseph Scholl, Peter School, William School, Wharton Schooler, William Scott, George Seeright, William Seeright, Charnock Self, Vincent Self, George Shepherd, Richard Shipley, Charles Shores, George Shortridge, John Shortridge, Samuel Shortridge, James Simpson, John Slavin, John Smith, John Snady, John South, Isaac Sparks, Joshua Spear, William Spencer, Thomas Spenor, William Spires, Martin Stafford, William Stafford, Robert Stannup, Edward Stean, Robert Steel, Richard Steele, Edward Steeves, James Stevens, Joseph Stevens, Nicholas Stoner, John Stout, Samuel Stout, Charles Stutterle, John Style, Daniel Swinney, Hercules Tanner, Zachary Taylor, George Tennell, John Tervey, James Thomas, John Thomas, Arthur Thomastant, James Thompsen, David Thompson, Francis Thorton, Jane Todd, Levi Todd, Robert Todd, Jane Tompson, William Tompson, Garrard Townshend, James Townshend, Andrew Tribble, William Trimble, James Trother, Michael Tumpart, Joseph Turner, Roger Turner, Abraham Venable, John Vivion, John Vivion, Jr., Richard Walker, Benjamin Ward, William

Ward, Markham Ware, John Warters, Robert Watson, David Watts, Dawson Weade, John Welch, James Wells, Peter Welty, Edward West, James Whaley, Benjamin Dod Wheeler, Marke Whiteiar, William Whitsitt, James Wilkerson, Moses Wilkerson, Alexander Willeby, Charles Williams, Edward Williams, Philip Williams, Frederick Willis, Mathew Wills, William Wills, James Wilson, Samuel Wilson, George Winn, Owen Winn, Owen Winn,Jr., Thomas Winn, Thomas Winn, Jr., Elisha Winters, Chesley Woodard, Joseph Woolf, Christopher Wools, Francis Wyatt, Frederick Wymoore, John Wymoore, Abner Young, John Young, Miner Young.

Floyd County, Kentucky, List of Names on the 1820 Census.

John Abshire, Arthur Adams, Benjamin Adams, Charles Adams, George Adams, Isaac Adams, Jesse Adams, Jesse Adams, John Adams, Lettis Adams, Moses Adams, Silvester Adams, Spencer Adams, Stephen Adams, Stephen Adams, William Adams, Bartlett Adkins, David Adkins, Elijah Adkins, Howard Adkins, Isham Adkins, James Adkins, James Adkins, Jesse Adkins Joel Adkins, John Adkins, Joseph Adkins, Lucas Adkins, Moses Adkins, Nathaniel Adkins, Nathaniel Adkins, Noton Adkins, Spencer Adkins, William Adkins, William Adkins, Winright Adkins Jonathan Akers, Solomon Akers, Valentine Akers, William Akers, David Aldridge, James Aldridge, Peggy Aldridge, Rovert Aldridge, George Allen, Isham Allen, Richard Allen, Samuel Allen, Sarah Allen, William Allen, William Allen, William Alley David Alley, Abraham Allington, David Allington, David Allington, Peter Amyx, Charles Anderson, Nimrod Anderson Abigail Ames, Reuben Arnett, Stephen Artnett, Daniel Auxer, JohnAuxer, Nathaniel Auxer, Samuel Auxer, Jacob Averall, Benjamin Bailey, John Bailey, Joseph Bailey, Joseph Bailey, Lemuel Bailey, Prior Bailer, James Baker, Moses Ball, William Banks, William Bannister, Gilbert Barnett, Nathaniel Barnett, Salley Barnett, Henry Barr, Samuel Bazil, David Beaty, Abraham Beavers, George Belcher, James Belshe, Benjamin Bentley, Daniel Bentley, John Bentley, Lewis Bentley, Solomon Bentley, Thomas Bentley, Isaac Berry, John Berry, Jubal Berry, Jesse Beshears, John Bivens, Thomas Biven, Hudson Blackburn, Thomas Blackburn, George Blair, Jesse Blair, John Blair, Obediah Blankenship, WilliamBlankenship, John Bolin, Charles Bond, Archibald, Borders, Catherine Borders, Hezekiah Borders, John Borders, Michael Borders, Joseph Bouney, Adam Bowen, Elijah Bowman, Elizabeth Braddon, Jessee Bradley, Samuel Brafford, Benjamin Branham, David Branham, David Branham, Edward Branham, Isham Branham, John Branham, Turner Branham, William Branham, Josiah Briant, Jacob Briggs, John Briggs, Berry Brown, Daniel Brown, Francis A. Brown, George R. Brown, James Brown, James W. Brown, John Brown, John

Brown, John Brown, John Brown, John Brown, Robert Brown, Thomas C. Brown, James Brush, Mary Bruster, Gabriel Bryant, Elijah Bunton, Isaac Bunton, John Bunyon, Armsted Burchett, Benjamin Burchett, Benjamin Burchett, Drury Burchett, John Burchett, Thomas Burchett, Adam Burchfield, Edward Burgess, Garland Burgess, Henry Burgess, William Burgess, John Burgess, David Burks, William Burnett, William Burton, William Burton, James Butler, Job Cains, Richard Cains, Robert Calhoun, Allen Campbell, William Campbell, James Camron, Can't Read, Ruth Cannaday, Abraham Cantrell, John Cantrell, David Carter, Jesse Casady, John Caskey, Thomas Caske, Bazil Castle, John Castle, Nathan Castle, Zedekiah Castle, Abner Caudill, Henry Caudill, Matthew Caudill, Sampson Caudill, Stephen Caudill, Stephen Caudill, Thomas Caudill, William Caudill, Kinsey B. Cecil, Christopher Chafin, David Chafin, James Chafin, John Chafin, Jourdan Chafin, Milley Chafin, Simon Chafin, Richard Chambers, Greenberry Chaney, IsaacChapman, John Chapman, Patience Chapman, Abraham Childers, Abraham Childers, Joel Church, Alexander Clark, Carter Clark, Daniel Clark, John Clark, Samuel Clark, Caleb Clay, Jourdan Clay, Benjamin Clemings, Alexander Clevenger, John Click, John Click, Jacob Coburn, Samuel Coburn, Jeremiah Cockrell, John Cody, Elijah Coffee, William Coffee, Isabella Cole, Alexander Coleman, Charity Coleman, Charlotte Coleman, Richard Coleman, Edward Colins, Jeremiah Collier, John Collier, Micajah Collier, Stephen Collier, Bradley Collins, George Collins, George Collins, James Collins, Meridith Collins, Reuben Collins, Valentine Collins, William Collins, Thomas Collinsworth, John Colvin, Jeremiah Combs, John Combs, Sally Combs, William Combs, William Congleton, David Conley, David Conley, Edmond Conley, Henry Conley, Henry Conley, John Conley, John Conley, Joseph Conley, Sampson Conley, Thomas Conley, Clayton Cook, Henry Cook, Isaac D. Cooksey, William Cooper, James Cope, James Copley, Joseph Copley, Nancy Copley, Thomas Copley, John Cornett, John Cornett, Reuben, Cornett, Joseph Cottle, Uriah Cottle, Levi Coun, Flory Cox, John Cox, John Cox, John Cox, Uelsill Cox, Reece Crabtree, George Crace, Peter Crace, Archelous Craft, James Craft, John Craft, James Craig, Robert Craig, Robert Craig, Nathaniel Crank, Ancil Crisp, Susanna Crisp, Adam Crum, Frederick Crum, Henry Crum, Jacob Crum, John Crum, Michael Crum, Polly Cumings, Uriah Cuning, Jonathan Cunningham, Thomas Cunningham, John Curzad, Aaron Cyphers, Moses Damron, Moses Damron, Richard Damron, Samuel Damron, George Daniel, Isham Daniel, Thomas Daniel, James Davis, John Davis, Thomas Davis, Evan Davis, Henry Davis, James Davis, James Davis, John Davis, John Davis, Joseph Davis, Mathias Davis, Robert Davis, Sally Davis, Samuel Davis, William Davis, Zachariah Davis, Vincent Dawson, Archibald Day, Jacob Day, James Day, John Day, John Day, John Day,

John Day, Joshua Day, Peter Day, Reuben Day, Travis Day, Dav
William Deal, Amos Dean, Job Dean, John Dean, George Delong
Derosett, Enos Derryfield, John Deskins, Henry Dickson, William
John Dixon, William Dixon, Edward Dorton, George Dradley, C
Drake, Michael Drake, Peter Drake, Daniel Duff, Alexander D ...,
Francis Dyer, Francis Dyer, William Dyer, Isham Dykes, James Dykes,
Cornelious Eastep, Elizabeth Eastep, James Eastep, Joel Eastep, Samuel
Eastep, Shadrack Eastep, William Easterling, Joseph Edwards, Meredith
Edwards, Jenny Edlridge, Elijah Ellidge, James Ellidge, Ephraim Elliott,
James Elliott, Thomas Ellis, Bradley Elswick, John Elswick, Joseph
Elswick, William Elswick, Wallis Elum, Joseph England, Abraham Enox,
Davis Evans, Evan Evans, Ferrell Evans, Isabella Evans, John Evans,
Richard Evans, Abid Fairchild, David Fannin, David Fannin, John
Ferguson, Richard Ferguson, William Ferguson, William Ferguson,
Preston Fields, William Fitspatrick, John Fitzpatrick, John Fitzpatrick,
John Fitzpatrick, Jonathan Fitzpatrick, Thomas Fitzpatrick, Adam
Fleetwood, Isaac Fleetwood, John Fleetwood, Robert Fleming, George
Fletcher, Mary Fletcher, Mary Ford, Reuben Fralye, Elizabeth Frances,
John Franklin, Haston Frazer, Jonathan Frazier, Micajah Frazier, Stedwix
Frazier, William Frazier, Isaac Friley, John Frisbey, Benjamin Fugit,
James Fugit, James Fugit, John Fulks, Elijah Gallion, John G. Galloway,
John Garehart, Joseph Garehart, William Garehart, Daniel Garrison, James
Garrison, William Garrison, Elimelich Garrott, Midleson Garrott, Adam
Gearhart, Aleacnder George, Jane George, Ancil Gerrald, Carrell Gerrald,
Jane Gerrald, Polley Gerrald, William Gerrald, John Ghost, Nathan H.
Gibbs, Archibald Gibson, Ezekial Gibson, Ezekial Gibson, James Gibson,
John Gibson, Martin Gibson, William Gibson, William Gibson, Zachariah
Gibson, Reuben Giddens, Richard Giddens, Enoch Gilmore, James
Gilmore, William Gilmore, Peter Gollihan John Graham, John V. Grant,
William Grant, William Graves, Abel Griffith, David Griffith, Jesse
Griffith, Robert Griffith, George Grubb, James Gullett, Jesse Gullett,
William Gullett, William Gullett, John Hackworth, Jeremiah Hackworth,
James Hagar, Mary Hagar, John Hagins, John Hagins, Thomas Hagins,
William Hagins, Benjamin Hale, John Hale, Jeseph Hale, Peter Hale,
Zachariah Hale, Anthony Hall, Isham Hall, Jesse Hall, Samuel Hall,
William Hall, Benjamin Hamilton, David Hamitlon, John Hamilton,
Samuel Hamilton, Thomas Hamilton, Joseph Hammon, William Hammon,
Edward Hammons, John Hamon, Livingston Hampton, Turner Hampton,
John Haney, William Haney, Fielding Hanks, Ebenezer Hanna, James
Hanna, Joseph Hanna, Samuel Hanna, Samuel Hanna, Andrew Hanshew,
John Hardin, Joseph Harless, Martin Harper, Stephen Harper, Samuel
Harris, David K. Harris, James P. Harris, John Harris, William Harris,
Rosanna Harrison, John Hatcher, Jeremiah Hatfield, Joseph Hatfield,

Samuel Hatfield, Valentine Hatfield, Nancy Hattton, Azriel Haws, John Haws, John Hays, Lewis Haywood, Abraham Hazle, Lewis Henry, John Henry, Elijah Hensley, George Hensley, Isaac Hensley, James Hensley, John Hensley, Enoch Herrell, Nathan Herrell, Robert Herrell, William Herrell, Edward Hill, Madison Hill, Spencer Hill, Benjamin Hilton, Jessee Hilton, Rhoderick Hilton, John Hitchcock, John Hoff, William Hoffman, James Hogg, Stephen Hogg, Randal Holbrook, John Holbrook, John Holbrook, Ranal Holbrook, William Holbrook, William Holiday, Henry Holt, John Holt, Nathan Holt, James Honaker, Garner Hopkins, George Howard, James Howard, James Howard, John Howard, Moses Howard, Thomas Howard, William Howard, Electius Howe, Stephen Howell, Thomas Howell, James Howerton, John Howerton, Nathan Howerton, William Howerton, John Hunt, Samuel Hurley, Elisha Hurst, Henry Hurst,John Iliff, Joseph Indicut, Henry Ingle, Hiram Ingram, Isaac Ingram, William Isaacs, Archibald Ison, Carter Jacobs, Claudias Jacobs, John Jacobs, Rowley Jacobs, William Jacobs, John James, Samuel James, Elizabeth Jameson, Johnathan, Janes, Thomas Janes, William Janes, Robert Jenkins, Thomas Johns, Andrew Johnson, Andrew Johnson, Barnabas Johnson, David Johnson, Eli Johnson, Elias Johnson, Jacob Johnson, Patrick Johnson, Patrick Johnson, Thomas Johnson, Thomas Johnson, Thomas Johnson, Thomas Johnson, William Johnson, William Johnson, Adis Jones, Ambrose Jones, John Jones, Joshua Jones, Nancy Jones, Richard Jones, William Jones, Christian Jost, Hiram Jourdan, Jesse Jourdan, Jonas Jourdan, George Justice, Archibald Justice, Edward Justice, Ezra Justice, Israel Justice, John Justice, John Justice, John Justice, Payton Justice, Simeon Justice, Simeon Justice, Simson Justice, Thomas Justice, Tubal Justice, William Justice, Caleb Kash, James Kash, Abraham Keeton, Barney Keeton, Isaac Keeton, John Keeton, Joseph Keeton, Nelson Keeton, William Keeton, Avara Keezee, Elias Keezee, Richard Keezee, John Kelley, John Kelley, John Kelley, Thomas Kelley, William H. Kelley, James Kennard, Jacob Kesner, John King, Samuel King, William King, Alexander Kirk, Mark Lacey, Alex-ander Lacey, James Lacey, John B. Lacey, William Lacey, Alexander Lackey, James Lain, James S. Lain, Samuel Lain, William Landsaw, Robert Large, Thomas Large, Dicea Lawhorn, James Lawson, John Lawson, Joseph Lawson, Travis Lawson, Peter Leadenham, Richard R. Lee, Francis Lemaster, Eliazer Lemasters, John Lemasters, John Lemasters, Lewis Lemasters, Robert Lesley, Abner Lester, Benjamin Lewis, Bracken Lewis, Charles Lewis, Charles Lewis, Charles Lewis, Francis Lewis, Gideon Lewis, John Lewis, John Lewis, Thomas Lewis, Thomas Lewis, William Lewis, William Lewis, William Lewis, Isaac Little, James W. Little, Peter Little, William Little, John Littral, James Logan, Joseph Logins, Stephen Lowe, Moses Munsford, David Lycan, Isaac Lycan, Jeremiah Lycan, John

Lycan, William Lycan, William Lycan, William Lycan, William Lyon,George Maddox, Nathaniel Maddox, Merriman Magee, Christopher Mainor, Christopher Mainor, David Mainor, James Mainor, James Mainor, Jesse Mainor, Lewis Mainor, Mark Mainor, Moses Mainor, William Mainor, Thomas Mallett, Thomas Mallett, Peter Mankins, Walter Mankins, Samuel Mann, William Mann, John Mannan, James Marcum, William Marcum, John Marshall, Reuben Marshall, David Martin, George Martin, James Martin, Joel Martin, William Martin, Reuben Mathews, Thomas Mathews, Caleb May, John May, Mial May, Samuel May, Thomas May, William I. May, Wilson May, Samuel Mayes, Henry B. Mayo, James Mays, James Mays, William Mays, Incabod McBrayer, Joseph McBroom, Thomas McCauley, Samuel McClintick, John McClintick, William McClintick, Robert McClintick, William McClure, Alexander McCown, Daniel McCoy, John McCoy, Richard McCoy, Samuel McCoy, William McCoy, John McCracken, Shadrack McDaniel, John McDowell, Westher McGuire, James McGuire, James McGuire, Solomon McGuire, Aron McHenry, Isaac McKinsey, Ambrose McKinster, Braxton McQuinn, Carlis McQuinn, Eli Mead, Moses Mead, Rhodes Mead, Robert Mead, Samuel Mead, Samuel Mead, William Mead, James Meeks, Charles Menix, Benjamin Miller, Benjamin Miller, Edward Miller, Phillip Miller, Robert Miller, Alexander Mont-gomery, Alexander Montgomery, John Montgomery, John Montgomery, Joseph Montgomery, William Montgomery, Andrew Moore, Chirstopher Moore, Isaac Moore, James Moore, John Moore, Obadiah Moore, Sampson Moore, Thomas Moore, William Moore, Mary Morehead, Anne Morgan, James Morgan, Jared Morgan, Nathaniel Morgan, Wells Morgan, Benjamin Morris, Benjamin Morris, Daniel Morris, Ezekial Morris, John Morrise, May Morris, John Mosley, Nathan Mullett, Booker Mullins, David Mullins, Isham Mullins, James Mullins, John Mullins, John Mullins, John Mullins, John Mullins, John Mullins, Joshua Mullins, Joshua Mullins, Marshall Mullins, Sherrard Mullins, Solomon Mullins, William Mullins, William Mullins, William Mullins, William Mullins, James Munsey, Samuel Munsey, Samuel Muncey, John Murphey, William Murphy, Samuel Murray, Thomas Murray, George Mutter, Imanuel Nelson, John Newcum, Harrison Newsom, William Newton, Isaac Nickel, Andrew Nickle, Henry Nickle, John Nickle, John Nickle, John Nickle, Joseph Nickle, Robert Nickle, Thomas Nickle, William Nickle, Samuel Nipps, John Nix, Isaac Nolin, Sinai Nolin, William Nolin, John Nosman, Herrell O'Brian, James O'Brian, John Oakley, Jesse Ogden, Stephen Ogden, James Ogles, Jesse Oldfield, Hiram Osborn, Jesse Osborn, Salley Osborn, Sherrad Osborn, Solomon Osborn, Eli Owens, Samuel Owens, Thomas Owens, Thomas Owens, William Owens, Charles Pack, George Pack, George Pack, Samuel Pack, Richard Packwood, David Page, Thompson Paplett, William

Parick, Gabriel Parsons, Simeon Parsons, Thomas Patrick, Elias Patrick, Hugh Patrick, James Patrick, John Patrick, Reuben Patrick, Robert Patrick, William Patrick, Christopher Patton, Florence Patton, Hanry Patton, John Patton, Samuel Patton, Joseph Peck, Alexander Pelfrey, Daniel Pelfrey, William Pelfrey, William Pelfrey, George Perkins, Lewis Perkins, Stephen Perkins, Arnold Perry, John Jerry, John Perry, Thomas Perry, Isaac Petty, Daviel Peyton, John Phillips, Daniel Phillips, Salley Phillips, Zachariah Phillips, Abraham Picklesimer, James Pigg, Obadiah Piggman, Aaron Pinson, Allen Pinson, Henry Pinson, Jered Pinson, John Pinson, Thomas Pinson, William Pinson, David Polley, Edward Polley, Henry Polly, John Porter, Joseph Porter, Polley Porter, Samuel Porter, William Porter, James Porter, Abraham Potter, Benjamin Potter, Levi Potter, Allen Powell, Cader Powell, Halloway Power, Lewis Power, Archibald Prator, Archibald Prator, Elijah Prator, John Prator, Thomas Prator, Thomas Prator, William Prator, William Prator, William Prator, James Pratt, Eliphas Preston, Geoffery, Isaac Preston, Isaac Preston, Moses Preston, Moses Preston, Nathan Preston, Uriah Prewit, Alfred Prewit, Henry Prewitt, Jesse Price, Thomas Price, John Prichett, John Pridemore, William Prince, Zachariah Pritchett, Samuel Procter, Joseph Proffit, Silvester Proffit, Elizabeth Puckett, Teague Quillan, Daniel Ramey, James Ramey, James Ramey, John Ramey, John Ramey, Moses Ramey, William Ramey, William Ramey, Charles Ramsey, Daniel Ramsey, Martin Ramsey, James Ratliff, Jeremiah Ratliff, John Ratliff, Richard Ratliff, William Ratliff, William Ratliff, Samuel Reagen, William Reid, Conrad Rice, John Rice, Samuel Rice, Martin Rice, Benjamin Ried, Joshua Ripey, Michael Risner, Ezekial Roberson, John Roberson, Solomon Roberson, John Robert, Cornelious Roberts, Isaac Roberts, James Roberts, James Roberts, Daniel Robins, William Rogers, David Rose, John Rose, David Ross, Thomas Rowan, James Rowe, James Rowe, John Rowe, Solomon Rowe, Thomas Rowe, Catey Ruffley, Andrew Rule, Henry Runnion, John Runyan, James Rutherford, John Rutherford, Reuben Rutherford, George Sadler, R and al Salineris, William Salineris, William Salsberry, William Salyers, John Sanders, Thomas Sanders, James Scott, Thomas Scott, William Scott, Garrett See, Samuel Sellards, John Sellards, Joseph Sewell, John Sexton, James Shannon, David Shepherd, Jacob Shepherd, John Shockey, Aaron Short, Adam Short, Benjamin Short, Charles Short, William Short, James Shropshire, George Simpkins, ??? Skaggs, John Skaggs, Lewis Skaggs, Peter Skaggs, Solomon Skaggs, Solomon Skaggs, James Skidmore, John Skidmore, Archibald Slone, George Slone, Hiram Slone, Isham Slone, Shadrack Slone, Shadrack Slone, Jacob Slusher, Elijah Smith Hardin Smith, James Smith, Jeremiah Smith, John Smith, Martin Smith, Moses R. D. Smith, Reuben Smith, William Smith, William Smith, William M. Smith, Hugh Smothers, John Smothers, Peter Snider, Leticia Sowards,

Francis Spaulden, John Spaulden, Robert Speers, Thomas Speers, Thomas Spencer, Benjamin Spradlin, James Spradlin, John Spradlin, Joseph Spradlin, Micajah Spradlin, Robert Spriggs, David Spurlock, Frances Spurlock, Hiram Spurlock, Matthew Spurlock, Simon Stacy, William Stacy, James Stafford, John Stafford, John Stambaugh, Phillip Stambaugh, Jr., Phillip Stambaugh, Sr., Jonathan Stamper, William Stanley, Joshua Stapleton, James Steel, William Steel, Barnett Steph, Gilbert Stephens, Thomas Steward, Thomas Steward, James Steward, Rebecca Stobuck, Cuthbert Stone, Enoch Stone, Ezekial Stone, James Stone, John Stone, Solomon Stone, John Stotts, Hannah Stratton, Harry Stratton, James Stratton, Richard Stratton, Salley Stratton, Tandy Stratton, Mark Stroud, David Sullivan, Peter Sullivan, Wilson Sullivan, John Sumner, Samuel Sumner, Abraham Swango, Samuel Swango, Levi Swanson, Neri Sweatman, John Sword, Jacob Syck, Francis Tackett, George Tackett, Lewis Tackett, Thomas Tackett, William Tackett, James Taylor, Isaac Terry, Leonard Terry, Miles Terry, William Terry, Absalom Thacker, Owen Thomas, Andrew Thompson, George Thompson, Richard Thompson, Samuel Thompson, Susanna Thompson, Isaac D. Tolby, William Tolby, James Tolby, Samuel Tolby, Elias Tolin, Joel Toliver, Thomas Tolson, Thomas Tolson, Lydia Trent, Mark Trimble, William Trimble, John Trout, William Trusty, John Turman, James Turner, Suddith D. Turner, Daniel Tyre, James Vanhoose, John Vanhoose, John Vanhoose, Levi Vanhoose, Alexander Varney, Andrew Varvil, Daniel Varvil, Ayres Vaughn, Ayres Vaughn, Patrick Vaughn, Gabriel Vaughn, Jesse Venters, John Venters, Edward Vess, Benjamin Wadkins, Thomas Wadkins, Moses Wagers, John Walker, Robert Walker, Jacob Waller, Jesse Waller, Nathan Walter, William Walter, Elizabeth Walters, James Ward, James Ward, Shadrack Ward, Solomon Ward, William Ward, William Ward, Peter Warden, Reuben Warren, Anna Watson, James Watson, George Watts, Benjamin Webb, William Webb, Henry Weddington, Bennett Wellmon, Elisha Wellmon, James Wellmon, Jeremiah Wellmon, Joseph Welmon, Michael Wellmon, William Wellmon, Edmond Wells, John Wells, William Wells, Lewis Welmon, James Wheeler, James Wheeler, Stephen Wheeler, Stephen Wheeler, William Wheeler, Price Whitaker, Charles White, Alexander Whitely, Bunyan Whitt, Richard Whitt, Francis Whittiker, Hezekiah Wiley, Jean Wiley, Alexander Williams, Coleman Williams, David Williams, Isaac Williams Isaac Williams, John Williams, John Williams, Joshua Williams, Mason Williams, Phillip Williams, Richard Williams, Thomas Williams, Thornton Williams, William Williams, Alden Williamson, Benjamin Williamson, Elizabeth Williamson, Hamon Williamson, Hiram Williamson, John Williamson, John Williamson, James Wills, Andrew Wilson, Andrew Wilson, Harris Wilson, Mary Winkles, David Winkless,

Abraham Wireman, Jacob Wireman, JohnWireman, Thomas Witten, Nancy Woods, George Wooton, Levi Wooton, Silas P. Wooton, Absalom Young, Alexander Young, Charles W. Young, James Young, John Young, Robert Young, Samuel Young, William Young, William Younts.

Carter County, Kentucky, Marriages, 1838-1839
George Buckner and Millie Pruitt, (MD) 31 Mar 1839
Henderson Burton and Rosa B. Sexton, (MD) 14 Apr 1839
Alfred Enochs and Mary Ann Miller, (MD) 18 Nov 1838
Joseph Fults and Elizabeth Smith, (MD) 22 Nov 1838
James Henderson and Margaret Henderson, (MD) 27 Sep 1838
Reuben Messer and Sarah Laws, (MD) 30 Jan 1839
William Sherman and Cynthiann Fults, (MD) 22 Nov 1838
William Smith and Catherine Evans, (MD) 29 May 1838
Andrew Stewart and Rachel Cook, (MD) 25 Dec 1838
Thomas Wooton and Nancy Henderson, (MD) 20 Dec 1838
Martin Zornes and Lucinda Horsley, (MD) 28 Nov 1839
Philip Zornes and Rachel Zornes, (MD) 12 Aug 1839

Fulton County, Kentucky, Alexander Family Cemetery, Two miles north of Jordon, Rock Creek Road.

| Name | Birth | Death |
| --- | --- | --- |
| Dr. John M. Alexander | May 28, 1818 | Oct. 18, 1878 |
| Mary Mott Alexander | Oct. 8, 1824 | Oct. 10, 1917 |
| Maj. Richard B. Alexander | Dec. 20, 1801 | Jun. 1, 1868 |
| Elizabeth M. Alexander | Jul. 14, 1822 | Sep. 26, 1887 |
| Wm. Lock Alexander | Aug. 13, 1775 | Dec. 21, 1851 |
| Susannah Allen Alexander | Jul. 18, 1784 | Npv. 29, 1850 |
| Wm. Fletcher Crenshaw | Nov. 3, 1821 | Aug. 9, 1896 |
| Moses Lawson | Jan. 21, 1776 | Nov. 30, 1852 |
| Columbia Washington Landrum | Sep. 10, 1833 | Oct. 16, 1859 |
| Horace Lawson | Jun. 4, 1800 | Jun. 30, 1883 |
| Lucie B. Lawson | Jul. 15, 1837 | Nov. 18, 1859 |
| Susan Ann Brevard | Oct. 24, 1823 | Sep. 1, 1851 |
| Cynthia A. Brevard | Aug. 29, 1838 | Aug. 11, 1887 |
| Alfred A. Brevard | Jan. 10, 1790 | Oct. 17, 1865 |
| Mary B. Brevard | Mar. 14, 1805 | Aug. 3, 1887 |
| Capt. W. W. Shuck | Apr. 16, 1839 | Aug. 7, 1926 |
| Wm. Lock Alexander | Jan. 9, 1822 | Dec. 2, 1901 |

Kentuckians listed in the Old Settler's Register, *"Shelby County Herald,"* 1899, Shelby County, Missouri.

John M. Alexander: (B) 1812, (ARVDMO) 1840, (ARVDCO) 1851, (A) 77Y.

George W. Bell: (B) 1824, (ARVDMO) 1837, (ARVDCO) 1837, (A) 65Y.

J. I. Bowles: (B) 1826, (ARVDMO) 1831, (ARVDCO) 1888, (A) 63Y.

C. M. Bohan: (B) 1824, (ARVDMO) 1834, (ARVDCO) 1880, (A) 64.

Eliza Blackford: (B) 1814, (ARVDMO) 1843, (ARVDCO) 1832, (A) 75.

Marshall Blackburn: (B) 1828, (ARVDMO) 1837, (ARVDCO) 1837, (A) 61Y.

J. M. Collier: (B) 1823, (ARVDMO) 1833, (ARVDCO) 1834, (A) 66Y.

Elijah S. Chinn: (B) 1825, (ARVDMO) 1834, (ARVDCO) 1834, (A) 64Y.

A. T. Chinn: (B) 1827, (ARVDMO) 1834, (ARVDCO) 1834, (A) 62Y.

John S. Chinn: (B) 1830, (ARVDMO) 1834, (ARVDCO) 1834, (A) 59Y.

J. W. Cochran: (B) 1828, (ARVDMO) 1832, (ARVDCO) 1833, (A) 61Y.

Jos. Chick: (B) 1813, (ARVDMO) 2830, (ARVDCO) 1849, (A) 76Y.

S. F. Dunn: (B) 1824, (ARVDMO) 1824, (ARVDCO) 1836, (A) 65Y.

J. W. Dunn: (B) 1820, (ARVDMO) 1824, (ARVDCO) 1836, (A) 69Y.

Gabriel Davis: (B) 1809, (ARVDMO), (ARVDCO) 1840, (A) 80Y.

Amelia Epperson: (B) 1817, (ARVDMO) 1840, (ARVDCO) 1849, (A) 72Y.

Mary Exline: (B) 1827, (ARVDMO) 1833, (ARVDCO) 1834, (A) 64Y.

John F. Finney: (B) 1837, (ARVDMO) 1837, (ARVDCO) 1837, (A) 52Y.

Jas. G. Glenn: (B) 1810, (ARVDMO) 1833, (ARVDCO)1833, (A) 79Y.

David W. Graham: (B) 1821, (ARVDMO) 1831, (ARVDCO) 1835, (A) 68Y.

James Gooch: (B) 1817, (ARVDMO) 1832, (ARVDCO) 1824, (A) 72Y.

M. J. Hawkins: (B) 1825, (ARVDMO) 1827, (ARVDCO) 1874, (A) 64Y.

G. Hoagland : (B) 1832, (ARVDMO) 1857, (ARVDCO) 1881, (A) 57Y.

W. O. Huston: (B) 1823, (ARVDMO) 1825, (ARVDCO) 1845, (A) 67Y.

T. W. Jones (B) 1827, (ARVDMO) 1837, (ARVDCO) 1869, (A) 62Y.

C. M. King: (B) 1826, (ARVDMO) 1832, (ARVDCO) 1833, (A) 63Y.

F. M. King: (B) 1835, (ARVDMO) 1838, (ARVDCO) 1839, (A) 54.

Addison Lair: (B) 1811, (ARVDMO) 1827, (ARVDCO) 1834, (A) 78Y.

A. S. McAfee: (B) 1826, (ARVDMO)1829, (ARVDCO) 1833, (A) 63Y.

J. C. Mayes: (B) 1826, (ARVDMO) 1833, (ARVDCO) 1833, (A) 63Y.

Thomas Mitchell: (B)1818, (ARVDMO) 1850, (ARVDCO) 1856, (A) 71Y.

C. G. Muldrow: (B) 1816, (ARVDMO) 1822, (ARVDCO) 1826, (A) 73Y.

Mrs. B. N. Melson: (B) 1825, (ARVDMO) 1827, (ARVDCO) 1846, (A) 64Y.

John E. McDaniel: (B) 1830, (ARVDMO) 1865, (ARVDCO) 1865, (A) 59Y.

W. T. Mayes: (B) 1831, (ARVDMO) 1833, (ARVDCO) 1833, (A) 58Y.

John F. McMurry: (B) 1828, (ARVDMO) 1835, (ARVDCO) 1842, (A) 61Y.

Elijah Pepper: (B) 1808, (ARVDMO) 1831, (ARVDCO) 1832, (A) 81Y.

B. Perry: (B) 1826, (ARVDMO) 1872, (ARVDCO) 1872, (A) 63Y.

John T. Pollard: (B) 1835, (ARVDMO) 1843, (ARVDCO) 1843, (A) 54Y.

Sarah A. Phillips: (B) 1834, (ARVDMO) 1857, (ARVDCO) 1857, (A) 55Y.

Jacob L. Pence: (B) 1818, (ARVDMO) 1860, (ARVDCO) 1860, (A) 71Y.

Mrs. Patsy Pickett: (B) 1813, (ARVDMO) 1835, (ARVDCO) 1835, (A) 76Y.

Henry Pickett: (B) 1838, (ARVDMO) 1853, (ARVDCO) 1853, (A) 62Y.

Eliza E. Rogers: (B) 1819, (ARVDM) 1824, (ARVDCO) 1840, (A) 70Y.

James Sanders: (B) 1819, (ARVDMO) 1830, (ARVDCO) 1831, (A) 70Y.

J. G. Swinney: (B) 1818, (ARVDMO) 1837, (ARVDCO) 1866, (A) 71Y.

Dr. Ben F. Stewart: (B) 1823, (ARVDMO) 1840, (ARVDCO) 1878 or 1880?, (A) 66Y.

H. D. Smith: (B) 1816, (ARVDMO) 1817 or 1818?, (ARVDCO) 1836, (A) 73Y.

S. J. Stevenson: (B) 1826, (ARVDMO) 1830, (ARVDMO) 1856, (A) 63Y.

J. M. Spencer: (B) 1835, (ARVDMO) 1838, (ARVDCO) 1854, (A) 54Y.

Martha Stalcup: (B) 1809, (ARVDMO) 1840, (ARVDCO) 1840, (A) 80Y.

John M. Simmons: (B) 1833, (ARVDMO) 1841, (ARVDCO) 1841, (A) 57Y.

John Thomas: (B) 1813, (ARVDMO) 1832, (ARVDCO) 1841, (A) 76Y.

F. P. Taylor: (B) 1829, (ARVDMO) 1829, (ARVDCO) 1835, (A) 60Y.

R. F. Taylor: (B) 1837, (ARVDMO) 1859, (ARVDCO) 1859, (A) 62Y.

Wilson Vaughn: (B) 1824, (ARVDMO) 1836 or 1837?, (ARVDCO) 1850 or 1851, (A) 65Y.

Alfred Vanskike: (B) 1825, (ARVDMO) 1829, (ARVDCO) 1850, (A) 64Y.

J. B. Wood: (B) 1820, (ARVDMO) 1829, (ARVDCO) 1834, (A) 69Y.

E. A. Wood: (B) 1826, (ARVDMO) 1830, (ARVDCO) 1836, (A) 63Y.

J. W. Wood: (B) 1832, (ARVDMO) 1833, (ARVDCO) 1833, (A) 57Y.

Mrs. Judith Weeden: (B) 1829, (ARVDMO) 1848, (ARVDCO) 1848, (A) 61Y.

Kentucky Connections: Rockbridge County, VA Deed Book B, pp. 498-509, 11 August 1792

James Wallace and Agness, his wife, Robert Wallace and, Sarah, his wife, and Robert Campbell, and, Rebeccah, his wife, of Fayette County, Kentucky to John Fulton of Rockbridge County, Virginia. By virtue of the last Will and Testament of John Wallace

Deceased, now of record in the Office of said County Court of Rockbridge, is devised said James Wallace, Robert Wallace, and Rebecca Campbell, their heirs, and assigns an equal share of all his lands by virtue of which and for and in consideration of the sum of 250 pounds current money of Virginia paid to them the said James Wallace and Agness, his wife, Robert Wallace and, Sarah, his wife, and Robert Campbell and, Rebeccah, his wife have bargained and sold to John Fulton a certain tract of land lying and being in said County of Rockbridge on Walker's Creek containing 250 acres including the pond spring and is bounded as follows: Beginning at a poplar tree and three hickory saplings near the top of a hill, S 35 deg., E 160 poles to 2 black oaks in a hollow, N 55 deg, E 200 poles to 2 small chestnuts in the barrens, N 35 deg, W 34 poles to a chestnut oak and black oak grub,N 9 deg, W 112 poles to a white oak and chestnut, N 50 deg, W 100 poles to a hickory and chestnut on the North side of the hill, S 38 deg, W 230 poles to the beginning.

Land with appurtenances to John Fulton, his heirs, and assigns forever. James Wallace and Agness his wife, Robert Wallace and Sarah his wife, and Robert Campbell and Rebeccah his wife forever warrant and defend by these present.

Signed Sealed and delivered James Wallace, Agness Wallace, Robert Wallace, Sarah Wallace, James Trotter, Robert Campbell,Will Morton, Rebecka Campbell
State of Kentucky to wit

At a Court held for the County of Fayette on the 12th day of March 1793. This Indenture was and ordered to be certified and admitted to record. March 14, 1793. Signed Levi Todd

At a Court held for Rockbridge July 2nd 1793 the foregoing Indenture from James Wallace Robert Wallace and Robert Campbell to John Fulton was acknowledged in the County Court of Fayette and State of Kentucky as appears by the above certificate and is ordered to be recorded here. A. Reid, Clerk
Rockbridge To wit

The Commonwealth of Virginia to James Trotter and William Morton,Gentlemen of the County of Fayette and State of Kentucky

Whereas James Wallace and Agness his wife, Robert Wallace and Sarahhis wife, and Robert Campbell and Rebeccah his wife by bargain and sale dated 11th August 1792 have sold and conveyed to John Fulton of Rockbridge County, Virginia 250 Acres of land more or less with appurtenances lying and being in said County of Rockbridge. Agness and Sarah Wallace and Rebecca Campbell cannot conveniently travel to one County Court of Rockbridge to make acknowledgement of the said conveyance therefore we do give unto you or any two of you power to receive the acknowledgement which the said Agness and Sarah Wallace and Rebecca Campbell shall be willing to make before you of the conveyances aforesaid contained in said Indenture. You are to personally go to the said Agness, Sarah and Rebecca and receive their acknowledgements of the same and Examine them privily and apart from the said James and Robert Wallace and Robert Campbell their husbands whether they do freely and voluntarily without the persuasion or threats of their husbands and whether they be willing the same should be recorded in our said County Court and when you have examined her as aforesaid that you distinctly and openly certify us thereof in our said County Court under your hands and seals sending there the said Indenture and this writ. Witness Andrew Reid, Clerk of our said Court, at the Courthouse of the said County the 11th day of August 1792 and the seventeenth year of the Commonwealth. A. Reid

By virtue of this Commission hereto annexed we the Subscribers Did on the twenty sixth Day of June 1793 and in the first year of the Commonwealth Personally did go to the within named Agness and Sarah Wallace and Rebecca Campbell and having examined them separately and apart from the within named Jas. and Robt. Wallace and Robert Campbell their Husbands do certify that they voluntarily acknowledged the conveyance contained in the Indenture hereto also annexed without the persuasion or threats of their said husbands and that they are willing the same should be recorded in the County Court of Rockbridge. Witness our hands and seals the day and year aforesaid James Trotter, Will Morton

Fayette County Kentucky to wit

Levi Todd Clerk of Court of the County aforesaid certifies that James Trotter ad William Morton esquires who have subscribed the foregoing acknowledgement are Justices of the Peace in the County foresaid duly commissioned and legally qualified to perform the duties appertaining to the said office. March 15, 1793. Levi Todd

At Rockbridge Court July 2, 1793

This Commission for the privy examination of Agness Wallace Sarah Wallace and Rebecca Campbell wives of James Wallace Robert Wallace and Robert Campbell touching the relinquishment of Dower in a certain tract of land conveyed by their husbands to John Fulton was this day returned with certificate of acknowledgement and ordered to be recorded. A. Reid Clerk.

James Wallace Robert Wallace and Rebeccah Campbell, Legatees of the Estate of John Wallace, deceased, as appears by his last Will and Testament of Record in County Court of Rockbridge, of Fayette County to Jno. Fulton of said County of Rockbridge .

James Wallace and Agness his wife, Robert Wallace and Sarah his wife, and Robert Campbell who intermarried with Rebecca Campbell previous to the making of the last Will and Testament but not mentioned therein as a legatee for and in consideration of the sum of four hundred pounds current money of Virginia to them in hand paid have granted bargained and sold by these presents do grant bargain and sell unto the said John Fulton one certain tract of land lying and being in the County of Rockbridge, bounded as follows: Beginning at a poplar tree and swamp oak in a fork of Walkers Creek, S 72 deg, E 228 poles, S 31 deg, W 298 poles to 3 chestnut oaks, N 30 deg, W 200 poles to a blazed chestnut, N 45 deg, W 130 poles to a walnut and small hickory on the said creek, Up several courses of the same to the beginning. land containing 322 1/2 acres being the half of 645 acres divided between Jno. Wallace, dec. and James Rutherford. To have and hold land with all appurtenances to said John Fulton and his heirs and assigns. James Wallace and Agness his wife, Robert Wallace and Sarah his wife, and Robert Campbell and Rebeccah his wife for themselves their heirs, Exors, and Admrs. covenant with the said John Fulton and his heirs that the said James Wallace and Agness his wife, Robert Wallace and Sarah his wife, and Robert Campbell and Rebecca his wife their heirs Exors and Admrs the land with all appurtenances unto the said John Fulton his heirs and assigns forever warrant and defend. Signed, sealed and, delivered James Wallace, Agness Wallace Robert Wallace, Sarah Wallace, Robert Campbell, James Trotter, Rebecca Campbell, Will Morton

State of Kentucky to wit

At a Court held for Fayette the 12th day of March 1793 This Indenture was produced in Court acknowledged by James Wallace Robert Wallace and Robert Campbell parties thereto which was ordered to be certified that the same may be admitted to record in the County where the lands lie. In Testimony whereof I hereto set my hand and affix the seal of the said Court this 15th day of March 1793 and in the first year of the Commonwealth. Levi Todd

At a Court held for the County of Rockbridge July 2nd 1793 this foregoing Indenture of Bargain and Sale for land from James Wallace Robt Wallace and Robert Campbell parties thereto to Jno Fulton was acknowledged in the County Court of Fayette and State of Kentucky as appears by the above certificate of the Clerk thereof and is ordered to be Recorded here. A. Reid, Clerk

Rockbridge To wit

The Commonwealth of Virginia to James Trotter and William Morton, Gentlemen of the County of Fayette and State of Kentucky

Whereas James Wallace and Agness his wife, Robert Wallace and Sarahhis wife, and Robert Campbell and Rebeccah his wife by bargain and sale dated 11 August 1792 have sold and conveyed to John Fulton of Rockbridge County, Virginia 322 1/2 Acres of land more or less with appurtenances lying and being in sd County of Rockbridge. Agness and Sarah Wallace and Rebecca Campbell cannot conveniently travel to one County Court of Rockbridge to make acknowledgement of the said conveyance therefore we do give unto you or any two of you power to receive the acknowledgement which the said Agness and Sarah Wallace and Rebecca Campbell and examine theme privly and apart from the said Jas. Robert and Robert their husbands whetheer they do freely and voluntarily without the persuasion or threats of their husbands and whether they be willing the same should be recorded in our said County Court and when you have examined them as aforesaid that you distinctly and openly certify us thereof in our said County Court under your hands and seals sending there the said Indenture and this writ. Witness Andrew Reid Clerk of our said Court at the Courthouse of the said County the 11th day of August 1792 and the seventeenth year of the Commonwealth. A. Reid

By virtue of this Commission, We the Subscribers Did on the twenty sixth Day of June 1793 and in the first year of the Commonwealth Personally did go to the within named Agness and Sarah Wallace and Rebeccca Campbell and having examined them privily and apart from the within named James and Robt. Wallace and Robt. Campbell their husbands do certify that they voluntarily acknowledged the conveyance contained in the Indenture here to also annexed without the persuasion or threats of their said husbands and that they was willing the same should be recorded in the County Court of Rockbridge. Witness our hands and seals the day and year aforesaid. James Trotter, Will Morton

Fayette County Kentucky to wit

Levi Todd Clerk of Court of the County aforesaid certifies that James Trotter and William Morton Esq who have subscribed the foregoing acknowledgement are Justices of the Peace in the County foresaid duly commissioned and legally qualified to perform the duties appertaining to the said office. March 15, 1793  Levi Todd

At Rockbridge Court July 2, 1793

This Commission for the privy examination of Agness Wallace wife of James Wallace, Sarah Wallace wife of Robert Wallace, and Rebecca Campbell wife of Robert Campbell touching the relinquishment of Dower in a certain tract of land conveyed by their husbands to John Fulton was this day returned with certificate of acknowledgement and ordered to be recorded. A. Reid, Clerk.

47

Kentucky Connections: Rockbridge County, VA Deed Book B, p. 547, 9 July 1793

William Blair and Mary his wife of Greenbrier County, Va and William Anderson and Catherine his wife of Fayette County, Ky, Heirs of Wm. Blair, decd. Previous to William Blair's death, he sold lot but made no legal conveyance. Beginning on Northwest side of Main St and fronting on same then bounded by out line of sd. Town on 1 square by line dividing same from Lot #28 and Nelson St., on the other squares.

Kentucky Connections: William Finley will, 25 February 1836, Will Book 21, page 291, Augusta Co., VA

I ,Wm. Finley, of the county of Augusta and State of Va. being of sound mind but weak of body and knowing that it is appointed for all men once to die, do hereby make and publish this my last will and testament thus making void all former acts of this kind done by me - and first I direct that my body be decently intered and that my funeral be conducted in a manner corresponding with my estate and situation in life and as to such worldly estate as it hath pleased God to intrust me with I dispose of the same as follows. First I direct that all my just debts and funeral expenses be paid - I next direct that my sister Sarah Finley be paid out of my estate fifteen hundred dollars said sum is to embrace all debts whatsoever due from me to her. the said Sarah Finley to her paid as follows viz in five equal anual payments the first to be made as soon after my decease as can be done but not to exceed one year and in addition to her above: I direct that my said sister have a full and sufficient support from my estate during life or so long as she is willing to continue a resident on my estate she must also be furnished with a good horse saddle and bridle. I direct that Margaret Mooney who is now residing with me a full and sufficient support on my estate during life. I next direct that my brother John Finley now residing in the State of Kentucky and my sister Jane Frazer late Jane Finley now residing in Ohio be paid each fifty Dollars said sums to be paid to my brother and sister three years after my decease. Next should my servants prove obstinate and ingovernable I direct that they be sold and the proseeds applyed to the payt of aforesd bequets reserving this priviledge for any man ??? that he have liberty of choosing his master next should the proseeds of my estate not be equal to the payt of my aforesd bequests I direct that my tract of land lying in said county lying below the turnpike in Rockfish gap and adjoining the land of ??? Bernard and others be sold another proseeds thereof be applyed to the pay of said legacys After the payment of all the above sd: I give and bequeath to Francis Marion Finley son to Margaret Mooney all the remainder of my estates whether real or personal to him the said Francis M. Finley and to his heirs forever and lastly I nominate my sister Sarah Finley and Hugh McClure to execute this my last will and testament In witness whereof I, Wm. Filey, the testator have to this my will set my h and and seal the 25th day of Feb. one thous and wight hundred and thirty six Signed, Sealed and delivered in presence of us who have subscribed hereto. Wm. Finley. James S. Bush Joseph Pick, Geo B. Keiser

Augusta County Court December Term 1836

This last will and testament of Wm. Finley, decd was presented in Court and proved by the oaths of Joseph Peck and George B. Keiser two of the subscribing witnesses thereto and ordered to be recorded and on the motion of Hugh McClure an executor therein named who made oath thereto according to law and with Joseph Peck and Samuel B. Kerr his securities entered into and acknowledged a bond in the penalty of eight thous and dollars conditioned as the law requires which bond is ordered to be recorded. certificate is granted to said Hugh McClure for obtaining a probate of said will in due force and leave is reserved to the execution therein named to qualify when she shall think proper to do so. Jefferson Kinney, Clerk.

Synod of Kentucky, Presbyterian Church, Established, 1802

The Synod was composed of the Presbyteries of Transylvania, West Lexington and Washington, as was petitioned for at the first meeting of the Washington Presbytery, when the Presbytery of Transylvania was divided into the three above named Presbyteries. The following is the roll of the first meeting:

Of the Presbytery of Transylvania, ministers present: David Rice, Samuel Finley, Matt. Houston, Saml. Robertson, Archibald Cameron; absent, Thomas Craighead, Terah Templin, James Balch, Wm. Hodge, James McGready, John Bowman, Wm. McGee, John Rankin, Saml. Donald, Wm. Mahon, Saml. McAdow, John Howe, James Vance and Jer. Abel, Elders: Andrew Wallace, James Bigham and Court Voris.

Presbytery of West Lexington, Ministers Present: James Crawford, Samuel Shannon, Isaac Tull, Robert Marshall, James Blythe, James Welsh, Joseph P. Howe, Samuel Rannels, John Lyle and Wm. Robinson. Absent: Barton W. Stone. Elders, James Bell, Robert Maffet, Malcolm Worley, Wm. Scott, Joseph Walker, Wm. McConnell, Samuel Hayden and Wm. Henry.

Presbytery of Washington, Ministers Present: James Kemper, John P. Campbell, Richard McNemar, John Thompson and John Dunlevy. Absent: John E. Finley and Matt. G. Wallace. Elders: Robert Gill and John Campbell.

Fulton County, Kentucky, Asbell Cemetery, southeast of Cayce, off State
Highway 239.

| Name | Birth | Death |
|---|---|---|
| Aaron S. Asbell | Aug. 4, 1800 | May 10, 1871 |
| Elizabeth Bonner Asbell | Dec. 9, 1811 | Feb. 3, 1843 |
| Wm. Nelson Asbell | Jan. 11, 1834 | Jul. 16, 1894 |
| Martha Alice Asbell Cruce | Sep. 24, 1832 | Jan. 15, 19-3 |
| Richard W. Cruce | Dec. 29, 1819 | Apr. 6, 1904 |
| Martha Cruce | Apr. 17, 1819 | May 19, 1854 |
| Elizabeth Boyd Cloyce | Sep. 10, 1821 | Nov. 9, 1902 |
| Henry Cloyce | 1823 | Sep. 20, 1861 |

Scott County, Kentucky, 1800, Tax List
    Ben Abbett, William Abbett, Charles Adams, Elijah Adams, Jacob
Adams, Moses Adams, Nathan Adams, James Adkins, John Adkins, Hugh
Alexander, Jacob Alexander, William Alexander, James Allen, Richard-
son Allen, Robert Allen, John Angleton, Richard Applegate, Zacheriah
Archer, Absolem Atkins, Goin Atkins, James Auford, William Bacon,
Hugh Baird, Joseph Baker, Joshua Baker, John Balding, George Ballard,
Mattehw Barclay, Henry Barlow, Henry Barlow, James Barlow, Thomas
Barlow, Daniel Barnhill, Robert Barnhill, Samuel Barnhill, Judson Ba-
sheers, Thomas Batts, James Baulden, Moses Baulden, Daniel Bauldin,
Jacob Baxter, Joseph Beates, Joseph Beates, Jr., James Beatey, William
Beatey, James Beaty, John Beaty, William Beauchamp, James Bell, Henry
Bellee, Solomon Bellow, Erasmus Benton, William Berry, Josiah Berry-
man, John Bertlet, Nicholas Betner, Lee Bird, Jonathan Blackburn, Julius
Blackburn, Henry Boaz, Daniel Boling, William Bond, John Bonds, Ro-
bert Bonds, Walker Bonds, Bartes Boots, Conrad Booyer, George Boswell,
John Boswell, John Bourn, Baptist Bowls, Hugh Boyd, Joseph Boyd,
Enoch Bradford, Benjamin Bradley, John Bradley, Robert Bradley,
Beverly Bradly, James Brady, Ben Branham, Gatin Branham, Harben
Branham, James Branham, Richard Branham, Spencer Branham, Tavenner
Branham, Thomas Branham, William Branham, William Brewer, William
Brewer, Charles Brian, Jacob Brindle, John Brock, Elijah Brockman, John
Brooken, Robert Brooken, Joseph Brooks, Thomas Brooks, John Brown,
Samuel Brown, Thomas Brown, Elias Brumagon, Samuel Buckley,
Abraham Buford, James Buford, George Burbridge, Joseph Burch, Ben
Burt, Moses Burt, Richard Burt, Moses Bussell, William Butler, Samuel
Caldwell, Jesse Calloway, Alex Campbell, Alexander Campbell, Allen
Campbell, Ben Campbell, David Campbell, David Campbell, John
Campbell, Samuel Campbell, William Campbell, Willis Cannon, John
Carnegy, William Carney, Daneil Carrel, Dempsey Carrel, Peter Cary,
Edmond Cason, William Cason, Henry Cave, William Cave, James

Chambers, Thomas Chesnut, Julius Christy, Francis Cirtley, Andrew Clark, William Clark, Henry Clevo, Paul Clutter, Samuel Cobb, William Cochril, John Cogwell, John Colbert, Presley Colbert, Joseph Colley, Bartlett Collins, Lewis Collins, Lewis Collins, Richard Collins, James Combs, James Conley, Tristram Conner, Joseph Conover, Benjamin Conyers, Colman Cook, Isaac Cook, John Cook, Natt Cook, Robert Cook, Samuel Cooper, Jonathan Cope, Isaac Coppage, John Coppage, Rhodin Coppage, James Cowden, Samuel Cowden, James Cox, John Cox, Lazarus Cox, William Cox, Alexander Cragmile, Elijah Craig, Elijah Craig, Jr., John Craig, Reubin Craig, Toliver Craig, William Craig, William Craig, James Craigmile, Matthew Craigmyle, Henry Creighton, Robert Creighton, Valentine Criss, Paul Cristian, David Criswell, George Criswell, Samuel Criswell, Jonathan Cropper, John Crouch, William Crowder, Benjamin Cruzan, Alexander Culbertson, Samuel Culbertson, Charles Cullins, James Cunningham, Archibald Curry, Bernard Daugherty, John Daugherty, James Daughton, John Dausen, Joseph Dausen, Thomas Dausen, Anne Davis, Benjamin Davis, Elijah Davis, John Davis, Joseph Davis, Phillip Davis, Phillip Davis, Solomon Davis, William Davis, Wood Davis, William Day, Simon Dearing, James Dehauney, Isaac Deheaven, Samuel Deheaven, James Denney, Fielding Denny, Lewis Denny, Andrew Deringer, Hugh Dickey, Michael Dickey, William Dickey, Edward Dingle, William Dinwiddy, Thomas Dolman, James Donaldson, John Douglass, Andrew Downey, John Downey, William Downey, Francis Downing, Thomas Drake, John Duitt, James Duley, Thomas Duley, Collin Dunkin, James Dunkin, Thomas Dunwiddy, Francis Durrit, William Duty, Cornelius Duvall, Nealy Duvall, Zachariah Duvall, William Eaden, Edward Ealey, Fielden Eastreag, Henry Edger, Robert Elder, John Ellerson, Moses Ellerson, Robert Ellerson, Benjamin Elliott, John Elliott, Richard Ellis, Henry Ely, Thomas Ely, Ash Emison, Hugh Emison, James Emison, Armstead Emmerson, Nathaniel Ennis, George Eve, Caleb Evins, Robert Evins, Robert Evins, James Ewing, Joseph Ewing, William Ewing, Christopher Eycoff, James Fargerson, Larken Fargerson, Hugh Farquer, John Fenal, John Ficklin, Thomas Ficklin, Abraham Fields, James Fields, Ree-son Fields, Abner Finnel, John Finnel, John Finton, John Fisher, Dennis Fitzpatrick, Lewis Flannegin, David Flournoy, Artha Forbus, John Ford, Nick Forkner, James Forquer, Robert Fortner, Christopher Forts, Arthur Foster, Thomas Foster, Jonathan Fothergill, Thomas Fothergill, Thomas Francis, Henry Gaines, Henry Gaines, Richard Gains, Robert Gale, Ruth Galloway, Samuel Galloway, Richard Ganoe, John Garnett, Elwell Garrison, Julius Gibbs, James Gibson, John Gibson, Thomas Gillam, Robert Gipson, Fleming Glass, Samuel Glass, Thomas Glass, William Glass, Jeremiah Glenn, Michael Goddard, Francis Golson, Adam Goodlet, Ignatius Gough, James Gough, John B. Gough, Susanna Grant,

George Gray, John Gray, William Gray, John Grayham, Charles Green, John Green, Joseph Green, Bennett Greenwell, Ignatius Greenwell, Robert Greer, Amos Gregg, Israel Gregg, Joseph Gregg, Samuel Gregg, Kindness Gresham, Ruth Grier, Isaac Griffith, Jesse Griffith, Robert Griffith, William Griffith, Nimrod Grimsley, Isaac Gruell, John Gruell, Richard Gunnel, Turner Haden, Edward Hall, John Hall, John Hall, Jr., John Hall, Sr., William Hall, Jessey Hambrick, Alexander Hamilton, Charles Hamilton, John Hammond, Abraham Hannah, Andrew Hannah, James Hannah, William Hardy, Robert Harkness, Elijah Harris, Thomas Harris, William Harris, Joseph Harrison, Robert Hastens, John Hawkins, Martin Hawkins, Nathan Hawkins, James Haws, Thomas Haws, John Hay, Joseph Hazelwood, John A. Head, William Head, Abraham Heath, Henry Helms, John Henderson, Bird D. Hendricks, John Henry, William Henry, David Herndon, Francis Herndon, Henry Herndon, James Herndon, Thomas Herndon, James Hinton, Jr., James Hinton, Sr., Solomon Hinton, James Hodins, John Holdon, William Holdon, Ann Holland , Ephraim Holland , George Holland, William Holland, Andrew Hood, John Hoop, James Hopkins, John Hornacher, Joseph Houston, Leonard Houston, John B. Howard, John Hoyle, Palson Hoyle, Kerby Hubbard, Robert Huey, Samuel Huey, Michael Hummer, John Hunter, John Hunter, Robert Hunter, Henry Hurst, John Hurst, Anthony Huston, Archibald Hutcheson, James Hutchison, Obediah Hutchison, John Ireland, Jr., John Ireland, Sr., William Ireland, Colby Jackson, Elliott Jackson, Mordecai Jackson, Phillip Jackson, Robert Jackson, Theodorus Jaco, William James, Henry Jenkins, Thomas Jenkins, William Jervis, Abraham John, Daniel John, David John, Jonathan John, Adam Johnson, Andrew Johnson, Bale Johnson, Charles Johnson, Daniel Johnson, Emanuel Johnson, Gabriel Johnson, George Johnson, James Johnson, James Johnson, Jr., John Johnson, Leavy Johnson, Robert Johnson, Thomas Johnson, William Johnson, Joseph Johnston, William Johnston, Abraham Jones, Ben Jones, Ben Jones, Jr., Charles Jones, James Jones, John Jones, John H. Jones, Joseph Jones, William Jones, Zadoc Jones, Daniel Kain, James Kee, Charles Keene, Hopewell Keene, Richard Keene, Samuel Keene, Samuel Y. Keene, Thomas B. Keene, Griffith Kelley, James Kelley, William Kelley, William Kendall, Robert Kendell, David Kerr, Simon Key, William King, James Lambert, Daniel Lamburt, John Lamburt, Joseph Lame, Thomas Landrum, Mary Laws, Randle Layforee, David Layton, Spencer Layton, John Leach, James Leak, John Leak, John Lebannon, Charles Lecount, David Lecount, Jeremiah Leetch, Walter Leetch, James Lemmon, Robert Lemmons, William Lemmun, John Lemon, Michael Leonard, Henry Lewis, Solomon Lewis, Thomas Lewis, Richard Libern, John Lindsay, John V. Lindsay, Henry Lindsey, James Lindsey, Oliver Lindsey, Anthony Linsey, Anthony Logan, Samuel Logan, William Logan,

Nicholas Long, Beverly Longdon, William Love, John Lowrey, Samuel Lowrey, Alexander Scott Lowry, Richard Lucas, Thomas C. Lucas, Elijah Lukers, John Lukers, Thomas Lukers, William Magaffock, Samuel Magary, Richard Magraw, Jerrit Manaffe, John Manning, Timothy Marker, George Marshall, Aaron Martin, Jacob Martin, Samuel Martin, Thomas Martin, William Massey, Benjamin Mattock, Sherwood Mattox, Thomas Mawhiney, James McCalister, Peter McCarty, Robert McCawley, John McCay, Daniel Mcclain, Benjamin McClennon, Abraham McClintock, John McClung, Samuel McClung, Thomas McClure, William McClure, Francis McConel, Hugh McCormack, George McCormick, Alexander McCoy, James McCrosky, Joseph McCulloch, William McCulloch, James McCutchen, Lavin McFarland, Charles Mc Grew, Alexander McHatton, John McHatton, John McHatton, Jr., James McManomy, Gardner McNemar, David Mefford, Jessey Melton, Joseph Messak, Andrew Mifford, Adam Miller, Henry Miller, John Miller, Katherine Miller, Robert Miller, Alvin Miner, Jeremiah Miner, John Miner, Thomas Mitchell, William Mithcel, John Montague, August Montgomery, John Montgomery, William Montgomery, Thomas Moody, Thomas Moody, Jr., William Moody, Barnet Moore, Charles Moore, George Moore, James Moore, John Moore, Thomas Moore, Alexander More, Robert More, Thomas More, Robert Morris, William Morris, Andrew Morrow, John Morrow, John Mosby, Abraham Mosley, Clement Mosley, Jacob Mosley, Mason Moss, Nathaniel Mothershead, Elijah Mounts, John Mounts, Jacob Mulbery, John Mulbery, Hance Murdock, Thomas Murdock, Charles L. Nall, Lewis Nall, Martin Nall, Jr., Martin Nall, Sr., William H. Nall, Daniel Neal, Jr., Rhodin Neal, John Neisbit, John Nelson, Joseph Nelson, Joshua Nevingham, Lewis Nuckles, David Nutter, James O. Harro, James Officer, John Ogdon, George Oldham, Joshua Ore, Bennet Osburn, James Osburn, John Osburn, Leavey Osburn, Richard Osburn, Thomas Osburn, Francis Otwell, Bartlett Overton, Charles Owins, Haroway Owins, Haroway Owins, Jr., John Owins, Owin Owins, Zedock Pain, Jacob Palsgrove, James Parke, Matthew Patterson, William Patterson, Robert Patton, John Payne, John Peak, Presley Peak, Hessey Peake, Richard Peck, Adam Pence, Adam Pence, Jr., John Pence, Shadrack Penn, John Perkins, Abraham Perry, Bartlet Perry, Edmund Perry, Henry Perry, John Perry, Larken Perry, William Pettet, Samuel Pettit, James Phillipe, John Picket, John Pierson, Josiah Pitts, Younger Pitts, George Plummer, Joseph Plummer, William Plummer, Fenbrey Plunket, Arthur Points, John Powell, Richard Power, William Pratt, James Price, Benjamin Quinn, Matthew Quinn, Nicholas Quinn, Amos Ragin, Abraham Rainey, Stephen Raizel, Thomas Ramsey, Robert Raney, Robert Raney, Jr., John Ransdell, Thomas Ravencraft, Elijah Readen, Joseph Readen, John Rease, Frederick Reaser, Aaron Reynolds, James Riley, John Ritchey, Stephen Ritchey, Ben

Roberson, William Roberts, Jonathan Robertson, Andrew Robison, Jacob Robison, John Rodes, Waller Rodes, John Rogers, Thomas Rolins, William Rolins, William Ross, Charles Rozel, James Rusk, John Rusk, Polly Russell, Robert Sale, Michael Salser, David Sampson, Thomas Samuel, Robert Sanders, Joseph Santee, Abraham Scott, Early Scott, John Scott, Thomas Scruggs, William Scruggs, Richard Seabrey, Lewis Sebastian, Reubin Seers, George Shannon, Hugh Shannon, Robert Shannon, Nathaniel Shanon, David Shelton, Medly Shelton, Robert Shelton, Samuel Shepard, Ezekiel Sherley, Colbey Ship, William Shirley, Eli Short, William Shortridge, Daniel Sinclair, Robert Sinclair, Berryman Smith, Henry Smith, James Smith, Joseph Smith, Lewis Smith, Oliver Smith, Roads Smith, Robert Smith, Samuel Smith, William Smith, John Snell, Joseph Snell, Louden Snell, John Snider, Robert Southward, Humphrey Sparks, Thomas Spence, Conrad Spoon, Jacob Sroyer, James Stafford, John Stafford, William Stafford, John Stearitt, William Steel, Archilles Step, Benjamin Stephens, Alexander Stephenson, Joseph Sterrett, John Stevens, James Stevenson, Adam Stifler, William Stodgell, Asa Stone, John Stone, Rufus Stone, William Story, Benjamin Stribling, John Strickler, Jacob Stucker, Henry Suddith, James Suggate, John Suggate, William Suggate, Stout Sutfin, John Sutton, John Sen Sutton, William Sutton, John Swann, George Swetnum, James Swigate, John Talbot, Jeremiah Talton, George Tangler, Francis Tansel, John Tapp, Caleb Tarlton, Bartholomew Taylor, James Taylor, William Taylor, Allen Tharp, William Theobalds, John Thomas, Solomon Thomas, William Thomas, Ann Thomason, Nelson Thomason, Richard Thomason, Samuel Thomason, David Thompson, Gilbert Thompson, Jarvis Thompson, John Thompson, Martin Thompson, Robert Thompson, Rodes Thompson, Watt Thompson, James Thorn, John Thornton, Peter Thrailkeld, Jessey Thrailkil, William Thrailkil, Alexander Tilford, David Tilford, Samuel Tilford, William Tilford, Barney Timpey, Samuel Todd, Samuel Todd, Sr., William Tomlin, William Tomlin, William Tomns, David Torrance, John Torrance, John Townsley, Thomas Townsley, James Tribeau, Hedgman Triplett, Agnes Trotter, James Trotter, Margaret Trotter, Margaret Troxel, Tatman Truitt, Benjamin Turner, John Turner, James Twyman, Richard Tyner, Jacob Ullis, Hankerson Utterson, Nancy Vann, John Vernum, George Viley, James Vinsant, John Vinsant, Garret Vorous, Mic Wainock, Aaron Walden, Alexander Walker, James Walker, Joseph Walker, Samuel Walker, William Walker, James Wallace, James Wallace, John Wallace, Samuel Walls, Jacob Ward, Samuel Ward, William Ward, William Warren, Wilson Warwick, James Weathers, John Weathers, Thomas Weathers, Christopher Weaver, John V. Webb, Thickor Webb, Vurn Webb, Robert Weir, Samuel Weir, Linn West, Andrew White, James White, John White, Lewis White, John Wiggins, Jonas Wiggins, Charles

Williams, Jeremiah Williams, Jeremiah Williams, John Williams, Joseph Williams, Robert Williams, David Williamson, James Williamson, Lewis Williamson, Roger Williamson, Thomas Williamson, Abraham Williamson, John Wills, Hill Willson, John Willson, Joseph Willson, Taply Willson, Nathaniel Wilson, Richard Wilson, William Wilson, Stephen Winters, Fielding Wood, Thomas Wood, William Wood, Elijah Woodfolk, Edmund Woods, Edward Wooling, Rosanna Wooling, Barneby Worland, Malcom Worley, Nathan Worley, Nathan Worley, Joseph Yeates, Samuel Young.

Military Pensioners Listed on the Kentucky 1840 Census.

| County | Name | Age | HD Household |
|---|---|---|---|
| Adair | James, William | 82 | Elijah Leech |
| | Warnock,William | 76 | |
| Allen | Stovall, George | 79 | |
| Barren | Cole, John | 88 | |
| Boone | Allen, Elizabeth | 65 | |
| Bourbon | Davis, James | 79 | |
| | Hayes, Thomas | 80 | Griffin Kelly |
| Bracken | King, John | 78 | |
| | King, Phillip | 53 | |
| | King, William Sr | 80 | |
| Butler | Wornock,Abner | 76 | |
| Campbell | Todd, Samuel | 83 | |
| Clinton | Davis, John | 83 | James David |
| Cumberland | King, George | 90 | |
| Daviess | Jones, James | 79 | |
| Fleming | Davis, Jesse | 76 | Matthew Lee |
| | Davis, William | 83 | John Swer |
| Garrard | Wormoth, Thaddeus | 79 | |
| Grant | Jones, Joshua | 71 | |
| Harlan | Jones, Stephen L | 99 | Sally Harlanes |
| Henry | Davis, Joseph | 77 | James Wentworth |
| | Mitchell, George K | 77 | |
| Hickman | Depositer, John | 86 | Gabriel Davis |
| Jessamine | Jenskins, Kesiah | 78 | Elisha Jenkins |
| | King, Jeremiah | 81 | |
| | Todd, Samuiel B | 47 | |
| Mason | Cole, Elizabeth | 81 | |
| | Owens, William | 77 | Albert Owens |
| McCracken | Jones, Benjamin | 79 | Isaac David |
| | Lovelace, Nancy B | 84 | Robert E Kester |
| Mercer | Fisher, Elias | 87 | |

| County | Name | Age | HD Household |
|--------|------|-----|--------------|
| Montgomery | Fisher, John F | 70 | |
| | Gray, William | 86 | |
| Muhlenburg | Elkins, Joshua | 86 | |
| Oldham | Austin, John | 102 | |
| Rockcastle | Farris, Moses | 78 | John Newcom |
| Russell | Sharp, Isham | 85 | |
| Shelby | Wiley, Henry | 95 | |
| Todd | Pannel, Benjamin | 83 | |
| Trimble | Gray, Isaac | 66 | |
| Washington | Farris, Elijah | 80 | |
| Woodford | Mitchell, John | 76 | |

Fulton County, Kentucky, Harmony Cemetery, Near Moscow.

| Name | Birth | Death |
|------|-------|-------|
| Rev. J. A. Rodgers | Oct. 18, 1838 | Jul. 10, 1903 |
| Nettie Mangrum | Jun. 16, 1839 | May 7, 1910 |
| J. S. Mangrum | Sep. 17, 1825 | Jan. 10, 1902 |
| Jacob A. Lannom | Nov. 29, 1839 | Aug. 15, 1915 |
| E. C. Linden | Aug. 31, 1826 | Apr. 1, 1894 |
| John H. Ramer | Oct. 15, 1837 | Sep. 11, 1914 |

Kentucky Connection: District No. 75, 1850 Census Ray, County, Missouri.

Household No. 446.

Goode, William: (A) 46, (SEX) M, (OC) Farmer, (BP) KY.
Goode, Susan: (A) 43 (SEX) F, (BP) KY.
Children: Margaret: (A)19, (BP) MO; Julia Ann: (A) 15, (BP) MO; Reuben: (A) 11, (BP) MO; Jane: (A) 8, (BP) MO; John: (A) 6, (BP) MO; Robert W.: (A) 2, (BP) MO.

Household No. 440.

Loyd, James: (A) 28, (SEX) M, (OC) Laborer, (BP) TN.
Loyd, Eliza: (A) 23, (SEX) F, (BP) KY.
Child: Harriett J.: (A) 1, (BP) MO.

Estill County, Kentucky, Index 1810 Census

| Name | Page No. |
|------|----------|
| Berry Abner | 5 |
| John Abner | 5 |
| William Abney | 7 |
| Jesse Adams | 5 |
| Ben Alexander | 4 |
| James Alexander | 4 |

| Name | Page No |
|---|---|
| David Evans | 7 |
| John Evans | 5 |
| John Evans | 7 |
| Peter Evans | 7 |
| John Evett | 7 |
| Peter Fe???el | 7 |
| Wm. Fielder | 2 |
| James Foley | 1 |
| Henry Fortner | 4 |
| John Fowler | 4 |
| Joseph Fowler | 4 |
| Valentine Fritts | 7 |
| Rodins Fuel | 5 |
| John Goosey | 3 |
| Peter Goosey | 5 |
| Henry Green | 2 |
| Patterson Griffith | 2 |
| Abram Groom | 1 |
| Abram Groom | 4 |
| Jacob Groom | 6 |
| McCajah Hall | 7 |
| Ben Halladay | 5 |
| Thomas Hardin | 1 |
| Francis Harris | 1 |
| William Harris | 1 |
| James Hathman | 5 |
| Adam Hattan | 2 |
| Wm. Hattan | 2 |
| John Hawkins | 2 |
| Danl. Henderson | 2 |
| Robt. Henderson | 2 |
| Moses Henry | 1 |
| Leroy Hightower | 4 |
| Humphrey Hill | 4 |
| Humphrey Hill | 4 |
| John Hix | 7 |
| Jacob Hockinsmith | 7 |
| Tandy Holeman | 5 |
| Mathew Horn | 7 |
| William Horn | 7 |
| William Horsley | 1 |

Some Miscellaneous Death Records for Kentucky.

Anna Vanhoose: (B) 1831ca, (D) Jan. 7, 1913, (A) 81Y, (CO) Johnson.

James A. Culwell: (B) 1838ca, (D) Jan. 5, 1915, (A) 76Y, (CO) Callaway.

Elizabeth Annis: (B) 1837ca, (D) Apr. 27, 1915, (A) 78Y, (CO) Ohio.

B. R. Musser: (B) 1831ca, (D) Dec. 7, 1913, (A) 82Y, (CO) Warren.

Catherine Musser: (B) 1831ca, (D) Dec. 31, 1914, (A) 65Y, (CO) Kenton.

Jane Green: (B) 1839ca, (D) Mar. 1, 1910, (A) 71Y, (CMTS) daughter of William and Sarah Lemaster, (CO) Johnson.

Peggy Waller: (B) 1829ca, (D) Nov. 14, 1910, (A) 81Y, (CMTS) daughter of Ambros and Nancy Lawson, (CO) Johnson.

H. F. Waller: (B) 1830ca, (D) Nov. 28, 1910, (A) 80Y, (CMTS) son of James and Hannah Waller, (CO) Johnson.

Mary E. Abbott: (B) 1834ca, (D) Dec. 6, 1911, (A) 77Y, (CO) Burboun.

Martha Collin: (B) 1836ca, (D) Feb. 6, 1926, (A) 90Y, (CO) Nelson.

Cathanie P. Dear: (B) 1836ca, (D) Apr. 14, 1914, (CO) Franklin.

Thomas M. Dear, Sr.: (B) 1836ca, (D) Jan. 1, 1911, (CO) Jefferson.

Lucy Gines: (B) 1837ca, (D) Jul. 16, 1912, (A) 75Y, (CO) Daviess.

Marquis D. Burns: (B) 1832ca, (D) Feb. 2, 1913, (A) 81Y, (CO) Boyd.

Courtney Askins: (B) 1833ca, (D) Dec. 7, 1912, (A) 79Y, (CO) Breckinridge.

Middleton Jameson: (B) 1833ca, (D) Feb. 29, 1916, (A) 83Y, (CO) Lee.

Hillard Wallace: (B) 1836ca, (D) Dec. 19, 1917, (A) 81Y, (CO) Daviess.

William M. Elder: (B) Jan. 28, 1802, (CO) Lincoln.

Marurice and riot: (B) 1837ca, (D) Apr. 19, 1916, (A) 79Y, (CO) Campbell.

Dr. Edward Alcorn: (B) Aug. 10, 1843, (CO) Lincoln.

Lidia Nolley: (B) 1832ca, (D) Aug. 3, 1916, (A) 85Y, (CO) Marion.

Jerome W. Ballance: (B) 1839ca, (D) Sep. 2, 1923, (A) 84Y, (CO) Campbell.

James H. McCampbell: (B) 1836ca, (D) May 20, 1915, (A) 79Y, (CO) Shelby.

Elizabeth B. Jefferson: (B) 1839ca, (D) Mar. 13, 1816, (A) 77Y, (CO) Trigg.

Dawson Anderson: (B) 1836ca, (D) May 1, 1911, (A) 75Y, (CO) Garrard.

Church Brooks: (B) 1830ca, (D) Jun. 30, 1914, (A) 84Y, (CO) Fayette.

B. F. Gordon: (B) 1832ca, (D) Sep. 24, 1921, (A) 89Y, (CO) Logan.

Elizabeth F. Gordon: (B) 1839ca, (D) Mar. 1, 1911, (A) 72Y, (CO) Muhlenbuerg.

Jerome Alrey: (B) 1828ca, (D) Mar. 15, 1920, (A) 92Y, (CO) Daviess.

Tammie Carter: (B) 1825ca, (D) Feb. 17, 1916, (A) 91Y, (CO) Jefferson.

Elizabeth A. Jefferson: (B) 1827ca, (D) Mar 23, 1912, (A) 85Y, (CO) Jefferson.

Upper Spottsvania Baptist Church Left In 1791 For Floyd County, Kentucky From Virignia Leading the Wagontrain was Rev. Lewis Craig and Capt. William Ellis

Allen, Elly Price, Asher, Eastin Robinson and wife, Bledsoe, Garrard, Ramsey, Bowman, Goodloe, Rucker, Barrow, Hunt, Shackelford, Burbridge, Hart, Shipp, Buckner, Hickman, Shotwell, Toliver Craig and wife, Hickerson, Singleton,Lewis Craig, Martin, Smith, Joseph Craig, Moore, Sanders, William Cave, Morton, Stuart, Curd, Marshall, Todd, Carr, Morris,Thompson, Creath, Mitchum,Walton, Dudley, Noel, Woolfolk, Dupuy, Payne,Watkins, Darnaby, Parrish, Timothy,Waller, Dedman, Parrish, James,Ware, Ellis, William, Pitman,Woolridge, Ellis' family of 5, Preston,Young. There were also other members

Floyd County, Kentucky, Land Warrant
        Surveyed on the 13th day of March 1827 for Robert Walker 50 acres of land by Virtue of one Kentucky land Office Warrant. No. 16816. Beginning on 3 birches on a point near Prewitts branch on the waters of Salt Lick Creed just below where James ? now lives on the east side of said branch in the county aforsaid. thence S52 W18 p.(poles) cropsing said branch to a Birch. N51 W70 polesto a white oak on the side of a hill N35 W138 p. to a Birch and Cucumber. N60 W58 p. to 2 birches stand ing near a drain near Prewitt's camp. N25 W75 p. to a stake N55 E18 p. to a stake S38 E250 p. to a stake S65 E69 p. to the beginning. Signed: James Patrick, John Pitts, J. Wadkins, Ro. Walker, D. S., John Graham, S. H. C., State of Kentucky.
        Surveyed on the 7th day of April 1828 for Thomas Collinsworth, Trustee for the Prestonsburg Academy 150 acres by virtue of 3 Kentucky land Office Warrants No. 16827-16820 and 16807. Lying and being in Floyd County aforesaid on the Burning Fork of Licking and bounded as followith. Beginning at a white oak on the north side of said fork corner to Richard Patricks 100 acre Survey Thence N36 W 198 piles to a white oak and Birch on a small branch. thence S60 W 66 poles to a Sugar tree Birch and Hickory same course continued 56 poles to a stake. Thence S36 E198 poles to a stake. Thence N60 E122 poles to the beginning . Signed: John Graham, S. H. C., Meredith Patrick, George Adams, Thomas Collinsworth.

Whitley County, Kentucky, Deed Index, 1818-1838
William Offield to John Pemberton, (D) 25 Apr 1818
Joseph Eve to Thomas Laughlin, (D) 7 Oct 1818
Nathaniel Ledger to James Campbell Sr., (D) 2 Nov 1818
Thomas Mahan and wife to James Mahan, (D) 10 Dec 1818
Aron Allen to Samuel Oosley, (D) 3 Nov 1818
Larken Jones to Thomas Swift, (D) 4 Apr 1818
Elizabeth Sharp, to Thomas Sharp, (D) 8 Oct 1819
James Stotts and wife to Isaac King, (D) 3 Jul 1819
James Stotts and wife to Benjamin Hammon, (D) 3 Jul 1819
David Wilson to James Sears, (D) 20 Dec 1819
Joseph Early to President and Director, (D) 18 Oct 1819

Benjamin Eaton to William Eaton, (D) 16 Oct 1819
John Day to Vincent Wyatt, (D) 17 Nov 1819
Joseph Early to Cornelius Gatliff, (D) 1 Jan 1819
John Faris and wife to Charles Gatliff, (D) 12 Jul 1819
William M. Bledso to John McHurg, (D) 1 Nov 1819
Joseph Earley to Presley Hunt, (D) 24 Feb 1820
James Mahan to Thomas Mahan, (D) 12 Oct 1819
Henderson to William Morgan, (D) 16 Mar 1819
Martin Beaty to William Morgan, (D) 16 Mar 1819
Martin Beaty to William Morgan, (D) 16 Mar 1819
Cornelius Gatliff to Charles Gatliff, (D) 17 Jan 1820
Joseph Early to Milton Eve, Wal, (D) 5 Jun 1820
Uriah Parks to brother George Parks, (D) 19 Jun 1820
William Gillreath to George Parks, (D) none
Rhodes Nuckolls to Ezra Nuckolls, (D) 24 Jun 1820
Joseph Parsons, to the Bank, (D) 18 Oct 1820
Trustees of Willia to John F. Sharp, (D) 27 Apr 1821
Benjamin Hamond to the Bank, (D) 5 Jun 1821
John Duncan to Elijah Girton, (D) 7 Aug 1821
George Lofftus to Joel Stow, (D) 13 Jul 1821
Hugh Munhollin to Andrew Higginbottom, (D) 23 Oct 1821
Milton Eve, heir to Isham G. Hamilton, (D) 24 Jan 1822
Joseph Parsons, to John Berry, (D) 10 Dec 1821
John Cox to William Cummins, (D) 29 Dec 1821
John Duncan and wife to John Sharp, (D) 4 Jul 1822
John Duncan and wife to John Sharp, (D) 4 Jul 1822
Jacob Sexson to Enoch Sexson, (D) 5 Jul 1822
John S. Laughlin to John Sharp, (D) 10 Aug 1822
Lewis Brown to William Tillison, (D) 22 Oct 1822
Joseph Duncan to Dela Fayette Berry, (D) 16 Dec 1822
Hugh French to William Duger, (D) 19 May 1823
Gardener L. Mullin to Joel Sto, Sr., (D) 12 Oct 1822
Thomas Brasfield to John Brasfield, (D) 21 Aug 1823
Thomas Mahan and wife to William Dryden, (D) 12 Mar 1824
Charles Gatliff to Cornelius Gatliff, (D) 14 Apr 1824
Rebecca Davisto Enoch Sexton, (D) 19 Apr 1824
Hugh French to Robert Finley, (D) 17 May 1824
James Mahan to daughter Pamelia, (D) 23 Feb 1824
James Gatliff to children, Charlotte, (D) 19 May 1824
James Gatliff to son Squire Gatlif, (D) 19 May 1824
Robert Stinson to John Storm Jr., (D) 7 Jul 1824
Samuel Cox, Sr. to son Levi Cox, (D) 6 Jul 1824
Joel A. Watkins to Baker E. Watkins, (D) 12 Jul 1824

Samuel Cox to Rutha Cox, (D) 16 Jul 1824
Samuel Cox to son William Cox, (D) 16 Jul 1824
Samuel Cox to daughter Sarah Co, (D) 16 Jul 1824
William Bledsoe to William Steel, (D) 13 Jul 1824
William Sceech to Joseph Screech, (D) 8 Sep 1824
B.S. Parsons to Walter R. Hunt, (D) 8 Nov 1820
Uriah Parks to Joseph J. Faris, (D) 21 Sep 1824
James Stotts and wife to Christopher Wampler, (D) 12 Sep 1815
William Richmond to John Richmond, (D) 13 Nov 1824
John Dunkin and wife to trusty friend Jos, (D) 11 Feb 1825
Abram Smith and wife to Gilbert Barnard, (D) 21 Mar 1825
Abraham Smith to Isaac King, (D) 21 Mar 1825
James Helton to Eliza Z. Helton, (D) 6 Jul 1825
John G. Crump to Mary Crump (D) 11 Jul 1825
Joseph D. Laughlin, (D) 22 Feb 1825
Joel A. Watkins, to Reuben Faulkner, (D) 5 Apr 1825
Nathan Cox and wife to Joseph J. Faris, (D) 9 Nov 1825
Joel A. Watkins, to Joseph D. Laughlin, (D) 6 Mar 1825
Nathan Cox and wifeif to Joseph D. Laughlin, (D) 10 Nov 1825
Simon Snider and wife to William Dugger, (D) 8 Aug 1825
Joseph D. Laughli to Walter R. Hunt, (D) 29 Oct 1825
Christopher Wampler to Michael Wampler, (D) 1 Oct 1825
William Brown to Samuel Carr, (D) 21 Nov 1825
Joseph D. Laughlin to Andrew Craig, (D) 22 Feb 1826
Timothy Perkins to John Grubb, (D) 23 Feb 1826
John Cox to James Sears, Jr., (D) 15 Sep 1822
Hawthon Hood of to Francis Faulkner, (D) 5 Aug 1822
James Litton and wife to Burton Litton, (D) 28 Sep 1825
Joseph D. Laughlin to Jesse Walker, (D) 22 Feb 1825
Joseph D. Laughlin to Timothy Perkins, (D) 22 Feb 1825
Joseph D. Laughlin to Francis Faulkner, (D) 22 Feb 1825
Zachariah Belshey to Richardson Herndo, (D) 1 Jun 1826
Edward Riley of to Walter R. Hunt,, (D) 15 Nov 1825
Joseph Eairley to Nathan Cox, Wil, (D) 19 May 1826
William M. Smyth to Robert Creekmore, (D) 1 Jul 1820
John White to Demcey White, (D) 28 Sep 1826
David Richmond to William Richmond, (D) 5 Oct 1826
Joel A. Watkins to Nathan Cox, (D) 15 Jun 1826
Polly Litton, (D) 7 Oct 1826
Burton Litton to William Brown, (D) 4 Dec 1826
Andrew Craig and wife to Jefrey Champlain, (D) 7 Sep 1826
Kesiah Meadors, (D) 14 Dec 1826
Solomon Litton to John Cardwell, (D) 16 Dec 1826

Jesse Walker and wife to Hiram Litton, (D) 20 Dec 1826
Joel A. Watkins, to Samuel G. Bayers, (D) 28 Dec 1826
Barton Gilreath to Benjamin Parks, (D) 5 Feb 1827
Daniel Twigg to John Smith of Wy, (D) 5 Mar 1827
Joel Sto, Sr. and wife to Joel Sto, Jr., (D) 13 Feb 1827
Elisha B. Creekmo to Benjamin J. Parks, (D) 4 Jun 1827
Francis Faulkner to Joel A. Watkins, (D) 5 Apr 1827
Thomas Adkins to son Jerry Adkins, (D) 20 Jun 1827
Andw. Craig to Mahlin Bishop, (D) 18 Jun 1827
Andw. Craig to Mahlin Bishop, (D) 18 Jun 1827
Malen Bishop and wife to Joseph Gillis, (D) 18 Jun 1827
Malin Bishop and wife to John H. Pemberton, (D) 18 Jun 1827
William McCoy to brother-in-law As, (D) 5 Aug 1827
Andrew Craig to Malin Bishop, (D) 18 Jun 1827
Andrew Craig to Charles Gatliff, (D) 2 Jul 1827
Joseph Gilliss to Samuel Boyd, (D) 7 Jul 1827
Jesse Fowler and wife to David Stansberry, (D) 13 Nov 1825
William Leforce to Hiram Litton, (D) 11 Dec 1827
Levi Pennington to Uriah Parks, (D) 15 Dec 1827
Milton Eve to William Bishop Sr., (D) 24 May 1827
William Bennet to Vincant Hamblin, (D) 12 Sep 1827
James Ellison to Elizabeth Ellison, (D) 29 Aug 1827
Nancy Ellison to Elizabeth Ellison, (D) 1 Oct 1827
Obedience Mays to Marmeduke Mays, (D) 2 Oct 1827
Daniel Faulkner to Nathan Cox, (D) 9 Oct 1827
Nathan Cox and wife to Daniel Faulkner, (D) 9 Oct 1827
Jesse Walker and wife to James K. Gallian, (D) 10 Nov 1827
Conrad Grubb and wife to Samuel Boyd, (D) 15 Feb 1828
Milton Eve and wife to Daniel Faulkner, (D) 7 Apr 1828
John Rogers to Daniel Twigg, (D) 25 Mar 1828
John Cordwell, to Nathan Cox, ass., (D) 23 Feb 1828
John Cordwell, to Nathan Cox, (D) 23 Feb 1828
Isaac Wilson and wife to Samuel Jones, (D) 18 Sep 1828
Abraham Stoe and wife to Robert Mayfield, (D) 20 Sep 1828
William McCoy to Asa McCoy, (D) 29 Sep 1828
Abraham Stoe and wife to Jacob Meadows, (D) 20 Sep 1828
James A. Brown to Oliver Steel, (D) 30 Sep 1828
David Hufft to Preston C. Berry, (D) 3 Oct 1828
Andrew Rodes to Joseph J. Faris, (D) 27 Dec 1828
Joseph D. Laughli to Joseph J. Faris, (D) 6 Jan 1819
Samuel Monhollan to John Davis who p, (D) 3 Feb 1829
James Monhollan to William Adams, (D) 3 Feb 1829
John Heaton to Joel Heaton, Na, (D) 30 Jan 1829

James Sears and wife to Samuel Boyd, (D) 6 Apr 1829
John S. Wilson to James Wilson, (D) 9 Apr 1829
John Cox to William F. Bishop, (D) 11 May 1829
Joel A. Watkins to Charles Gatliff, (D) 6 Apr 1829
James Mahan to Thomas Mahan, (D) 22 Sep 1825
Thomas Mahan to Nathan Cox, (D) 17 Feb 1821
Andrew Rodes to William Rodes, (D) 10 Jul 1829
William Vanoy Sr. to Samuel Vanoy, (D) 3 Aug 1829
William Bishop to James Rogers, Jr., (D) 6 Aug 1829
John Cox and wife to "our father" James, (D) 30 Sep 1829
Elijah Durham to Richard Botkin, (D) 5 Oct 1829
Joseph Screech to William Russle, (D) 7 Nov 1829
Isaac Leabo and wife to John Richmond, (D) 5 Oct 1829
Thomas Laughlin to Harvey B. Duncan, (D) 8 Feb 1828
John Cardwell to Joseph J. Faris, (D) 25 Aug 1829
James Helton, Sr. to William Bishop, (D) 31 Oct 1829
Joel Stoe and wife to James Calavan, (D) 6 Sep 1829
Hirum Litton to Joseph J. Faris, (D) 8 Dec 1829
Milton Eve and wife to Frank Ballinger,, (D) 23 Dec 1829
Milton Eve and wife to Andrew Craig, (D) 23 Dec 1829
Archilus Blake to Abraham Smyth, (D) 2 Dec 1829
John Wilson and wife to Abraham Wells, (D) 22 Aug 1829
Walter D. Hunt to Andw. Craig, (D) 16 Jan 1830
Samuel C. Jones to Charles Gatliff, (D) 18 Mar 1830
James Sears, Sr. to James Sears, Jr., (D) 27 Mar 1830
James Sears, Jr. to Samuel Boyd, (D) 5 Apr 1830
David Middleton to Joseph J. Faris, (D) 4 Jun 1830
Joseph J. Faris to David Middleton, (D) 8 Jun 1830
Joseph J. Faris to Thomas Faulkner, (D) 8 Jun 1830
Joseph Duncan of to John S. Laughlin, (D) 11 Feb 1829
Joseph Duncan of to Joel Stoe, (D) 21 Jun 1830
James Mahan, Sr. to James Mahan, Jr., (D) 13 Feb 1830
James Mahan and wife to John Mahan, (D) 13 Feb 1830
Vincent Hamblin to Solomon Wilder, (D) 5 Mar 1830
David Middleton to David Caddle, (D) 25 Jul 1830
Mary Harmon, adm to Jeremiah Harmon, (D) 25 Oct 1830
William Dugger to Andrew Hash, (D) 30 Sep 1830
William Dugger to Andrew Hash, (D) 30 Sep 1830
William Dugger to Andrew Hash, (D) 30 Sep 1830
Stephen Hubbs to William Floyd, (D) 5 Apr 1830
David Middleton to Jesse Walker, (D) 23 Sep 1830
James Mahan and wife to Francis Berry, (D) 13 Feb 1830
Ballinger Boyd to James Love, (D) 20 Sep 1830

Richard Ballinger to Richardson Adams, (D) 17 Apr 1828
William Dryden to Charles Gatliff, (D) 20 Sep 1830
Joel A. Watkins to John Heaton, (D) 21 Sep 1830
Edmond Steel and wife to Samuel Aegnour, (D) 15 Nov 1830
Michael Wampler to Christopher Wampl, (D) Sep 1829
Abraham Smith to John Smith, (D) 15 Oct 1830
Stanly Hatfield to Elisha Solomon, (D) 5 Jun 1825
Stanly Hatfield to Joseph Hatfield, (D) 15 Jun 1825
Joseph Hatfield to Stephen Hart, (D) 30 Dec 1830
Demcy White to Joseph J. Faris, (D) 23 Mar 1831
Joseph Gillis to Samuel Boyd, (D) 7 Apr 1829
James McGee and wife to Oliver Steel, (D) 3 Feb 1831
Andrew J. Margrov to Joseph J. Faris, (D) 6 Jun 1831
Francis Berry to James Mahan, (D) 4 Oct 1830
Moses Warner to Benjamin Siler, (D) 29 Jun 1831
Joseph J. Faris to Joseph L. Gatliff, (D) 9 Aug 1831
Joseph J. Faris to Joseph Duncan, (D) 9 Aug 1831
Joel Stow, Jr. to James Callivan, (D) 10 Sep 1831
Joel Stow, Sr. to James Callivan, (D) 10 Sep 1831
Abraham Stow and wife to James Callivan, (D) 10 Sep 1831
William Newton to Israel Newton, (D) 9 Mar 1825
Israel Newton to James Barnard, (D) 4 Oct 1831
Jesse Walker and wife to John C. Brown, (D) 17 Oct 1831
Thomas Faulkner to Jess Walker, (D) 17 Oct 1831
Joseph J. Faris to Levy Cox, (D) 31 Oct 1831
Hiram Litton to Jesse Walker, (D) 17 Oct 1831
Joseph J. Faris to David Evens, (D) 24 Dec 1831
John Sears to Samuel Cox, Sr., (D) 15 Feb 1819
Isaac Davis to Henry O. Middleto, (D) 2 Oct 1831
James Brown to Thomas McKehan, (D) 19 Mar 1832
Daniel Faulkner to Joseph J. Faris, (D) 8 Apr 1832
Joseph J. Faris to George Bowen, (D) 23 Mar 1832
Levi Cox and wife to Joseph J. Faris, (D) 23 Jan 1832
Middleton Meadors to Nicholas White, (D) 9 Jan 1832
Charles Gatliff to Joseph J. Faris, (D) 9 May 1832
Joseph J. Faris to Charles Gatliff, (D) 9 May 1832
Joseph J. Faris to Charles Gatliff, (D) 9 May 1832
Thomas Rockhold, to James G. McKinny, (D) 16 Apr 1832
John Mahan and wife to Robert Findley, (D) 26 May 1832
James Girton and wife to Joseph Sulivan, (D) 2 Mar 1832
William Bishop to Samuel Kerr, (D) 20 Feb 1831
George W. Craig to Isaac King, (D) 11 May 1832
Thomas Rockhold, to E.C. Faris, (D) 17 Sep 1832

Thomas Rockhold, to John Craig, (D) 19 Sep 1832
James Sears, Sr. to John Sears, (D) 9 Apr 1832
Caleb M. David to Joseph J. Faris, (D) 12 Nov 1832
John Craig and wife to Andw. Craig, (D) 31 Jan 1833
Harison White to Frank Ballenger, (D) 21 May 1833
Joel A. Watkins, to Cornelius Gatliff, (D) 24 Sep 1832
Nathan Cox and wife to William Johnson, (D) 5 Mar 1828
Hugh Cummins to William Johnson, (D) 15 Jan 1826
John Berry and wife to Joseph Johnson, (D) 28 Sep 1822
Joseph J. Faris to Cornelius Gatliff, (D) 21 May 1832
Joseph J. Faris to Francis Faulkner, (D) 12 Nov 1832
Patrick Burk and wife to John Hood, (D) 1 Jan 1833
Jesse Walker and wife to Jesse Austin, (D) 5 Jan 1833
Joseph Eve and wifeif to Leighton Ewel, (D) 16 Feb 1833
John Edwards and wife to James Cummins, (D) 12 Mar 1833
John C. Brown to ? (no date)
John C. Brown to ? (D) (no date)
James G. McKinny to Thomas Cox, (D) 7 Dec 1832
James Mahan and wife to William Anderson, (D) 10 Aug 1833
Daniel Lebo and wife to James Campbell, (D) 6 Dec 1832
James Mahan and wife to Stephen Hart, (D) 10 Aug 1833
Joseph Jonson to Isriel Mayfield, (D) 16 Sep 1833
Henry A. Early to William Stephenson, (D) 20 Aug 1833
William Anderson to Jacob Engle, (D) 9 Oct 1833
Henry P. Brown to Isaac King, (D) 18 Nov 1833
William Stephenson to William Morgan, (D) 23 Aug 1833
David Evans to Squire Gatliff, (D) 22 Dec 1833
Andrew Rods to Isaac King, (D) 25 Nov 1833
Leighton Ewel to Joseph Eve, (D) 5 Oct 1833
John Goodin to Joseph J. Faris, (D) 10 Nov 1833
Duncan Mcfarlan to Timothy Ward, (D) 24 Dec 1833
Rosanah Hackler to "my grand children, (D) 31 Jan 1834
Solomon Bunch to sons Jesse Bunch, (D) 18 Feb 1834
John G. Early to William Stephenson, (D) 3 Mar 1824
Augustus Tillison to James Hill, (D) 3 Oct 1833
Leah Sexon to Enoch Sexon, (D) 7 Dec 1833
Free Sexon to Enoch Sexon, (D) 7 Dec 1833
Free Sexon to Nathaniel Ward, (D) 17 Feb 1834
Charles Gatliff to G.M. Churchwell, (D) 10 Sep 1833
Ann Hatfield to Joseph Steel, (D) 31 Mar 1834
Elijah Girton to John Duncan, (D) 15 Mar 1819
Margaret Mulky to Clabourne Griffen, (D) 21 Jun 1819
Nathan Osburn to Ezekiel Baley, (D) 29 May 1819

Samuel Cox and wife to Milton Eve, (D)  20 Dec 1819
Thomas Rains to Viney Griffet, (D)  20 Apr 1819
Isam Wright and wife to Samuel Prewet, (D)  21 Feb 1820
Brook Smith to Joseph Smith, (D)  20 Mar 1820
Nathan Cox to Jesse Sears, (D)  7 Dec 1816
B.S. Parsonsto Milton Eve, (D)  7 Jun 1820
Nathan Osbourne to Angus Ross, (D)  29 May 1819
Benjamin S. Parsons to John F. Sharp, (D)  10 Jul 1820
Benj. S. Parsons to John F. Sharp, (D)  10 Jul 1820
Hugh Allison and wife to John Archer, (D)  21 ??? 1820
Aron Allen to Francis Faulkner, (D)  21 Aug 1820
Jacob Nicholson to Samuel Woosley, (D)  21 Aug 1820
Ezekial Baley to Daniel Neil, (D)  29 May 1819
Isham Meadors to Elisha Blevins, (D)  18 Sep 1820
William Ellison to William Richmond, (D)  21 May 1821
Henry Sanders to Sampson Wilder, (D)  25 Nov 1820
Martin Branham to William McCoy, (D)  6 Oct 1821
Martin Branham to James Falkner, (D)  6 Oct 1821
John Keer and wife to Elijah Smith, (D)  10 Dec 1821
Larkin Jones and wife to James Lawson, (D)  11 Jan 1822
Larkin Jones and wife to Danl Falkner, (D)  11 Jan 1822
Larkin Jones and wife to David Richmond, (D)  11 Jan 1822
J. D. Laughlin, to Jesse Walker, (D)  27 Apr 1821
Joseph D. Laughlin to Benj. S. Parsons, (D)  11 May 1822
Tolbert Adkin to Daniel Oak, (D)  20 Nov 1820
Saml. G. Boyers to Solomon Litton, (D)  19 Aug 1822
James Falkner to Robt. Haislip, (D)  18 Aug 1822
James Faulkner to Henry Haislip, (D)  18 Aug 1822
John F. Sharp to Sampson David, (D)  9 Sep 1822
George Smith to Hiram L. Faris, (D)  29 Nov 1822
Josiah Smith and wife to Isaac Criscelliou, (D)  16 Jun 1823
Samuel Sutton to John Heaton, (D)  18 Apr 1823
Hiram L. Faris to Robert Findly, (D)  19 May 1823
Viney Griffetts to William Briant, (D)  24 Aug 1822
John Richmond to Joshua Moses, (D)  17 Mar 1823
Charles Gatliff to William Manning, (D)  9 Oct 1823
John Richmond to Joshua Moses, (D)  30 Dec 1823
Archibald Jacoway to John Neil, (D)  8 Dec 1823
Elisha Blevins to William B. Creekm, (D)  22 Sep 1823
John Prewett and wife to Enoch Cox, (D)  19 Apr 1824
Samuel Cox, Sr. to Nathan Cox, (D)  22 Jun 1824
Samuel Cox, Sr. to Levi Cox, (D)  6 Jul 1824
Nathan Cox and wife to Joel A. Watkins, (D)  6 May 1824

B.S. Parsons to Walter R. Hunt, (D)   8 Nov 1820
Uriah Parks to Joseph J. Faris, (D)   21 Sep 1824
James Sams  and  wife to ??, (D)  2 Aug 1824
Thomas M. Meadows to William Smith, (D)   15 Nov 1824
Hiram L. Faris  to Joseph Sullivan, (D)   5 Jan 1825
Samuel G. Boyers to Francis Faulkner, (D)   6 Jan 1825
Hiram L. Faris  to Samuel G. Boyers, (D)   5 Jan 1825
William Sears  to Daniel Faulkner, (D)   19 Mar 1825
William Sears  to John Conner, (D)   19 Mar 1825
Solomon Reed to Daniel Faulkner, (D)   17 Apr 1825
Solomon Reed to Daniel Faulkner, (D)   17 Apr 1825
Joseph Eve to Joel Walker, (D)   19 Jul 1825
John Tye to Joshua Tye, (D)   6 Mar 1825
Hiram L. Faris  to Gabriel P. Shackl, (D)   22 Feb 1825
David Wilson, Sr. to Peter Wilson, (D)   5 Mar 1825
William Solomon to Tunstall Quarles, (D)   5 Sep 1825
Joel A. Watkins, to William Solomon, (D)   2 Sep 1825
Joel Walker  and  wife to Thomas Bird, (D)   23 Sep 1825
Samuel Petre  and  wife to Daniel Petre, (D)   Dec 1824
Nathan Cox  and  wife to Joseph J. Faris, (D)   9 Nov 1825
Nathan Cox  and  wife to Joseph D. Laughli, (D)   10 Nov 1825
Tunstall Quarles to Levi Cox, (D)   9 Oct 1825
James Faulkner, Sr., to William Smith, (D)   17 Oct 1825
Joseph D. Laughlin to Walter R. Hunt,, (D)   29 Oct 1825
Joshua Teague to John Siler, (D)   16 Dec 1820
Samuel Reed, assignee to John Siler, (D)   8 Dec 1825
Samuel Reed  and  wife to John Siler, (D)   8 Dec 1825
Jacob Day to Jesse Walker, (D)   16 Jan 1826
Heathon Hood, as to Samuel Reed, (D)   26 Nov 1822
Harton Hood  and  wife to Samuel Reed, (D)   26 Nov 1822
Henry Haislip  to Joel Haislip, (D)   14 Sep 1825
Joseph D. Laughlin to Andrew Craig, (D)   22 Feb 1826
Timothy Perkins to John Grubb As, (D)   23 Feb 1826
Hawthon Hood to Francis Faulkner, (D)   5 Aug 1822
Joseph D. Laughlin to Jesse Walker, (D)   22 Feb 1825
Joseph D. Laughlin to Timothy Perkins, (D)   22 Feb 1825
James Murphy  and  wife to James Blakely, (D)   24 Feb 1826
Joseph D. Laughlin to Francis Faulkner, (D)   22 Feb 1825
Daniel Oak  and  wife to Francis Faulkner, (D)   20 Mar 1826
Dant Hamblin  and  wife to Samuel Sutton, (D)   9 Jan 1826
Ambrose Garlan  to James Smith, (D)   1 May 1826
Isham Meadors  to Uriah Parks, (D)   18 Sep 1820
Viney Griffets to the heirs of John, (D)   13 Dec 1825

James Sulivan to Gallant Ranes, (D)  9 Aug 1826
James Blakely to Jesse Walker, (D)  14 Sep 1826
James Blakely to William Lay, (D)  14 Sep 1826
Joel A. Watkins to Nathan Cox, (D)  15 Jun 1826
Solomon Litton to Stephen Bolin, (D)  16 Dec 1826
Harvey B. Duncan to Thomas Prewett, (D)  11 Jan 1827
Hiram L. Faris to Squire Gatliff, (D)  19 Dec 1826
Henry H. Tye and wife to Reace Brummet, (D)  15 Apr 1826
Jesse Walker and wife to Elijah Smith, (D)  19 Dec 1826
Jesse Walker and wife to Hiram Litton, (D)  20 Dec 1826
Solomon Litton to John Cardwell, (D)  16 Dec 1826
Jesse Walker and wife to Hiram Litton, (D)  20 Dec 1826
Joel A. Watkins to Samuel G. Bayers, (D)  28 Dec 1826
Samuel G. Boyer to Joel A. Watkins, (D)  28 Dec 1826
G. P. Shackleford to Samuel Cox, (D)  27 Dec 1826
Jabes Perkins, Jr. to John Hichcock, (D)  25 Sep 1826
Peter Snider and wife to Cornelius Gatliff, (D)  5 Feb 1827
Thomas Flanigan to Jeremiah Adkins, (D)  3 Aug 1826
Francis Faulkner to Joel A. Watkins, (D)  5 Apr 1827
Timothy Perkins to Nathan Richardson, (D)  4 Jun 1827
Pleasant Meadows to James Tackett, (D)  7 Aug 1827
John Hichcock to Nathan Richardson, (D)  11 Oct 1826
Levi Cox and wifee to Nathan Cox, (D)  21 Aug 1826
Andrew Craig to Malin Bishop, (D)  18 Jun 1827
Joshua Tye and wife to Chelton Parton, (D)  25 Aug 1827
John Archer and wife to William Sears, (D)  17 Oct 1827
James Tackett to George Tackett o, (D)  18 Sep 1827
Claibourn Griffin to Daniel Oak, (D)  10 Feb 1827
George Tacket to William Davis, (D)  6 Oct 1827
Daniel Faulkner to Nathan Cox, (D)  9 Oct 1827
Thomas Adkins to Jeremiah Adkins, (D)  30 Jun 1827
Thomas Adkins, Sr. to Thomas Adkins, Jr., (D)  30 Jun 1827
Thomas Adkins to David Adkins, (D)  30 Jun 1827
Nathan Cox and wife to Daniel Faulkner, (D)  9 Oct 1827
Jesse Walker and wife to James K. Gallian, (D)  10 Nov 1827
William Sears to Clabourn Griffen, (D)  22 Dec 1827
Hiram L. Faris to Joseph L. Gatliff, (D)  11 Apr 1828
Milton Eve and wife to Daniel Faulkner, (D)  7 Apr 1828
William Bryant to Thomas Foley, (D)  11 Feb 1828
Thomas Foley and wife to Andrew Evans, (D)  16 Nov 1827
Francis Faulkner to Ruben Faulkner, (D)  28 Jan 1828
Tolbert Adkins to Christopher Natio, (D)  7 Feb 1828
John Heaton and wife to Thomas Foley, (D)  11 Feb 1828

Joel A. Watkins to John Ervin, (D)  5 May 1828
Joseph Gillis to Nathan Cox, (D)  8 Jul 1828
John Cordwell, to Nathan Cox, assi, (D)  23 Feb 1828
John Cordwell, to Nathan Cox, (D)  23 Feb 1828
James Murphy and wife to Henry Skean, (D)  23 Sep 1826
Hugh Johnson and wife to William Monhollan, (D)  1 Sep 1828
David Chitwood to Murry King, (D)  17 May 1828
Gallant Ranes to Elizabeth Ranes, (D)  19 Sep 1828
William Sears to Claiborne Griffen, (D)  7 Oct 1828
William Sears to Claibourn Griffen, (D)  7 Oct 1828
James Sulivan to Ephraim Rose, (D)  9 Oct 1828
Jesse Sears and wife to William Evans, (D)  13 Sep 1828
Francis Faulkner to George Faulkner, (D)  23 Jan 1828
Daniel Faulkner to Claibourn Griffen, (D)  9 Oct 1828
Joseph J. Faris to Joseph Sulivan, (D)  19 Dec 1828
Joseph D. Laughlin to Joseph J. Faris, (D)  6 Jan 1819
Thomas Prewit to Andrew Craig, (D)  4 Feb 1829
Andrew Craig to William T. Meadow, (D)  6 Apr 1829
John S. Wilson to James Wilson, (D)  9 Apr 1829
James Wilson to Stephen Bolen, (D)  22 Apr 1829
James Wilson and wife to Stephen Bolin, (D)  9 Apr 1829
Joel A. Watkins to Charles Gatliff, (D)  6 Apr 1829
Samuel Pruit and wife to Henry Haislip, (D)  6 Dec 1828
Thomas Mahan to Nathan Cox, (D)  17 Feb 1821
Ezekial Bealy to John Ross, (D)  29 Jan 1827
Ezekial Bealy to John Ross, (D)  27 Aug 1827
Francis Faulkner to Reuben Faulkner, (D)  29 Dec 1828
Esau Prewit and wife to Daniel Strunk, (D)  7 Jul 1829
Esau Prewit and wife to Daniel Strunk, (D)  7 Jul 1829
Esau Prewit and wife to James Murphy, (D)  7 Jul 1829
Esau Prewit and wife to Mark Jones, (D)  22 Jun 1829
Roads Nuckolls to William Hays, (D)  25 Jul 1829
Whitmell Stephens to Sherrard Cid, (D)  10 Jun 1829
Joel Hayslip and wife to William Lay, (D)  6 Oct 1829
Thomas Adkins, Jr. to Jesse Adkins, (D)  Sep 1829
Joel Haislip and wife to Bird Lay, (D)  6 Oct 1829
John Stanfield to Isom Jones, (D)  26 Sep 1829
Isaac Leabo and wife to John Richmond, (D)  5 Oct 1829
Joel Hayslip and wife to Moses Warner, (D)  6 Oct 1829
John Cardwell to Joseph J. Faris, (D)  25 Aug 1829
William T. Meders to Sherrod Stanfield, (D)  2 Nov 1829
Joel Hayslip and wife to Peter Purkins, (D)  6 Oct 1829
John Ervin to Joel A. Watkins, (D)  18 Oct 1829

Hirum Litton to Joseph J. Faris, (D)  8 Dec 1829
Milton Eve  and  wife to Frank Ballinger,, (D)  23 Dec 1829
Eleanor Cadwell, to Johnathan Lovet, (D)  2 Jan 1830
Milton Eve  and  wife to Andrew Craig, (D)  23 Dec 1829
Isham Jones Sr. to James Jones, (D)  10 Dec 1828
Walter D. Hunt  to  and w.  Craig, (D)  16 Jan 1830
James Murphy  and  wife to Jesse Blakly, (D)  1 Mar 1830
James Murphy  and  wife to Jessee Blakely, (D)  1 Mar 1830
Samuel Pruet  and  wife to John Ross, (D)  20 Dec 1828
James S. Sears  to Daniel  Anderson, (D)  5 Apr 1830
John Sears  and  wife to William Lambdon, (D)  17 Apr 1830
Amos Bennet  and  wife to Claibourn Rundles, (D)  8 May 1830
Joseph J. Faris to David Middleton, (D)  8 Jun 1830
Joseph J. Faris to Thomas Faulkner, (D)  8 Jun 1830
William Davis  to Thomas Cox, (D)  19 Nov 1830
Joshua Tye  and  wife to Reece Brumet, (D)  14 Jun 1830
Mark Jones  and  wife to William Murphy, (D)  1 Sep 1830
Claiborn Griffin to Daniel Faulkner, (D)  23 Sep 1830
David Middleton to Jesse Walker, (D)  23 Sep 1830
John Heaton  and  wife to James Veach, An, (D)  20 Sep 1830
Robert Findley  to Joseph Sulivan, (D)  27 Oct 1830
Richard Goggin  to Henry Roberts, (D)  24 Sep 1829
Joshua Tye  and  wife to Reace Brummet, (D)  14 Jun 1830
Leonard S. Swenk to William Riddle, (D)  20 Sep 1830
John Flanigan  to William Reynolds, (D)  27 Nov 1826
Stephen Blevins to James Richmond, (D)  18 Jun 1830
Stephen Blevins to James Richmond, (D)  18 Jun 1830
Reace Brumett  to John Tye, (D)  14 Jun 1830
David Girdner  to Jesse Adams, (D)  1 Apr 1830
Powel Sharp  and  wife to Jacob Sowder, (D)  1 Aug 1830
William Richmond to William Elison, (D)  25 Nov 1830
Moses Warner  and  wife to James Faulkner, (D)  27 May 1831
Mathias Reed  and  wife to James Sears, Jr., (D)  2 Oct 1830
Moses Warner  and  wife to John Hamblin, (D)  Jun 1831
Moses Warner  and  wife to John Hamblin, (D)  Jun 1831
Nathan Richeson to Sally Richmond, (D)  18 Jul 1831
William Richmond to Daniel Caddell, (D)  1 Sep 1830
Joseph J. Faris to Joseph L. Gatliff, (D)  9 Aug 1831
Joseph J. Faris to Joseph Duncan, (D)  9 Aug 1831
Pleasant Meadows to Allen Marler, (D)  12 Aug 1831
Benjamin Gilreath to Whitmill Stephens, (D)  16 July 183
William S. Porter to Lafayette Berry, (D)  13 Sep 1831
William Porterfield to Reuben Meadows, (D)  21 Sep 1831

Jesse Walker and wife to John C. Brown, (D) 17 Oct 1831
Thomas Faulkner to Jess Walker, (D) 17 Oct 1831
Joseph J. Faris to Levy Cox Will, (D) 31 Oct 1831
Hiram Litton to Jesse Walker, (D) 17 Oct 1831
Hiram Litton to Jesse Walker, (D) 31 Oct 1831
Joseph Screach to Bri and Patric, (D) 29 Jan 1831
Joseph J. Faris to David Evens, (D) 24 Dec 1831
John Sears to Jesse Sears, (D) 9 Jan 1831
Joseph J. Faris to James T. Curd, (D) 24 Jan 1832
Daniel Faulkner to Joseph J. Faris, (D) 8 Apr 1832
Levi Cox and wife to Joseph J. Faris, (D) 23 Jan 1832
Levi Cox and wife to Joseph J. Faris, (D) 23 Jan 1832
Joseph Screech to Simon Jones, (D) 3 Oct 1831
Isaac Davis to William Penington, (D) 18 Feb 1832
Isaac Davis to Jesse Walker, (D) 18 Feb 1832
Isaac Davis to Joel A. Watkins, (D) 22 Feb 1832
Isaac Davis to William Beams, (D) 22 Feb 1832
Isaac Davis to Isaiah Bird, (D) 18 Feb 1832
Isaac Davis to Levi Cox, (D) 29 Feb 1832
Isaac Davis to Joseph J. Faris, (D) 2 Mar 1832
Isaac Davis to Isam Jones, (D) 5 Mar 1832
Isaac Davis to Absalom Cox, (D) 18 Feb 1832
David Wood to Jeriah Wood, (D) 10 Dec 1831
John Ross and wife to Elijah Stephens, (D) 28 July 183
Samuel Ross and wife to James Angel, (D) 22 Oct 1831
Isaac Davis to James Cutbirth, (D) 18 Feb 1832
Joseph J. Faris to Levi Cox, (D) 24 May 1832
Joseph J. Faris to Richard Potter, (D) 24 May 1832
Thomas Rockhold to James G. McKinny, (D) 16 Apr 1832
Thomas Rockhold to James G. McKinny, (D) 16 Apr 1832
Isaac Davis to William Skean, (D) 8 May 1832
Isam Jones and wife to Thomas Adkins, (D) 31 Mar 1832
Isaac Davis to William Bodkin, (D) 25 Feb 1832
John Moses and wife to Robert Thomas, (D) 19 Jun 1832
Benjamin Richards to John Prewit, (D) 14 Jul 1832
Daniel Strunk to John Oliver, (D) 14 Jul 1832
Isaac Davis to Frederick Snyder, (D) 18 Feb 1832
Stephen Bolin to James Lawson, (D) 30 Jul 1832
Stephen Bolin to Nathan Lawson, (D) 30 Jul 1832
James Girton and wife to Jesse Sears, (D) 11 Aug 1832
Jesse Sears and wife to William Evans, (D) 18 Aug 1832
Jesse Sears and wife to Jesse Powers, (D) 15 Aug 1832
Jesse Sears and wife to William Harp, (D) 15 Aug 1832

Jesse Sears and wife to Abraham Stoe, (D) 17 Aug 1832
Thomas Rockhold, to John Craig, (D) 19 Sep 1832
Caleb M. David to Joseph J. Faris, (D) 12 Nov 1832
John Craig and wife to Andw. Craig, (D) 31 Jan 1833
Joel A. Watkins to Cornelius Gatliff, (D) 24 Sep 1832
Nathan Cox and wife to William Johnson, (D) 5 Mar 1828
Isaac Davis to Samuel Cox, (D) 5 Mar 1832
James Cutbirth to Joseph Duncan, (D) 9 Jul 1833
Sherard Kidd and wife to James Kerrell, (D) 11 Oct 1832
Joseph J. Faris to Cornelius Gatliff, (D) 21 May 1832
Joseph J. Faris to Francis Faulkner, (D) 12 Nov 1832
James Veach and wife to Johnithan Foley, (D) 31 Dec 1832
Joshua Bird and wife to John Cox, (D) 3 Mar 1833
Joel A. Watkins to Cornelius Gatliff, (D) 19 Sep 1832
Hiram J. Faulkner to Nathan Cox, (D) 21 Mar 1833
Francis Faulkner to Hiram Faulkner, (D) 12 Aug 1832
Richard Potter to William Lawson, (D) 8 Jun 1833
Richard White to Simon Jones, (D) 7 Aug 1833
Richard Potter to Charles Potter, (D) 8 Jun 1833
James G. McKinny to Thomas Cox, Nat, (D) 7 Dec 1832
William Mannon to Andrew Patrick, (D) 7 Aug 1833
Absolam Cox and wife to Jeremiah Anderson, (D) 20 Sep 1833
Henry A. Early to William Stephenson, (D) 20 Aug 1833
Jesse Perkins to Joseph Duncan, (D) 7 Sep 1833
Isaac Sexson and wife to James Sears Jr., (D) 9 Nov 1833
John Polly to William Polly, (D) 22 Aug 1833
Sampson Wilder to Jesse Wilder, (D) 7 Sep 1833
Jesse Perkinswi to heirs John Dun, (D) 7 Sep 1833
Daniel Richardson to Nathan Richarson, (D) 25 Dec 1833
Clabrin Griffin to Daniel Faulkner, (D) 2 Mar 1833
Samson Wilder to William Adams, (D) 20 Nov 1833
Claborn Reynolds to Jesse Powers, (D) 16 Sep 1833
Sherard Standfield to James Smith ,(D) 16 Mar 1833
Jesse Adkins and wife to Stephen Bolin, (D) 29 Oct 1833
James Harp and wife to Daniel Hamblin, (D) 12 Oct 1833
Wilson Oliver to John Lovet, (D) 29 Jan 1833
John Richardson to John C. Brown, (D) 8 Oct 1833
John Richardson to John C. Brown, (D) 8 Oct 1833
Isaac Davis to Elizabeth Allison, (D) 25 Feb 1832
Reuben Faulkner to George Faulkner, (D) 31 Mar 1832
Brooks Smith and wife to Alexander Campbell, (D) 12 Sep 1833
Joshua Teague to Jacob Nicholson, (D) 27 Jul 1833
Robert Thomas to Andrew Penington, (D) 17 Mar 1834

Daniel Lebo to Daniel Taylor, (D)  30 Sep 1833
Isaac Davis to Mary Bird, (D)  23 Feb 1832
Thomas Bird and wife to Stephen Cox, (D)  26 Sep 1833
Rachel Mayfield to Hiram Litton, (D)  1 Nov 1833
Silas Teague and wife to Jacob Nicholson, (D)  7 Mar 1833
William C. Martin to Jesse Powers, (D)  22 Feb 1834
Isaac Smith and wife to Joseph Richmond, (D)  30 Sep 1833

Woodward County, Kentucky, 1800 Tax List
Jonathan Abbay, Larkin Abbet, Robert Abbet, William Abbet, William
Adams, Elizabeth Addams, Edwin Alexander, Robert Alexander, Hugh
Allen, John Allen, David Allin, Francis Allin, Henry Allison, William
Alloway, John Anderson, Thomas Anderson, William Anderson,
James Annold, John Armstrong, John Arnold, Lewis Arnold, John
Ashford, Thomas Ashford, Joel Ashley, Henry Atkinson, William
Atwood, Jr., William Atwood, Sr., Ann Aynes, John Ayres, Benjamin
Babb, George Bain, Johnson Ballard, Nathan Bardune, William Barns,
Thomas Bartlett, Thomas Bates, Asael Battleton, Adam Beatty, Julianna
Beavis, Catharine Beazley, Edmund Beazley, Philip Beazley, Robert
Beazley, Thomas Bell, John Bently, Benjamin Berry, Henry Berry,
Samuel Berry, Absolam Binbridge, Robert Black, George Blackburn,
Isiah Blackford, Eli Blades, John Blakemore, James Blankenship, Lewis
Blankenship, James Blanton, John Blanton, John Blanton, Thomas
Blanton, Jr., Thomas Blanton, Sr., Larkin Bohanan, Elliott Bohanon,
John Bohanon, Joseph Bonderant, Josiah Boone, Benjamin Boston,
James Bowdery, Lewis Bowdery, William Bowland, Charles Bowles,
Jane Bowles, Harman Bowmar, Robert Bowmar, William Bridgford,
Leonard Brisby, Ezekiel Brisco, James Bristow, George Brooke, Samuel
Brooking, Dawson Brown, Elliott Brown, George Brown, John Brown,
Preston Brown, Wilson Brown, Daniel Brumly, Peter Bryant, Philip
Buchannon, Alexander Buckhannon, William Buckley, Thomas Bullock,
Benjamin Burbridge, Elijah Burbridge, Susanna Byers, Allen Caldwell,
Dan Caldwell, Henry Caldwell, James Caldwell, John Calhoon, Jr., John
Calhoon, Sr., Marquis Calms, George Campbell, Gilbert Campbell,
Joanna Campbell, Robert Campbell, John Canady, Joseph Canady,
Martha Canady, Archibald Cannon, Reubin Cannon, Jacob Caplinger,
William Carlan, George Carlisle, Edward Carr, Thomas Carson,
Richard Case, Lewis Castleman, Edward Cathers, Reubin Cave, Richard
Cave, John A. Chapman, John A. Chapman, Sally Chapman, Jonas
Christman, John Christopher, William Christopher, Thomas Claggett,
Easton Cark, Joshua Claxton, Michael Cliford, John Clinton, George
Cloak, Jacob Cochron, Richard Cole, Richard Cole, Sr., James
Coleman, Thomas Coleman, Jeremiah Collins, Joel Collins, John

Collins, Joseph Collins, John Cook, George Cotter, John Cotton, William Coulson, Daniel Covenhoven, Peter Covenhoven, Rachel Covenhoven, James Cox, Thomas Cox, Lewis Craig, Lewis Craig, John Crittenden, Joshua Cromwell, Bela Cropper, James Cropper, Noble Cropper, Isaac Crutcher, Joseph Culbertson, Hugh Cunningham, Thomas Cunningham, John Curry, Abraham Dale, Ailsey Dale, George Dale, Jr., George Dale, Sr., Ignatius Dale, Robert Dale, Roley Dale, William Dale, William Daniel, Aaron Darnell, Joseph Darnell, Lewis Darnell, Ely Davis, Henry Davis, John Davis, Richard Davis, Solomon Davis, Thomas Davis, William Davis, George Dawkins, John Dawkins, Sr., John Dawson, Richard Dawson, William Dawson, Nathan Dedman, Catharine Derringer, Joseph Derringer, Michael Derringer, James Dickey, James Dickey, Jr., John Dickey, Michael Dickey, William Dickinson, Joseph Dictum, Richard Dictum, Thomas Donnell, James Dougherty, Hezekiah Douglass, Elijah Driskell, Priscilla Driskell, Alexander Dunlap, James Dupuy, Joel Dupuy, John Dupuy, Jr., John Dupuy, Sr., George Duvall, Thomas Duvall, John Eaton, Joseph Eaton, Joseph Edrington, Edmond Edwards, John Edwards, Joseph Edwards, Joseph Edwards, Sr., Mildred Edwards, Moses Edwards, Simeon Edwards, Isiah Elkin, Maryan Elkin, John Elliott, Robert Elliott, William Elliott, Jesse Ellis, Sr., Jonathan Ellis, Leonard Ellis, William Ellis, Sr., Robert Elliston, George Eplear, Samuel Evans, Thornton Farrow, John I. Felix, Hugh Ferguson, William Filson, William Finch, John Finn, James Finnie, John Finnie, Daniel Fitzgerald, Leonard Fleming, Spencer Fletcher, William Florence, Levy Floyd, William Floyd, Obediah Fogg, Absalom Ford, James Ford, John Ford, Richard Fox, George Francisco, John Francisco, Jacob Frowman, John Frowner, Stephen Fur, Abner Gaines, Everitt Galloway, James Garner, James Garnett, William Garnett, William Garrett, Hugh Garrott, Nicholas Gassaway, Charles Gatewood, James Gatewood, Jr., John Gatewood, Sr., John Gay, Robert Gay, Robert Gay, Joseph George, Edward Gibbany, John Gibbs, Spencer Gill, Jr., Spencer Gill, Sr., Tyre Glenn, William Glenn, Thomas J. Glover, Vivion Goodloe, Jesse Grady, Benjamin Graves, John Graves, Jonathan Gray, Ely Green, Paul Green, William Green, Abram Gregory, Stephen Gregory, George Grimes, Robert Groom, Andrew Gudshall, Alexander Guthery, Benjamin Guthery, Thomas Guthrie, Jr., Thomas Guthrie, Sr., John Gwin, Jonathan Gwin, Moses Gwin, Robert Gwin, Jr., Robert Gwin, Sr., James Halbert, Andrew Hamilton, John Hamilton, John Hamilton, William Hamilton, John Hancock, Obediah Hancock, Simon Hancock, Tene Hancock, William Hancock, Abner Hanks, John Hanks, David Hannah, Martin Hardin, James Harlin, William Harman, Adam Harper, George Harper, Henry Harper, Jacob Harper, Jacob Harper, Sr., John Harper, Nicholas Harper,

William Harper, David Harris, John Harris, Nathaniel Harris, Randolph Harris, Davis Harrison, Henry Harrison, Jeremiah Harrison, Luke Harrison, Robert Harrison, Moses Hawkins, William Hawkins, Henry H. Hazard, John Hazard, Grace Head, Edward Hearn, Jacob Hearn, Jacob Hearn, Sr., Reuben Hedger, William Hedger, Jonathan Hicklin, Thomas Hicklin, Harriss Hicks, William Hicks, Lewis Hieatt, Thomas Hill, Luke Hilton, Abraham Himpenstall, Thomas Hinton, Thomas Hinton, Sr., Charles Hiter, James Hiter, Sr., John Hitt, James Hoge, Daniel Holeman, Edward Holeman, Edward Holeman, Sr., Isaac Holeman, James Holeman, Jane Holeman, Edward Holland, John Hollingsworth, George Holloway, Hugh Holmes, James Holmes, William Hopkins, Elijah Hotton, Isaac Howard, James Howard, Leroy Howard, Thomas Howard, John Hudson, Roley Hudson, John Hufford, Rowlin Hughes, John Hunt, Jr., John R. Hutcherson, James Hutcheson, William Hyter, Robert Irwin, William Irwin, John Jack, Francis Jackson, John Jackson, Ann James, Samuel January, Francis Johnson, William Johnson, Elizabeth Johnston, Robert Johnston, John Jones, Thomas Jones, Uriah Jones, John Jouitt, Alexander Keeth, Robert King, Archibald Kinkead, Guy Kinkead, James Kinkead, John Kinkead, William Kinkead, Elliott Kirtley, Samuel Kyle, Daniel Lamkin, Edward Lane, Felix Lane, Robert Langford, Francis W. Lay, Henry Lee, John Lee, Leonard E. Leland, John Lever, Fielding Lewis, William Lewis, James Ligget, William Lisenby, David Lock, Robert Lockridge, Burton Loftiss, Garrard Long, James Long, John Long, Mary Long, Alexander Loughery, Abram Lowderback, Henry Lurton, William Lurton, Adam Lynn, Thomas Maddux, William Maddux, William Maham, Alexander Major, John Malone, James Mann, Samuel Mansfield, John Marshall, Lewis Marshall, William Marshall, Henry Martin, James Martin, John Martin, Samuel Martin, William Martin, James Matthews, James McBride, Hugh McCammon, Joseph McClane, Samuel McClane, John McClary, Alexander McClure, Samuel McClure, James McConnell, William McCoy, Virgil McCrackin, Elizabeth McCrakin, Hugh McCrary, William McCuddy, Jr., William McCuddy, Sr., Archibald McCulloh, John McCumsey, William McCumsey, Charles McDonald, George McDonnel, James McDowell, Darby McGannon, Patrick McGowan, John McGuier, Thomas McIlroy, Moses McIlvain, Robert McKee, Daniel McKinny, Andrew McKnight, John McQuade, Thomas McQuady, Jr., James Meek, Archibald Milam, Enos Miles, Isaac Miles, Jacob Millar, Joseph Minter, Charles Mitchel, Frederick Mitchel, George Mitchel, John Mitchel, Michael Mitchel, Robert Mitchel, Rosanna Mitchel, Thomas Mitchel, James Mitchell, Dudley Mitchum, Dudly Mitchum, George Moffitt, James Moffitt, John Moffitt, Robert Moffitt, William Monro, Benjamin Moore, Francis Moore, James

Moore, John Moore, William Moore, William F. Moore, John Morgan, Morgan Morgan, William Morris, Jeremiah Morton, John Morton, Edward Mosby, John Mosby, Nicholas Mosby, John Moss, Jr., John Moss, Sr., William Moss, Amos Mounts, John Mullikin, Jesse Musick, John Musie, George Muter, Christian Myers, George W. New, James Norris, Gabriel Nourse, Alexander O'Bannon, John O'Bannon, William O'Bannon, Jabez Ozburn, William Page, Isaac Palmer, James Patterson, John Paul, Charles F. Payne, George Payton, Francis F. Peart, Elijah Peppers, Elijah Perry, Lewis Perry, Sameul Perry, Thomas Perry, Jacob Peter, James Peters, Nimrod Peters, Charles Peyton, Ransford Peyton, Jacob Philips, John Philips, William Phillips, Israel Pierson, Fielding Pilcher, Richard Pitman, William Poak, William Poindexter, James Porter, Susanna Porter, William Porter, Charles Pouly, William Powel, James Powers, Mary Praul, Daniel Preston, Isaac Price, John Pry, Joseph Pryer, Samule Pryer, George Puff, William Pulham, Tunstall Quarles, Charles Railey, Isham Railey, R and olph Railey, Thomas Railey, William Railey, James Rainey, John Ramsay, Seth Ramsey, Mary Rankin, Thomas Rankin, Joseph Ransford, Dennis Rardin, Samuel Ratcliff, Hankinson Read, Berry Rearden, Joseph Rearden, Henry Reardon, John Redd, Mordecai Redd, Thomas Redd, Armistead Reding, Ely Reding, Jesse King Redman, John Reed, Sarah Reeves, William Reid, Robert Render, James Rennick, Thomas Reynolds, William Rice, Rezin Rickets, Abram Ritter, Joseph Ritter, John Robarts, Spencer Robinson, Turner Rogers, Peter Romine, Rodeham Rout, David Rowlin, Sr., Richard Rowlin, Abner Rucker, Ahmend Rucker, Ephraim Rucker, James Rucker, James Rucker, Sr., Jeremiah Rucker, John Rucker, Jr., John Rucker, Sr., Cornelius Ruddell, Stephen Ruddell, Isaac Ruddle, Peter G. Runyan, Reubin Runyan, Alice Sample, Hannah Sample, William Sample, Lucy Samuel, Larkin Sandidge, John Scarce, William Scarce, Archelous Scott, Charles Scott, Fanney Scott, John Scott, Moses Scott, William Scott, Robert Scrogin, David Searce, James Searce, Sr., John Searce, Robert Searce, William Searce, Edmund Searcy, John Searcy, Reubin Searcy, Richard Searcy, John Sellars, Joseph Shannon, Robert Shannon, Armistead Sharp, Judith Sharp, James Shaw, John Shaw, William Shaw, William Sheets, John Shepherd, William Shepherd, Richard Ship, Richard Shipp, Jr., Peyton Short, Henry Shouse, Joseph Shropshire, Samuel Shroutt, John Simonis, William Simonis, John Sims, Jeconias Singleton, Pleuright Sisk, Samuel Small, Elijah Smith, Henry Smith, Humphrey Smith, Joel Smith, John Smith, John T. Smith, William Smith, Reubin Smythey, Benjamin Snelling, Elizabeth Snelling, Daniel Spangler, Martin Sparks, William Spaulden, James Spilman, James Standford, James Stapp, Harvey Starlings, Frederick Starn, David Steele, Sr., Samuel Steele, Thomas

Steele, William Steele, William Stephenson, Benjamin Stevenson, Isaac
Stevenson, James Stevenson, John Stevenson, Samuel Stevenson,
William Stevenson, Robert Stewart, John Stinson, Sebastian Stone,
Thomas Stone, Voluntine Stoner, John Story, Elijah Stout, Elijah
Stout, Jr., James Stout, John W. Stoutt, Nehemiah Stoutt, Peter Stoutt,
William Stroher, Jacob Stucker, John Stucker, Michael Stucker, Lewis
Sublett, Mary Sullenger, Lewis Sullivan, Jesse Suter, John Suter, Thomas
as Suter, William Suter, John Tanner, Aaron Taurence, Robert Tawbert,
bert, Alexander Taylor, Argoile Taylor, Chapman Taylor, Henry Taylor,
John Taylor, Joseph Taylor, Richard Taylor, Robert Taylor, William
Taylor, Zachariah Taylor, Richard M. Thomas, Tapley Thomas, Tapley
Thomas, Nathaniel Thompson, Anthony Thomson, David Thomson,
Susanna Thomson, William T. Thomson, Moses Tibbs, William Tillory,
Elijah Tinder, James Tinder, Lewis Todd, William Todd, James Torbet,
Edward Trabue, James Trimble, William Trousdale, Henry Tucker,
Ellinder Tull, Joshua Tull, Samuel Tull, Alexander Turner, Arthur
Turner, Branham Turner, Joseph Turner, George Turpin, George
Twyman, Reubin Twyman, John Usleton, Benjamin Utterback, Jacob
Utterback, Lewis Utterback, Martin Utterback, Nimrod Utterback, Philip
Varvel, David Vaughan, Edmund Vaughan, John Vaughn, William
Vawter, Daniel Veach, Jr., Daniel Veach, Sr., James Vincin, Augustine
Violet, Hanson Violet, Thomas Violet, William Violet, Joseph Walden,
Daniel Walker, Henry Walker, Jane Walker, John Walker, Margaret
Walker, Richard Walker, Samuel Walker, William Walker, Caleb
Wallace, Joseph Wallace, Patrick Wallace, William Warren, Walkin
Warwick, Benjamin Watkins, Henry Watkins, John Watkins, Joseph
Watkins, Philip Watkins, Nathan Watson, Jeremiah Weaver, Tilman
Weaver, Aaron Webb, Jr., Aaron Webb, Sr., William Webb, Theodore
Welmon, Charles Wendling, John West, Daniel White, John White,
Robert White, John Whiteker, William Whitington, Littleton Whittington,
ton, James Wickersham, Ekillis Wilhite, John Wilhite, Charles Wilkins,
Stewart Wilkins, Daley Williams, David Williams, John Williams, John
F. Williams, John T. F. Williams, Josiah Williams, William Williams,
Absolam Wilson, Benjamin Wilson, David Wilson, Isaac Wilson, James
Wilson, Jeremiah Wilson, John Wilson, Joseph Wilson, Joshua Wilson,
Thomas Wilson, Peter Winebriner, Daniel Wolcoxon, David Woodson,
Elisha Wooldridge, Josiah Wooldridge, William Woolfaulk, Sowel
Woolfolk, Tho.Worland, Jas. Wright, Roert Yancy, John Young, Leonard
Young, Lewis Young, Rich. Young, Wm. Young, Wm. Young, Sr.

Hardin County, Kentucky, White Mills Baptist Church Cemetery.

| Name | Birth | Death |
|---|---|---|
| Mary W. Anderson | Jan. 12, 1803 | Feb. 13, 1863 |

| Name | Birth | Death |
|---|---|---|
| Dr. Robert L. Ashlock | Aug. 1, 1824 | Jun. 26, 1878 |
| M. G. Ashlock | Nov. 1, 1832 | May 1, 1891 |
| Thomas Daugherty | Jul. 11, 1836 | Apr. 30, 1908 |
| Mary Jane Daugherty | Nov. 22, 1838 | Feb. 13, 1890 |
| George H. Cook | Apr. 26, 1799 | Mar. 27, 1876 |
| Houson Duncan | Feb. 27, 1815 | Jan. 27, 1890 |
| Lucretia F. Duncan | Nov. 19, 1818 | Mar. 20, 1899 |
| Adam R. Graham | Mar. 4, 1804 | Sep. 19, 1876 |
| Susan M. Graham | May 4, 1820 | Sep. 10, 1891 |
| Sarah Greenwalt | 1781 | 1852 |
| William K. Hart | Oct. 11, 1818 | Apr. 7, 1874 |
| Malem Hatfield | Jan. 31, 1819 | May 29, 1890 |
| Susannah Hayden (Age: 78Y) | | 185 (?) |
| William Hogan | Jul. 21, 1814 | Apr. 23, 1856 |
| Sarah Hoover | Aug. 8, 1824 | Jul. 10, 1894 |
| William Littrell | Mar. 18, 1821 | Nov. 13, 1904 |
| Sophronia Catherine Littrell | Mar. 9, 1839 | Mar. 1, 1889 |
| James Mallen | Oct. 7, 1838 | Mar. 16, 1887 |
| Eliza Morrison | Aug. 31, 1831 | Aug. 15, 1902 |
| William C. Morrison | Jul. 29, 1825 | Jul. 4, 1887 |
| Mary Scott Nelson | Nov. 26, 1839 | Aug/ 21, 1872 |
| Henry Payne | Nov. 13, 1811 | Oct. 3, 1893 |
| Mahala J. Payne | Mar. 10, 1817 | Feb. 21, 1885 |
| Thomas Redman | Nov. 16, 1791 | Dec. 16, 1877 |
| Joseph Duncan Richardson | 1833 | 1922 |
| Samuel Scott | Feb. 23, 1798 | Mar. 16, 1873 |
| Lucretia Ellen Duncan Scott | May 27, 1838 | Dec. 2, 1876 |
| Bailey S. Tabb | Oct. 12, 1834 | Jan. 3, 1917 |
| Susan D. Tabb | Jul. 8, 1821 | Nov. 18, 1916 |
| Lydia Ann Taylor | Oct. 8, 1820 | Mar. 25, 1875 |
| Moses Terry | Jan. 26, 1817 | Jan. 27, 1879 |
| Harriett S. Terry | Dec. 6, 1828 | Sep. 23, 1862 |
| Barbara Terry | Nov. 9, 1815 | Jan. 30, 1869 |
| Eldridge Ventress | 1834 | 1904 |
| Sophronia Ventress | Jul. 22, 1837 | May 3, 1910 |
| Martin E. White | 1833 | 1906 |
| J. P. Woolridge | 1831 | 1909 |
| Rhoda A. Woolridge | 1838 | --- |
| D. F. Wortham | Aug. 20, 1818 | Jul. 11, 1898 |
| Susan Wortham | Oct. 6, 1823 | Apr. 7, 1903 |

| Name | Birth | Death |
|------|-------|-------|
| Mary Wortham | 1824 | 1909 |

Adair County, Kentucky, Death Register.

Aaron (Slave): (D)Apr. 24,1857, (BP) Unknown, (A) 65, (B)1792ca, (CMTS) No Owner Given

Elizabeth Aaron: (D) Aug. 25,1852, (BP) Adair Co., KY, (A) 47, (B)1805ca, (CMTS) No Parents Given

Margaret Allen: (D) Mar. 30,1858, (BP) Pulaski Co., KY, (A) 42, (B)1816ca, (CMTS) John and Ann Mcclister

Robert Anderson: (D)Dec. 22,1858, (BP) Virginia, (A) 65, (B)1793ca, (CMTS)Verdman and Verney Anderson

Anne (Slave): (D) Feb., 1858, (BP) Butler's Branch, (A)19, (B)1839ca, (CMTS) Owner: Winfield Squires

Anthony (Slave): (D) Sep.,1859, (BP) Unknown, (A) 19, (B)1840ca, (Cmts) Owner: Alben Bradshaw

Prudence Mantle: (D) Nov. 11,1858, (BP) Russell Co., Ky, (A) 23, (B)1835ca, (Cmts) Milton and Jane Woldord

Armenius (Slave) : (D) May 18,1858, (BP) Glens Fork, (A) 45, (B)1813ca, (Cmts) Owner: William Waggener

Ceny Autle: (D) Jul. 2,1859, (BP) Dry Fork, (A) 71, (B)1788ca, (Cmts) Henry and Polly Autle

Avis (Slave): (D) Dec.,1852, (BP) Virginia, (A) 48, (B)1804ca, (Cmts) Owner: Eli Wheat

Elizabeth Bault: (D) Mar. 18,1853, (BP) Germany, (A) 75, (B)1778ca, (Cmts) John and Catherine Bault

Rial D. Bell. (D) Aug. 16,1858, (BP) Casey Creek, (A) 21, (B)1837ca, (Cmts) Jacob and Catherine Bell

Walker J. Blades: (D) Nov. 23,1859, (BP) Virginia, (A) 72, (B)1787ca, (Cmts) Johnson Blades

George W. Blair: (D) May 19,1858, (BP) Harrold Fork, (A) 26, (B) 1832ca, (Cmts) William and Lucy Blair

Benjamin Bomer: (D) Jul. 25,1858, (BP) Virginia, (A) 83, (B)1775ca, (Cmts) Robert and Mary Bomer

Gideon Bradshaw: (D) Sep. 8,1856, (BP) Adair Co., Ky, (A) 24, (B) 1832ca, (Cmts) Gideon and Mar y Bradshaw

??? Breeding : (D) Jul. 9,1853, (BP) Adair Co., Ky, (A) 35, (B)1818ca, (Cmts) Robert Leftwich

Elizabeth Breeding: (D) Sep. 26,1859, (BP) Sulphur Fork, (A) 22, (B) 1837ca, (Cmts) Obediah and Ann Crimer

George Breeding: (D) May 29,1859, (BP) Virginia, (A) 86, (B) 1773ca, (Cmts) George and Rachel Breeding

John H. Breeding: (D) Aug. 25,1853, (BP) Virginia, (A) 81, (B) 1772ca,

(Cmts) John Breeding

Martha A. Breeding: (D) Jan. 28,1858, (BP) Virginia, (A) 36, (B) 1822ca, (Cmts) Robert and Catherine Leftwich

Rhody Bryant: (D) Apr. 22,1858, (BP) French River, Tn, (A) 59, (B) 1799ca, (Cmts) JoSeph and Frances Hardon

Elizabeth Burton: (D) Apr. 5,1858, (BP) Green River, (A) 38, (B) 1820ca, (Cmts) John and Mary Harmon

Elizabeth B. Butler: (D) Aug. 22,1854, (BP) Adair Co., Ky, (A) 41, (B) 1813ca, (Cmts) Zidner and M. Butler

Ann Caldwell: (D) Aug. 8,1856, (BP) Adair Co., Ky, (A) 24, (B) 1832ca, (Cmts) Ann Workman

Wm. Caldwell: (D) Jan. 10,1854, (BP) Virginia, (A) 77, (B) 1777ca, (Cmts) John Caldwell

Caroline (Slave): (D) Mar., 1859, (BP) Virginia, (A) 55, (B) 1804ca, (Cmts) Owner: David Griffith

Caroline (Slave): (D) No Date, (BP) Unknown, (A) 35, (B)?, (Cmts) Owner: Samuel Bridgewater

Catherine (Slave): (D) Jan.,1854, (BP) Adair Co., Ky, (A) 50, (B) 1804ca, (Cmts) Owner: R. W. McWhorter

Barnett Chapman: (D) Oct. 2,1858, (BP) Lincoln Co., Ky, (A) 39, (B) 1819ca, (Cmts) James and Mary Chapmancharles

Martha Jane Coats: (D) Nov. 14,1852, (BP) Adair Co., Ky, (A) 21, (B) 1831ca, (Cmts) Zidner and Ann Coffey

George W. Coffee: (D) Aug. 28,1856, (BP) Adair Co., Ky, (A) 55, (B) 1801ca, (Cmts) No Parents Given

Mary Collison: (D) Sep. 8,1852, (BP) Adair Co., Ky, (A) 37, (B) 1815ca, (Cmts) Parents Unknown

Polly Compton: (D) Jan. 15,1857, (BP) Adair Co., Ky, (A) 65, (B) 1792ca, (Cmts) Thomas Kelsoe

Richard Condiff: (D) Nov. 12,1854, (BP) Adair Co., Ky, (A) 20, (B) 1834ca, (Cmts) G. W. and M. Cundiff

Dorinda Cooksey: (D) Feb. 10,1853, (BP) Virginia, (A) 53, (B) 1800ca, (Cmts) No Parents Given

Melinda Coomer: (D) Jan. 29,1859, (BP) North Carolina, (A) 42, (B) 1817ca, (Cmts) William and Nancy Gregory

James Cox: (D) Aug. 4, 1853, (BP) Adair Co., Ky, (A) 78, (B) 1775ca, (Cmts) Parents Unknown

Martha Cundiff: (D) Jun. 1,1859, (BP) Green River, (A) 43, (B) 1816ca, (Cmts) John and Sally Damron

Richard Cundiff: (D) Nov. 12,1854, (BP) Adair Co., Ky, (A) 21, (B) 1833ca, (Cmts) G. W. and M. Cundiff

Kissiah Curry: (D) Jun. 16,1858, (BP) Sulphur Fork, (A) 56, (B) 1802ca, (Cmts) John and Polly Judd

Rebecca J. Dehoney: (D) Apr. ,1858, (BP) Adair Co., Ky, (A) 19, (B)
    1839ca, (Cmts) Paten and Polley Dehoney
Louisa Demurnbrim: (D) Aug. 19,1852, (BP) Adair Co., Ky, (A) 17, (B)
    1835ca, (Cmts) Jno. F. and Sallie Demurnbrim
Depha (Slave) : (D) Sep. 27,1856, (BP) Adair Co., Ky, (A) 30, (B) 1826ca,
    (Cmts) Owner: John Hendrickson
Rebecca Diddle: (D) Aug. 25,1852, (BP) Adair Co., Ky, (A) 65, (B)
    1787ca, (Cmts) Parents Unknown
Thomas Dohoney: (D) Jun. 18,1859, (BP) Adams Creek, (A) 67, (B)
    1792ca, (Cmts) Rodes and Jane Dohoney
John B. Dooley: (D) Nov., 1859, (BP) Alabama, (A) 56, (B)1803ca,
    (Cmts) William and Nancy Dooley
Dicey Dooly: (D) Nov. 12,1852, (BP) Adair Co., Ky, (A) 50, (B) 1802ca,
    (Cmts) Uriah and J. Stone
Mrs. Dooly: (D) Nov. 12,1852, (BP) Adair Co., Ky, (A) 46, (B) 1806ca,
    (Cmts) Parents Unknown
Thomas Edrington: (D) Aug. 16,1859, (BP) Unknown, (A) 82, (B) 1777ca,
    (Cmts) No Further Information
Polly Elliott: (D) Sep. 5,1852, (BP) Adair Co., Ky, (A) 75, (B) 1777ca,
    (Cmts) Parents Unknown
Ule and er Elliott: (D) Aug. 23,1852, (BP) Unknown, (A) 89, (B) 1763ca,
    (Cmts) No Parents Given
Martha Ellis: (D) Feb18,1852, (BP) Adair Co., Ky, (A) 34, (B) 1818ca,
    (Cmts) Parents Unknown
Emmanual (Slave): (D) 1856, (BP) Adair Co., Ky, (A) 65, (B) 1791ca,
    (Cmts) Owner: Jonathan Jones
William Epperson: (D) Sep.,1852, (BP) Virginia, (A) 80, (B) 1772ca,
    (Cmts) No Parents Given
Ermine (Slave): (D) Jun. 20,1859, (BP) Russell's Creek, (A) 23, (B)
    1836ca, (Cmts) Owner: James Page
Deborah Estes: (D) Jun. 26, 1857, (BP) Adair Co., Ky, (A) 50, (B) 1807ca,
    (Cmts) Benjamin and Deborah Naylor
Etter (Slave): (D) Feb. 16,1859, (BP) Unknown, (A) 17, (B) 1842ca,
    (Cmts) Owner: James G. Turk
John Field: (D) Dec. 15,1857, (BP) Bedford Co. Va., (A) 80, (B) 1777ca,
    (Cmts) John and Sarah Field
William L. Fletcher: (D) Jan. 16,1859, (BP) Cumberland Co., Ky, (A) 44,
    (B) 1815ca, (Cmts) John and Catherine Fletcher
Lucy Flowers: (D) Oct. 20,1859, (BP) Logan Co, (A) 54, (B) 1805ca,
    (Cmts) Harrison and Ann Townsend
Stephen C. Floyd: (D) Oct. 30,1852, (BP) Pulaski Co., Ky, (A) 30, (B)
    1822ca, (Cmts) M. and L. Floyd
Sarah Frazer: (D) Jun. 28,1854, (BP) Fairfax Co. Va., (A) 63, (B) 1791ca,

(Cmts) L. and S. Hiskin

Elizabeth Free: (D) Jul. 7,1854, (BP) Adair Co., Ky, (A) 50, (B) 1804ca, (Cmts) No Parents Given

Charlotta Furquin: (D) Jul. 3,1857, (BP) Cumberland Co., Ky, (A) 24, (B)1833ca, (Cmts) William and Elizabeth Furquin

Gemima (Slave): (D) Oct. 27,1858, (BP) Virginia, (A) 80, (B) 1778ca, (Cmts) Owner: John Gilmer

Job Gibson: (D) Jul. 23,1853, (BP) Adair Co., Ky, (A) 75, (B) 1778ca, (Cmts) Parents Unknown

Harrison M.Gill: (D) Apr. 7,1858, (BP) Maryland, (A) 72, (B) 1786ca, (Cmts) Charles and Rebecca Gill

Jane Grant: (D) Jan. 4,1858, (BP) Pennsylvania, (A) 85, (B) 1773ca, (Cmts) Samuel Mear

James B. Grider: (D) Aug. 25,1852, (BP) Russell Co., Ky, (A) 35, (B) 1817ca, (Cmts) Wm. and Nancy Grider

Nancy Grider: (D) Aug. 13, 1852, (BP) North Carolina, (A) 35, (B) 1817ca, (Cmts) Momanauke Hare

Emily Grissom: (D) Nov. 13, 1854, (BP) Adair Co., Ky, (A) 47, (B) 1807ca, (Cmts) Jno. and Lucy Grissom

Benjamin Hamilton: (D) Aug. 2,1854, (BP) Adair Co., Ky, (A) 21, (B) 1833ca, (Cmts) W. and P. Hamilton

Elizabeth Harvey: (D) Oct17,1852, (BP) Pennsylvania, (A) 88, (B)1764ca

Margaret Harvey: (D) Nov. 8,1856, (BP) Adair Co., Ky, (A) 41, (B) 1815ca, (Cmts) Christopher and Nancy Lewis

Margaret Hickman: (D) Sep., 1853, (BP) Adair Co., Ky, (A) 63, (B) 1790ca, (Cmts) Parents Unknown

William Holladay: (D) Aug. 26,1859, (BP) Sulphur Fork, (A) 22, (B) 1837ca, (Cmts) William and Polly Holliday

Margaret Holt: (D) Sep. 30,1853, (BP) Adair Co., Ky, (A) 25, (B) 1828ca, (Cmts) Parents Unknown

Rizens Holt: (D) Dec. 12,1859, (BP) Cedar Creek, (A) 16, (B) 1843ca, (Cmts) William and Elizabeth Holt

James M. Huggard: (D) Aug. 25,1858, (BP) West Fork, (A) 19, (B) 1839ca, (Cmts) Cambell and Mary Huggard

William Hughes: (D) Nov. 27,1859, (BP) Big Creek, (A) 19, (B) 1840ca, (Cmts) Turner and Nancy Hughes

Mary A. Janes: (D) Aug. 31,1854, (BP) Adair Co., Ky, (A) 18, (B) 1836ca, (Cmts) Thomas J. and Martha Janes

Zachariah Janes: (D) Sep. 30,1859, (BP) Jefferson Co., Ky, (A) 20, (B) 1839ca, (Cmts) Samuel and Elizabeth Janes

Martha Johnson: (D) Apr. 22,1859, (BP) Pettets Fork, (A) 46, (B) 1813ca, (Cmts) James and Elizabeth Morrison

Eliza J. Jones: (D) Jun. 1,1859, (BP) Butler's Fork, (A) 28, (B) 1831ca,

(Cmts) Elijah and Nancy King

Margaret Jones: (D) Jun. 28,1858, (BP) Green River, (A) 28, (B) 1830ca, (Cmts) Sims A. and Margaret Winfrey

Mary Jones: (D) Jun. 6,1857, (BP) Adair Co., Ky, (A) 47, (B) 1810ca, (Cmts) John Neat

Mary J. Jones: (D) Dec. 31,1859, (BP) East Fork, (A) 40, (B) 1819ca, (Cmts) William J. and Nancy Hancock

Nancy Jones: (D) Aug. 27,1858, (BP) Green Co., (A) 17, (B) 1841ca, (Cmts) Green R. and Rachel Jones

Harrison Judd: (D) Dec. 31,1858, (BP) Sulphur Fork, (A) 45, (B) 1813ca, (Cmts) Salley Judd

Judy (Slave): (D) Feb17,1859, (BP) Unknown, (A) 24, (B) 1835ca, (Cmts) Owner: Rice Morgan

Sarah Kelter: (D) Nov., 1854, (BP) Wythe Co. Va., (A) 60, (B) 1794ca, (Cmts) Wm. Rogers

Mary Leach: (D) Mar. 22,1858, (BP) Unknown, (A) 63, (B) 1795ca, (Cmts) Benjamin and Elizabeth Powell

Mary Ledington: (D) Aug. 29,1854, (BP) Wythe Co. Va., (A) 54, (B) 1800ca, (Cmts) John and Noami Moncey

Kitty F. Leftwich: (D) Aug. 29,1858, (BP) Prices Creek, (A) 16, (B) 1842ca, (Cmts) Robert and Catherine Leftwich

Jane S. Lewis: (D) Apr. 9,1857, (BP) Pittsylvania Co.Va., (A) 24, (B) 1833ca, (Cmts) John and Elizabeth Curry

Lytha Loy: (D) May 5,1853, (BP) Adair Co., Ky, (A) 18, (B) 1835ca, (Cmts) Jacob and Jane Loy

Lucy (Slave): (D) Mar. 31,1857, (BP) Adair Co., Ky, (A) 40, (B) 1817ca, (Cmts) Thomas J. Smillis

Mahaly (Slave): (D) Apr. 5,1859, (BP) Jessamine Co. Ky?, (A) 57, (B) 1802ca, (Cmts) Owner: Nancy Reynolds

Martha Ann (Slave): (D) Dec,1859, (BP) Casey's Creek, (A) 18, (B) 1841ca, (Cmts) William Mcwhorter

Anderson McGinis: (D) Jan. 7,1859, (BP) Harrolds Fork, (A) 18, (B) 1841ca, (Cmts) Anderson and Nancy Mcginis

Paschal L. McGlasson: (D) Oct. 2,1854, (BP) Virginia, (A) 43, (B) 1811ca, (Cmts) Wm. M. Mcglasson

Peter McKinney: (D) Jul. ,1852, (BP) Adair Co., Ky, (A) 16, (B) 1836ca, (Cmts) Charles and Emily Mckinney

Emma Melson: (D) Nov. 23,1854, (BP) Adair Co., Ky, (A) 36, (B) 1818ca, (Cmts) Wm. and C. Jackman

Luving Miller: (D) Aug. 26,1859, (BP) Cabin Fork, (A) 52, (B) 1807ca, (Cmts) Zachariah and Nancy Taylor

Milly (Slave): (D) Nov. 6,1858, (BP) Green Co., (A) 55, (B) 1803ca, (Cmts) Owner: John Hendrickson

Aim (Slave) Milton: (D) Mar. ,1859, (BP) Pettes Creek, (A) 21, (B)
1838ca, (Cmts) Owner: Jacob Goodson

Elizabeth P. Moore: (D) Oct. 25,1854, (BP) Adair Co., Ky, (A) 42, (B)
1812ca, (Cmts) No Parents Given

Elizabeth Moran: (D) Dec. 21,1854, (BP) Adair Co., Ky, (A) 37, (B)
1817ca, (Cmts) No Parents Given

Martha E. Morgan: (D) Aug. 22,1856, (BP) Adair Co., Ky, (A) 18, (B)
1838ca, (Cmts) Rice and Caroline Morgan

Berry Morris, Sr.: (D) Sep. 21,1858, (BP) Cumberland River, (A) 29, (B)
1829ca, (Cmts) Wm. and Mar. garet Morris

Julia A. Morrison: (D) Jun. 12,1857, (BP) Adair Co., Ky, (A) 32, (B)
1825ca, (Cmts) Robert and Mar. tha Morrison

Almirah L. Murray: (D) Apr. 10,1858, (BP) Adair Co., Ky, (A) 48, (B)
1810ca, (Cmts) Thomas T. and Polly Bailey

Martha Murrell: (D) Sep. 6,1859, (BP) Russells Creek, (A) 17, (B)
1842ca, (Cmts) Elijah and Mar. y Murrell

Nancy (Slave): (D) Aug. 5,1859, (BP) Sulphur Fork, (A) 56, (B) 1803ca,
(Cmts) Owner: William P. Williams

John Nell: (D) Nov. 3,1852, (BP) Maryland, (A) 90, (B) 1762ca,

Hamilton Nelson Owens: (D) Dec15,1853, (BP) Columbia, Ky, (A) 45,
(B) 1808ca, (Cmts) Wm. and Mary Owens

Charles S. Page: (D) Apr. 29,1859, (BP) Virginia, (A) 43, (B) 1816ca,
(Cmts) Nicholas and Ann Page

Ellen Page: (D) Apr. ,1856, (BP) Adair Co., Ky, (A) 28, (B) 1828ca,
(Cmts) George R. Page

Frances Page: (D) Jul. 15,1858, (BP) Adair Co., Ky, (A) 19, (B) 1839ca,
(Cmts) Shelton and Jenetta Page

Frances Page: (D) Oct. 10,1856, (BP) Adair Co., Ky, (A) 39, (B) 1817ca,
(Cmts) James and Nancy Humphries

Patty (Slave): (D) Sep. 20,1854, (BP) Adair Co., Ky, (A) 70, (B) 1784ca,
(Cmts) Owner: Otho Wheat

Catherine Peck: (D) Apr. ,1858, (BP) South Fork, (A) 18, (B) 1840ca,
(Cmts) John and Elviry Peck

John Pendleton: (D) Oct.,1856, (BP) Virginia, (A) 63, (B) 1793ca, (Cmts)
John and Elizabeth Pendleton

Salley Petty: (D) Apr. 25,1858, (BP) Virginia, (A) 57, (B) 1801ca, (Cmts)
Elijah and Tabitha King

Phebe (Slave): (D) Jul. ,1856, (BP) Virginia, (A) 43, (B) 1813ca, (Cmts)
Owner: Clayton Miller

James H. Pike: (D) Sep. 13,1858, (BP) Green Co., Ky, (A) 53, (B)
1805ca, (Cmts) Thomas and Sarah Pike

Margaret Pile: (D) 1853, (BP) Adair Co., Ky, (A) 20, (B) 1833ca, (Cmts)
J. B. and Emily Craig

Rachel (Slave): (D) Apr. 15,1858, (BP) Cumberland Co., Ky, (A) 33, (B) 1825ca, (Cmts) Owner: Clayton Miller

Philip Read: (D) Jul. 6,1858, (BP) Pennsylvania, (A) 88, (B) 1770ca, (Cmts) Philip and Mary Read

Nancy Reynolds: (D) Dec. 5,1859, (BP) Virginia, (A) 76, (B) 1783ca, (Cmts) Jacob and Milley Sallee

Elizabeth A. Rice: (D) May 8,1854, (BP) Adair Co., Ky, (A) 29, (B) 1825ca, (Cmts) Nathan and Mary England

George W. Rice: (D) Jul. 18,1852, (BP) Missouri, (A) 33, (B) 1819ca, (Cmts) David and Elizabeth Rice

Sarah A. Rice: (D) Aug. 18,1858, (BP) Green Co., Ky, (A) 38, (B) 1820ca, (Cmts) Anderson and Sarah Rice

Jane Roach: (D) May 2,1854, (BP) Henry Co., Va., (A) 60, (B) 1794ca, (Cmts) John and Talitha Hampton

Robert (Slave): (D) Jun. 10,1857, (BP) Unknown, (A) 19, (B) 1838ca, (Cmts) Owner: Joshua A. Hatcher

Mary Rogers: (D) Nov.,1858, (BP) Virginia, (A) 74, (B) 1784ca, (Cmts) Chesley and Ellor Rogers

Nancy Row: (D) Feb. 1,1854, (BP) Virginia, (A) 46, (B) 1808ca, (Cmts) Jno. and Ann Garmon

Sarah Ann Rowe: (D) Apr. 7,1856, (BP) Adair Co., Ky, (A) 24, (B) 1832ca, (Cmts) B. Mar tin

Polly Rutherford: (D) Dec. 15,1859, (BP) Wythe Co. Va., (A) 70, (B) 1789ca, (Cmts) William and Letty Rodgers

Joseph Sampson: (D) Aug. ,1856, (BP) Adair Co., Ky, (A) 18, (B) 1838ca, (Cmts) N. and R. Humphreys

Thomas H. Sanders: (D) Oct. 16,1852, (BP) Adair Co., Ky, (A) 37, (B) 1815ca, (Cmts) James and Mary Sanders

Salley Sexton: (D) Mar. 9,1859, (BP) Butlers Fork, (A) 24, (B) 1835ca, (Cmts) William and Emeline Williams

Am and a Shepherd: (D) Jul. 6,1856, (BP) Adair Co., Ky, (A) 31, (B) 1825ca, (Cmts) Jobidiah Shepherd

Harriet Shirley: (D) May 1,1857, (BP) Adair Co., Ky, (A) 20, (B) 1837ca, (Cmts) James B. Craig

Franklin Simpson: (D) Aug. 3,1852, (BP) Adair Co., Ky, (A) 25, (B) 1827ca, (Cmts) Bernard Simpson

Mary Susan Sinclair: (D) ? (BP) ? , (A) 76, (Cmts) Joseph and C. Curry

Charity Smith: (D) Jul. 8,1853, (BP) Adair Co., Ky, (A) 50, (B) 1803ca, (Cmts) Joseph Callison

Mary Smith: (D) Aug. 31,1852, (BP) Adair Co., Ky, (A) 17, (B) 1835ca, (Cmts) Parents Unknown

Mrs. Smith: (D) Jul. 25,1852, (BP) Adair Co., Ky, (A) 80, (B) 1772ca, (Cmts) R. I. B. Sexton

Samuel Stephens: (D) Sep. 16,1856, (BP) Adair Co., Ky, (A) 28, (B) 1828ca, (Cmts) William J. and Susan Collins

Malinda Stephenson: (D) Jan. 20,1858, (BP) Russell Co., Ky, (A) 44, (B) 1814ca, (Cmts) Joseph and Agness Hopper

John Stewart: (D) Aug. 25,1852, (BP) Virginia, (A) 54, (B) 1798ca, (Cmts) Parents Unknown

Charlotte Stone: (D) Nov. 29,1857, (BP) Farquiar Co. Va, (A) 74, (B) 1783ca, (Cmts) William Viola

Zuly Ann Stotts: (D) May 15,1859, (BP) Harrolds Fork, (A) 42, (B) 1817ca, (Cmts) Solomon and Milinda Stotts

Susan (Slave): (D) May 7,1858, (BP) Virginia, (A) 30, (B) 1828ca, (Cmts) Owner: Lucy Allen

Benjamin F. Taylor: (D) Nov. 18,1852, (BP) Adair Co., Ky, (A) 20, (B) 1832ca, (Cmts) G. W. and Frances Taylor

Sarah Morgen Taylor: (D) Sep. 16,1856, (BP) Adair Co., Ky, (A) 26, (B) 1830ca, (Cmts) Joseph and Susan Mclain

Thomas (Slave): (D) Apr. 14,1857, (BP) Unknown, (A) 76, (B) 1781ca, (Cmts) Owner: Richard Wallace

James Thomas: (D) Aug. 4,1859, (BP) Rockbridge Co. Va., (A) 50, (B) 1809ca, (Cmts) Charles and Polly Thomas

Judith Ann Thomas: (D) Jul. 27,1852, (BP) Adair Co., Ky, (A) 28, (B) 1824ca, (Cmts) Wm. and Mary Workman

William H. Thomas: (D) Apr. 4,1859, (BP) Russells Creek, (A) 27, (B) 1832ca, (Cmts) Hugh and Martha Thomas

Alexander Thompson: (D) Oct. 30,1858, (BP) Green Co., Ga., (A) 30, (B) 1828ca, (Cmts) Permalus Wintmerth

John R. Tilman: (D) Oct. 14,1856, (BP) Adair Co., Ky, (A) 34, (B) 1822ca, (Cmts) John and Nancy Tilman

George Henry Townsend: (D) Apr. 3,1857, (BP) Adair Co., Ky, (A) 18, (B) 1839ca, (Cmts) Henry and M. Townsend

Henry Townsend: (D) Dec. 18,1859, (BP) Milltown, (A) 44, (B) 1815ca, (Cmts) William and Mary Townsend

Martha Jane Turner: (D) Dec. 6,1854, (BP) Adair Co., Ky, (A) 16, (B) 1838ca, (Cmts) Hiram and M. Turner

John Claiburn Vance: (D) May 7,1856, (BP) Adair Co., Ky, (A) 20, (B) 1836ca, (Cmts) Wm. and Elvira Vance

Sally Jane Vigers: (D) Jan13,1854, (BP) Adair Co., Ky, (A) 30, (B) 1824ca, (Cmts) W. and Polly Compton

Wade ????: (D) Apr. 3,1853, (BP) Adair Co., Ky, (A) 50, (B) 1803ca, (Cmts) Archibald Wheeler

Rosana Waggoner: (D) Aug. 27,1854, (BP) Adair Co., Ky, (A) 36, (B) 1818ca, (Cmts) Simeon and B. Creel

Polly W. Alburt: (D) Dec. 1,1859, (BP) South Fork, (A) 40, (B) 1819ca,

(Cmts) John and Jane Anderson

James B. Walbut: (D) Aug. 3,1854, (BP) Rutherford Co. N.C., (A) 52, (B) 1802ca, (Cmts) J. and E. Walbut

Robert M. Walkup: (D) Oct. 10,1854, (BP) Adair Co., Ky, (A) 40, (B) 1814ca, (Cmts) Jos. and L. Walkup

Sioaty Wesley: (D) Oct29,1858, (BP) Pulaski Co., Ky, (A) 31, (B) 1827ca, (Cmts) John and Ann Higens

Agnes C. Wheat: (D) Sep. 11,1854, (BP) Albemarle Co., Va, (A) 44, (B) 1810ca, (Cmts) Thomas B. and S. Johnston

Melissa Wilkerson: (D) Oct. 20,1859, (BP) Crocus Creek, (A) 32, (B) 1827ca, (Cmts) Nathaniel and Polly Morgan

Merry Willis: (D) Jan,1857, (BP) Virginia, (A) 66, (B) 1791ca, (Cmts) Edwen and F. Willis

Elijah Wilson: (D) Jun. 25,1859, (BP) Augusta Co., Va., (A) 70, (B) 1789ca, (Cmts) William and Nancy Wilson

Margaret Wismerland: (D) Jun25,1859, (BP) Clinton Co., (A) 28, (B) 1831ca, (Cmts) John and Franky Asberry

Mary Workman: (D) Nov. 27,1852, (BP) Virginia, (A) 75, (B) 1777ca, (Cmts) Fannie Mullins

Amsterd York: (D) Jun. 25,1859, (BP) Orange Co., Va, (A) 88, (B) 1771ca, (Cmts) John and Nancy York

Margaret Young: (D) Nov. 1,1859, (BP) Iredell Co., N. C., (A) 94, (B) 1765ca, (Cmts) John and Jane Young

Rachel Young: (D) Aug. 1,1856, (BP) Adair Co., Ky, (A) 78, (B) 1778ca, (Cmts) Sam and Mary Young

Greenup County, Kentucky, 1811 Tax List.

John Alexander, John Allison, Gabriel Anglin, John Anglin, Benedict Bacon, Thomas Bainfield, James Ball, Robert Ballk, Henry Bar, Ruth Barklow, Wiatt Barley, Robert Barnes, John Bartley, Joshua Bartley, Amos Baset, Stephen Bean, Thompson Bell, George Benough, Douglas Biggs, William Blackburn, Kenneth Blake, Jesse Boone, Nathan Boone, George Bradshaw, William Bradshaw, Armstead Bragg, Skinner Broomfield, Davis Brown, John Brown, Nelson Brown, Abraham Brubaker, John Bruce, William Bruce, John Bryan, Zephaniah Bryan, William Bryson, William Buchannon, Robert Buckles, Robert Burbridge, John Cain, Jacob Cain, Job Cam, Thomas Cam, Jesse Cambell, Johnson Cambell, John Cannon, Benjamin Canterbury, John Canterbury, Nimrod Canterbury, Reuben Canterbury, George Carter, Hebe Carter, Thomas Cartwright, Robert Cathwell, Alex Catlett, Alex Catlett, Jr., Horatio Catlett, Elisha Catlett, John Chadwick,Christopher Chaffin, Nancy Chaffin, Reuben Chapman,Benjamin Chinn, John R. Chitwood, John Clark, John Clark, Jr., John Cob, Gideon Cohlin, John Colvin, Samual Colvin, Austin Cornelius,

Wm. Craig, Jacob Crank, John Crank, Joseph Crank, Charles Craycraft, Michell Creekpaun, Conlas Culp, Tilman Culp, Joseph Curren, Henry Curry, Henry Cummings, George N. Davis, Rezin Davis, Samual Davis, Josiah Davisson, Anthony Deering, Richard Deering, Samual Demint, John Downs, Salson Drury, Alexander Duncan, Charles Duncan, William Dummit, William Dupuy, Amos Durbin, Edward Eason, John Edwards, John Ellington, Pleasant Ellington, William Evans, Jacob Everman, John Everman, Jeremiah Farmer, Joshua Farmer, Christian Flaugher, Job Foster, Andrew Friend, Jacob Friend, Jonas Friend, David Fuqua, Mary Fuqua, Moses Fuqua, Samual Fuqua, Wlliam Fuqua, Frances H. Gaine, Richard Gammon, Ignatius Garrett, Joseph Garden, William Gholson, James Gibson, Edward Gilkey, Abram Goble, Daniel Goble, Ephraim Goble, William Gorman, Alfred Grayson, George Grayson, Robert Grayson, Robert H. Greene, John Greenslate, Jacob Hamm, Gabriel Hannah, Robert Hannah, Edward Hatch, William Hatton, Elijah Hatton, George Hardwick, John Hargus, Soloman Hedges, Robert Henderson, Robert Henderson, Jr., George Hensley, Calab Hitchcock, Wright Holland , John Hockaday, Andrew Hood, Thomas Hood, Taylor Horseley, James Howe, John Howe, Joseph Howe, Jacob Huffman, James Huson, Charles Jackson, Levi Johnson, Peter Jones, William Jordan, Amos Kibbee, Moses Kibbee, David Kilgour, Jacob Kiser, James Kite, Joshua Knap, Jacob Kouns, John Kouns, John Lacy, Thomas Lawson, Charles Lewis, John Littlejohn, Valentine Littlejohn, Jacob Lockwood, James Lowry, John Lowry, Melvin Lowry, William Lowry, Hezekiah Lyons, Ezra Mathew, Elijah Mayhew, John Mackoy, Nathan Madden, James McAlester, James McCallister, Luke McCallister, Andrew McGlone, Owen McGlone, James McGuire, John McGuire, William McLaughlin, James Meadow, James Meek, Samual Meek, John Miller, William Miller, Jonathon Morton, Josiah Morton, Cassandra W. Nicholls, John Nicholls, Joseph Norman,James Norton, William Osborne, James Oscar, David Parker, Elias Parker, Robert Parker, Daniel Parry, Matthew Pettit, Samual Pettit, Younger Pickett, Allen Pogue, James Pogue, John Poguek, Mary Pogue, Jacob Porter, Joseph Powell, Edmond Price, Mordacai Price, Sampson Price, Daniel Radcliffe, Lewis Reason, James Rice, Thomas Richards, John Riddle, Jesse Roberts, Winslow Robertson, Ambrose Rucker, Ephraim Rucker, Reuben Rucker, David Scott, James Scott, John Scott, Thomas Scott, Joseph Shelton, John Shields, Aaron Short, Levi Shortridge, Margaret Shortridge, Joseph Skidmore, Polly Skidmore, Samual Skidmore, Samual Slawter, Martin Smith, Robert Smith, Randell Smith, Samual Smith, Thomas Smith, Samual Solliday, James Sperry, Samual Sperry, Samual Spriggs, Koonrad Starr, Richard Stephenson, Charles Stewart, Matthew Stewart, John Storey, Seriah Stratton, Jeremiah Stratton, Christopher Stump, Thomas Terry, William Terry, Andy Thompson,

James Thompson, Samual Thompson, Waddy Thompson, Joseph Throckmorton, William Throckmorton, Oba Timberlake, Thomas Tolbert, William Tyree, Benjamin Ulen, Jacob Van Bibber, James Van Bibber, Peter Van Bibber, Enoch Vice, Rexin Virgin, Thomas Virgin, James Ward, John Ward, Thomas Ward, Clement H. Waring, Frances Waring, James Waring, Thomas Waring, Thomas Truman Greenfield Waring, James Warnock, Johnson Warnock, Samual Warnock, William Warnock, John Wells, Richard Wheatley, David White, Soloman White, William White, Lewis Wilcox, Eli Williams, Joseph Willit, Alexander Wilson, Thomas Wilson, Andrew Woods, John Woolford, Charles Wooton, Silas Wooton, Archer Womack, Fountain Young, John Young, Andrew Zane, Phillip Zane.

## Livingston County, Kentucky 1806 Delinquent Tax List

| Name | Comments |
| --- | --- |
| Morton Askey | Gone to Tennessee |
| John Brazzel | Removed out of state |
| James Best | Removed out of state |
| James Best | Removed out of state (sic) |
| Daniel Bridgeway | Removed out of state |
| Jessee Cockram | In the Indianna |
| Jacob Craft | Removed to Carolinia |
| John Campbell | Gone to Carolinia |
| John Craig | Not found |
| Abraham Dean | Not found |
| Wm. Davidson | Removed to Tennessee |
| David Evins | Removed out of state |
| Thos. Edwards | Not found |
| Wm. Galaspie | Insolvent |
| Hugh Gibbs | |
| John Harden | Not found |
| William McCluskey | Gone to Georgia |
| John Martin | Insolvent |
| Josh McClemurry | Gone to Indianna |
| Joshua Moore | Not found |
| Josiah Moore | Removed to Tennessee |
| Elisha McLain | Not found |
| Baalam Maulden | Gone to Tennessee |
| John Noye | Gone to Nashville |
| Walter Pool | Gone to Tennessee |
| Thos. Page | Not found |
| John Phelps | Gone to Indiannia |
| William Robins | Gone to Georgia |

| Name | Comments |
|---|---|
| Wm. Reed | |
| Robert Smith | Gone to Indiannia |
| Francis Smith | Not found |
| Lewis Shirey | Insolvent |
| John Taylor | Not found |
| Eldac Taylor | Not found |
| John Word | Insolvent |
| Jeremiah Wilson | In the Indiannia |

Franklin Academy, Trustees, 1795

Thomas Waring, Thomas Sloo, John Coburn, Nathaniel Wilson, David Broderick, Edward Harris, George Lewis, William Ward, Robert Rankin, John Johnson, John Machin, William Wood, Basil Duke, William Goforth, William Roe, George Stockton, Alexander Marshall, Philip Buckner, Lewis Moore, Richard Durrett, Winslow Parker, Alexander D. Orr, Thomas Marshall, Philemon Thomas

Union County, Kentucky, County Order Book, 1821 - 1822

Sibley, Enos: (CMTS) Will depostion
Alvey, Robert: (CMTS) Will depostion
Alvey, Robert heirs: (CMTS) Guardian appointed
Allen, Hugh: (CMTS) Deed of emanapation
Blakley, William: (CMTS) Stock br and recorded
Buck, Charles: (CMTS) Tavern licenses granted
Branbarger, Frederick : (CMTS) Administrator appointed
Beverly, Mackenzieland : (CMTS) Deed
Blue, Johnlands : (CMTS) Transaction
Bealmear, John heirs: (CMTS) Division of Slaves
Bishop, John B. orphans: (CMTS) Guardian appointed
Blue vs Kibby: (CMTS) Court Case
Blue vs Dyer: (CMTS) Court Case
Buck, William C: (CMTS) Deed
Catlett, Robert: (CMTS) Property tax
Chapman, Johnland : (CMTS) Transaction
Cook, Benjamin: (CMTS) Will depostion
Crosby, John M. vs K. Lawrence: (CMTS) Court Case
Carlen, William H.: (CMTS) Honesty established
Casey, Peterland : (CMTS) Deed
Carr, Charles W.: (CMTS) Estate settlement
Catthy, Elizabeth: (CMTS) Bound out
Cambron, Zephamal: (CMTS) Taxable property
Cowan, Jeremiah: (CMTS) Will depostion

Clements, Edward H.: (CMTS) Estate settlement
Cook, Robert: (CMTS) Summons
Catlett, Thomas: (CMTS) Summons
Davis, William: (CMTS) Guardian appointed
Davis, James: (CMTS) Estate Appraisal
Davis, John D. (CMTS) Stock br and recorded
Davenport, Adrian: (CMTS) ?
Dodge, Richard: (CMTS) Will depostion
Floyd, Nathaniel vs Peter Betty: (CMTS) Court Case
Fisher, Meredith: (CMTS) Will depostion
Floyd, John: (CMTS) Tavern licenses
Givens, Samuel: (CMTS) Payment to support a slave
Grundy, Will iam: (CMTS) Deed field
Graham, Jane: (CMTS) Will depostion
Guilky, Betsy: (CMTS) Will depostion
Green, John orphans: (CMTS) Guardian appointed
Henshaw, Adam: (CMTS) Tavern license
Higgins, James vs John McCrasby: (CMTS) Court case
Hooper, James: (CMTS) Administrator named
Hall, James: (CMTS) Honesty certified
Hart, Soloman: (CMTS) Administrator appointed
Hewett, Russell: (CMTS) Property tax
Higgins, James: (CMTS) Tavern license
Hudson, Mary: (CMTS) Bound out
Hampton, Collins: (CMTS) Orphan, bound out
Harris, Thomas: (CMTS) Will depostion
Hudson, Baxter: (CMTS) Guardian appointed
Hite, James C.: (CMTS) Administrator appointed
Jones, James M. vs Jesse Burch: (CMTS) Court Case
Jefferson Simmary vs John Waggoner: (CMTS) Court Case
James, Thomas: (CMTS) Stock br and filed
Johnson, Balwin: (CMTS) Heir
Keirman, Lawrence vs John M. Crosby: (CMTS) Court Case
Kerney, Thomas: (CMTS) Guardian appointed
Kibby vs Blue: (CMTS) Court Case
Kerley, Samuel, heirs: (CMTS) Settlement
Latham, James: (CMTS) Ferry established
Lash, David: (CMTS) Tavern licenses
Luttrell, John: (CMTS) Estate appraisal
Luttrell, John: (CMTS) Will depostion
Leach, Humphrey, heirs: (CMTS) Guardian appointed
Lancer, Benjamin: (CMTS) Estate settlement
Mills, Frances: (CMTS) Estate settlement

McKenny-Waggoner-Bryant: (CMTS) land dispute
McCoutry, William: (CMTS) Tax release
McClure, Alexander: (CMTS) Stock brand filed
Maddox, William : (CMTS) Administrator appointed
Miller, Peter: (CMTS) Guardian appointed
Norley, Samuel: (CMTS) Widow applied for help
Onroiee, Daniel M.: (CMTS) Tax release
Oakley, Wiliam L.: (CMTS) Tavern licenses
Oard, John: (CMTS) Administrator appointed
Oaard, Nancy and Polly: (CMTS) Administrator appointed
Pool, Benjamin: (CMTS) Administrator appointed
Peters, John: (CMTS) Estate appraisal
Pennell, Thomas M: (CMTS) Administrator appointed
Purnell, John: (CMTS) Administrator appointed
Rice, John: (CMTS) Estate settlement
Ramsey, William: (CMTS) Administrator appointed
Rice, George: (CMTS) Record 1787 military land grant
Rice, George, heirs: (CMTS) Administrator appointed
Rice vs Gibbens: (CMTS) Court Case
Russell, John C.: (CMTS) Will depostion
Sugg, William: (CMTS) Stock brand filed
Seinarter, John: (CMTS) Estate settlement
Saliaferr, John W. vs. Jesse F. Smith
Sibley, Isaac: (CMTS) Administrator appointed
Sibley, David: (CMTS) Administrator appointed
Sprague, John: (CMTS) Tavern licenses
Sprague, Jonathan: (CMTS) Estate settlement
Sibley, Enos: (CMTS) Estate settlement
Scanland, Margaret: (CMTS) Administrator appointed
Scandland's heirs: (CMTS) Guardian appointed
Townsend, James: (CMTS) Tavern licenses
Vaughn, Thomas: (CMTS) Tax release
Vaughn, James: (CMTS) Tax release
Waggenor, John: (CMTS) Land division
Waggenor, Nancy: (CMTS) Dower settlement
Waller, John: (CMTS) Will depostion
Weir, Turner: (CMTS) Taxable property
Young, Peter: (CMTS) Land addition
Young, Christian: (CMTS) List of taxable property

P. 557 Corban Dyer of Christian County, Kentucky and Isaac Dyer of Grainger County, Tennessee. land formerly owned by Robert Dyer, Deceased. Marvel Wickliff, witness.

P. 558 Hardin Cleake and wife Elizabeth of Christian county, Kentucky. Others mentioned: William McGee and Wm. Hury.

P. 557 and 558 Corbin Dyer to Isaac B. Dyer

This indenture made and entered into the first day of January in the year of our lord one thousand eight hundred and thirty three by and between Corban Dyer of County of Christian and State of Kentucky of one part and Isaac B. Dyer of the county of Grainger and State of Tennessee of the other part.

Witnessed that the Corban Dyer for and in consideration of the sum of five hundred dollars to him will the receipt and payment is hereby hath this day bargained sold unto the said Isaac B. Dyer two tracts of land County of Grainger aforesaid on the waters of Flat Creek containing one hundred and twenty nine acres more or less owned by Robert Dyer deceased. Mentioned: John Smith 's line to Silas McGee 's line, Monrow's line. Signed Corban Dyer, Witnesses: P.D. Cocke and M. M. Wickliff

P. 558 Bottom: Hardin Cleake and wife to Claiborne Johnson this indenture made and entered into this fourth day of December in the year of our Lord one thous and eight hundred and twenty between Hardin Cheake and Elizabeth his wife of the county of Christian and State of Kentucy of the one part and Claibourne Johnson of County of Grainger and State of Tennessee of the other part . Witnesseth that for and in consideration of the sum of eighty seven dollars to the said. Hardin and Elizabeth Cheake in hand paid the receipt whereof thus hereby acknowledged and hath granted bargained and sold alinated and confirmed unto the said Claibourn Johnson. Signed Hardin Cleake and Elizabeth Cleake. Christian County Kentucky, William McGee and William Heury, Justices of the peace County do hereby certify that Hardin Cheake and Elizabeth Cheake parties to the withnin deed personally appeared before us and acknowledged the same to be their act and deed... oath of said Elizabeth Cheake apart from her husband and her own free will and consent relinquished her right of dower.

Kentucky Connection: Tennessee Pension Roll Of 1835

John Bartlett: Davidson County, TN; Private; Virginia Contl. Line; $96.00 Annual Allowance; $1,210.93 Amount Received; May 23, 1822 Pension Started 70Y; Transferred from Jefferson County, Ky on March 4, 1825.

James McDaniel: Morgan County, TN; Private; Kentucky Militia

$76.66 Annual Allowance; $229.98 Amount Received; July 10, 1834
Pension Started 76Y.

Kentucky Connection: Osage County, Ridgeway Township, Kansas, 1865
Census
Knowles: John E.: (A) 40, (OC) Farmer, (BP) KY.
Household Members: Elizabeth: (A) 42, (BP) IN; John Wm.: (A)
12, (BP) IN; Juliet A.: (A) 3, (BP) KS.

Union County, Kentucky, Little Bethel Cemetery, South of Morganfield
on Bethel Church Road.

| Name | Birth | Death |
|---|---|---|
| Alford J. Cullen | Apr. 21, 1839 | Aug. 7, 1906 |
| W. H. Cullen | Sep. 5, 1819 | 1877 |
| Misstia J. Cullen, wife of | | |
| W. H. Cullen | Jan. 15, 1820 | Apr. 17, 1881 |
| Frederick Cullen | Aug., 1799 | Aug. 10, 1879 |
| James P. Clements | 1832 | 1908 |
| Elizabeth Clements, wife of | | |
| James P. Clements | 1836 | 1906 |
| Bennie Omer | Jan. 7, 1834 | Oct. 19, 1916 |
| Harriet Omer, wife of | | |
| B. S. Omer | Oct. 19, 1937 | Aug. 23, 1900 |
| Thomas Omer | Apr. 11, 1810 | Jan. 5, 1898 |
| L. Theopoles Tucker | 1834 | 1929 |
| William M. Tucker, son of | | |
| A. T. and M. Tucker | Feb. 17, 1812 | Nov. 23, 1872 |
| Ann Perkins, wife of | | |
| W. H. Perkins | May 14, 1824 | Oct. 16, 1876 |
| William A. Henry | Dec. 25, 1810 | May 13, 1882 |
| Mary T. Henry | Jan. 17, 1819 | Dec. 13, 1864 |
| Mary J. Henry, wife of | | |
| T. F. Henry (Age: 59Y 9M) | | Nov. 6, 1845 |
| Mary F. Henry | 1815 | Oct. 26, 1876 |
| Harriet T. Henry | Jul. 24, 1830 | Oct. 11, 1898 |
| Samuel Shrote | May 24, 1827 | Oct. 4, 1909 |
| Mary E. Shrote | Oct. 4, 1833 | Jun. 20, 1913 |
| James A. Hall | Oct. 8, 1838 | Aug. 2, 1903 |
| Norman Hall | Feb. 11, 1815 | Nov. 23, 1900 |
| Josie Quinn | Mar. 9, 1819 | Jun. 20, 1907 |
| F. H. Shouse | Aug. 6, 1808 | Mar. 10, 1882 |
| Joseph G. Vance | Jul. 15, 1815 | May 2, 1899 |
| Nicholas Briscoe | Aug. 16, 1820 | Nov. 18, 1870 |

| Name | Birth | Death |
|---|---|---|
| William J. Hager | May 1, 1819 | Feb. 10, 1885 |
| Minerva Hager | Mar. 2, 1830 | Jun. 7, 1895 |
| Mary A. Book, wife of | | |
| M. A. Booker | Sep. 4, 1808 | Oct. 2, 1879 |
| Permelia Boston | 1835 | 1923 |
| V. H. Smith | Aug. 12, 1820 | Oct. 2, 1898 |
| Lewis Davis | Aug. 1, 1822 | Dec. 12, 1877 |
| Samuel J. Quick | Sep. 6, 1816 | Mar. 26, 1899 |
| John W. Quick | Mar. 9, 1819 | Jun. 20, 1907 |
| Nelson Fuller | Dec. 16, 1816 | Nov. 27, 1881 |
| Susan Gregg, wife of | | |
| John S. Gregg | Apr. 9, 1836 | Feb. 7, 1877 |
| A. M. J. Holt, wife of | | |
| A. J. Holt | Oct. 22, 1824 | Apr. 29, 1869 |
| Joseph A. Nash | Mar. 4, 1804 | Nov. 8, 1886 |
| Sarah Moore, wife of | Aug. 18, 1819 | Feb. 14, 1866 |
| William Moore | | |
| Malinda Scott | May 19, 1808 | Jul. 9, 1880 |
| Sarah M. Markham | Aug. 27, 1825 | Dec. 19, 1897 |
| William A. Markham | May 15, 1816 | Sep. 24, 1899 |
| A. J. Young | 1837 | --- |
| Elizabeth Farmer Sale, born | | |
| Jefferson County | Jul. 23, 1838 | May 19, 1924 |
| Nancy Paris, wife of | | |
| W. W. Paris | Mar. 15, 1821 | May 27, 1874 |
| Rebecca Reasoner | Dec. 20, 1814 | Sep. 12, 1899 |
| Thomas Reasoner | May 12, 1811 | Nov. 21, 1891 |

Woodford County, Kentucky, Some of the first Catholic settlers from Maryland of the Diocese of Covington Settling on the Forks of the Elkhorn in 1786.
   Robert Combs, James Combs, James Gough, Ignatius Gough, John B. Gough, Bennet Greenwell, Henry S. Greenwell, Mrs. Ann James, Thomas Courtney Jenkins, James Leak, Jeremiah Tarlton, George W. Tarlton, Thomas Worland, Bernard Worland.

Grayson County, Kentucky, 1810 Census
| Name | Census Data |
|---|---|
| Lewis Willis | 0 0 0 0 0 0 0 0 0 0 0 |
| Owen Willis | 0 1 1 0 2 0 0 1 0 0 5 |
| Jas. Hornback | 0 2 1 0 1 1 0 1 0 0 0 |
| John Doran | 0 0 1 0 0 0 0 1 0 0 0 |

| Name | Census Data |
|---|---|
| John Artman | 2 0 1 0 2 0 0 1 0 0 0 |
| John Bozarth | 0 1 0 2 1 0 1 1 1 0 2 |
| Jerry Bozarth | 0 2 0 0 1 0 2 0 0 0 0 |
| William Shaw | 0 0 1 0 4 1 1 0 0 0 0 |
| John Miller | 0 0 1 0 0 0 0 0 0 0 0 |
| James Shields | 0 1 1 0 5 2 0 1 0 0 3 |
| John Keller | 0 1 0 0 0 0 1 0 0 0 0 |
| Thomas Taylor | 1 1 0 1 4 2 1 1 0 0 0 |
| James Stuliville | 0 0 1 0 2 0 0 1 0 0 0 |
| Richard Downs | 4 2 0 1 3 2 1 1 0 0 0 |
| Andrew Burtle | 0 1 0 1 0 0 1 0 1 0 4 |
| Ben Stoddert | 0 1 0 0 0 0 1 0 0 0 0 |
| James Harrel | 0 0 1 0 4 0 0 1 0 0 0 |
| John Litsey | 0 0 1 0 2 1 1 1 0 0 0 |
| Uriah Purtle | 0 1 1 0 2 0 1 0 0 0 0 |
| William Ewing | 1 0 0 2 2 1 2 0 0 0 0 |
| George Keller | 1 2 0 1 1 1 0 1 0 0 0 |
| Randle Rose | 1 1 0 0 1 1 0 0 0 0 0 |
| Theoshirley Barton | 0 0 0 1 0 0 0 0 1 0 0 |
| Jacob Miller | 1 2 0 1 2 1 0 0 1 0 0 |
| John Watkins | 0 0 1 0 2 1 0 1 0 0 0 |
| Phenes Cox | 0 1 0 0 1 0 1 0 0 0 0 |
| Daniel Cox | 0 1 0 0 0 0 1 0 0 0 0 |
| Thomas Fisher | 0 1 0 0 1 0 1 0 0 0 0 |
| James Husten | 2 0 1 0 2 0 0 1 0 0 0 |
| John Hays | 2 0 1 0 2 0 0 1 0 0 0 |
| Henry Decker | 0 0 1 0 3 2 1 0 1 0 0 |
| Calep Decker | 0 0 1 0 0 0 1 0 0 0 0 |
| Laving Ballard | 0 0 1 0 3 1 0 1 0 0 0 |
| Ezehiel Decker | 0 1 0 0 2 0 1 0 0 0 0 |
| John Decker | 0 1 0 0 0 0 1 0 0 0 0 |
| Jacob Miller | 0 2 0 0 1 0 1 0 0 0 0 |
| John White | 0 1 0 0 2 0 1 0 0 0 0 |
| Jacob Paul | 0 0 0 1 1 0 1 0 1 0 0 |
| John Paul | 1 0 0 0 3 0 0 1 0 0 0 |
| David Chanceller | 1 0 1 0 2 1 0 1 0 0 0 |
| Nancy Taylor | 1 1 0 0 1 1 0 1 0 0 0 |
| James Hays | 1 0 1 0 2 1 0 0 1 0 0 |
| Rene Napper | 1 2 1 0 1 0 0 1 0 0 0 |
| Thomas Barns | 1 1 0 1 2 1 0 1 1 0 0 |
| Edward Fletcher | 0 1 0 0 0 0 1 0 0 0 0 |

| Name | Census Data |
| --- | --- |
| Obediah Howerton | 2 0 1 0 2 1 0 0 1 0 0 |
| Marling Davis | 1 0 1 1 2 2 0 0 1 0 0 |
| John Davis | 0 0 0 1 1 0 0 0 1 0 0 |
| Luces Davis | 0 1 0 0 1 2 0 1 0 0 0 |
| William Phelps, Sr. | 0 0 1 1 0 0 0 0 1 0 0 |
| William Phelps | 0 0 1 0 1 2 0 1 0 0 0 |
| William Britt | 0 0 1 0 1 0 0 1 0 0 0 |
| Abner Blanten | 0 0 1 0 1 0 0 1 0 0 0 |
| John Galling | 2 1 1 0 1 2 1 0 1 0 0 |
| Fredrick Galling | 0 0 1 0 2 0 1 0 0 0 0 |
| Thomas Jones | 0 0 1 0 2 0 1 0 0 0 0 |
| James Jones | 2 0 0 1 3 1 0 0 1 0 0 |
| Philip Jones | 0 1 0 0 1 0 0 1 0 0 0 |
| Henry Ness | 1 1 0 1 3 1 1 0 1 0 0 |
| David Sunning | 1 0 1 0 1 0 1 0 0 0 0 |
| Abram Ramer | 1 0 0 1 0 0 1 0 1 0 0 |
| John Yearly | 0 0 1 0 1 0 0 1 1 0 0 |
| Christn. Narsley | 1 0 1 0 1 1 0 1 1 0 0 |
| William Dennis | 2 0 1 0 1 0 0 1 0 0 0 |
| Derum Turner | 3 0 1 0 2 0 0 1 0 0 0 |
| Christopher Brunk | 0 1 0 1 2 3 0 1 0 0 0 |
| James Riley | 0 0 1 0 2 0 0 1 0 0 0 |
| Josiah Dennis | 0 0 1 0 0 0 0 1 0 0 0 |
| William Armes | 0 1 0 0 0 0 1 0 0 0 0 |
| John Vanmatre | 0 2 0 1 0 2 1 0 1 0 0 |
| Joseph Worley | 0 0 1 0 1 0 0 0 1 0 0 |
| Garry Morris | 0 0 1 0 1 0 0 1 0 0 0 |
| Josiah Bass | 1 1 1 0 4 0 0 1 0 0 0 |
| William Richeson | 0 0 1 0 3 0 1 0 0 0 0 |
| Thomas Richeson | 0 1 0 0 1 0 1 0 0 0 0 |
| John Brunk | 0 1 1 0 0 0 1 1 0 0 0 |
| Martin Stuteville | 0 0 1 0 2 0 1 0 0 0 0 |
| Isaiah Watkins | 1 0 1 0 3 2 0 0 1 0 0 |
| James Higdon | 0 1 0 0 1 2 0 1 0 0 5 |
| Shadrick Souder | 0 1 0 0 1 1 0 1 0 0 0 |
| John Morgan | 0 1 0 0 0 0 0 0 0 0 0 |
| Christopher Stone | 0 1 0 0 2 0 1 0 0 0 0 |
| Edmund King | 0 0 1 0 0 0 1 0 0 0 0 |
| David Edward | 0 0 1 0 4 1 0 1 0 0 0 |
| Targen Powter | 0 0 1 0 0 0 1 0 0 0 0 |
| Peter Fuches | 0 2 1 0 0 0 0 1 0 0 0 |
| James Ferry | 1 0 1 0 0 2 0 1 0 0 0 |

| Name | Census Data |
|------|-------------|
| William Harrison | 0 0 0 1 1 3 0 1 0 0 0 |
| James Holman | 0 0 1 0 1 0 1 0 0 0 0 |
| John Bozarth | 0 1 0 0 0 0 1 0 0 0 0 |
| Benjamin Malden | 0 0 1 0 1 0 1 0 0 0 0 |
| Daniel Payton | 0 0 1 0 3 0 1 0 0 0 0 |
| Elisha Payton | 1 1 1 0 2 3 1 1 0 0 0 |
| Robert Watson | 1 0 0 1 0 1 1 0 1 0 0 |
| Stephen Cleaver | 4 0 1 0 1 0 0 1 0 0 21 |
| John Oldham | 1 3 1 0 2 2 0 1 0 0 0 |
| Jacob Myers | 0 1 1 0 0 0 0 1 0 0 9 |
| Robert Esten | 0 1 0 0 0 0 1 0 0 0 1 |
| James Lands | 1 0 1 0 2 1 0 1 0 0 0 |
| John Shain | 0 0 1 0 2 0 0 1 0 0 0 |
| William Bracher | 1 0 0 1 0 0 0 0 1 0 0 |
| John Holman | 0 0 0 1 0 0 0 0 1 0 1 |
| Jacob Vertrees | 0 1 0 0 0 0 1 0 0 0 1 |
| Philip Turpin | 0 0 1 0 2 0 0 1 0 0 1 |
| Thomas Shain | 0 0 1 0 0 0 1 0 0 0 0 |
| Henry Turpin | 0 0 0 1 0 0 0 0 0 0 4 |
| Edward Shain | 0 0 0 1 0 0 3 0 2 0 0 |
| Thomas Sullinger | 0 1 0 0 1 0 1 0 1 0 13 |
| James Shain | 0 1 0 0 1 0 1 0 0 0 0 |
| Thomas Fries | 0 1 0 0 0 0 0 0 0 0 0 |
| William Cuertin | 1 1 1 0 3 1 0 1 0 0 0 |
| Abner Edwards | 0 1 0 0 1 0 1 0 0 0 0 |
| Reubon Brown | 0 1 0 0 1 0 1 0 0 0 0 |
| William Steel | 0 1 0 0 0 0 0 0 0 0 0 |
| William Meeks | 1 0 1 0 1 0 0 1 0 0 0 |
| Samuel Putt | 1 0 1 0 0 0 0 1 0 0 0 |
| John Sutton | 2 0 0 1 2 0 1 1 0 0 0 |
| William Walker | 0 0 1 0 1 0 1 0 0 0 0 |
| George Mathis | 0 0 1 0 2 0 1 0 0 0 0 |
| Daniel Mathis | 0 1 0 0 0 0 1 0 0 0 0 |
| David Atterberry | 0 1 0 0 0 0 1 0 0 0 0 |
| Mary Mathis | 1 1 1 0 0 1 0 0 1 0 0 |
| Edward Wilson | 0 0 1 0 1 1 1 1 0 0 0 |
| John Wilson | 0 0 1 0 4 0 0 1 0 0 0 |
| Edmund W. More | 0 0 0 1 0 0 0 0 1 0 0 |
| Joseph Willson | 0 0 1 0 2 1 0 1 0 0 0 |
| Jessy Wilson | 0 0 1 0 1 0 0 1 0 0 0 |
| Sara Cummins | 0 0 0 0 3 0 0 1 0 0 0 |
| James Willson | 0 0 1 0 3 0 1 0 0 0 0 |

| Name | Census Data |
|---|---|
| William Willson | 0 2 1 1 2 0 1 0 1 0 0 |
| Hannah Suttle | 0 0 0 0 0 0 0 1 0 0 0 |
| Joseph Willson | 1 1 0 1 0 0 1 0 1 0 0 |
| Robert Preston | 0 0 1 0 1 0 1 0 0 0 0 |
| William Bracher | 2 0 1 0 2 2 1 1 0 0 0 |
| Harry Ryley | 2 0 0 1 0 0 1 0 1 0 0 |
| Samuel McGee | 1 0 2 1 0 0 2 1 1 0 0 |
| Edward Davison | 0 0 1 0 2 1 0 1 0 0 0 |
| Collins McDanuel | 0 0 1 0 0 0 1 0 0 0 0 |
| Philip Davison | 0 1 0 0 1 0 1 0 0 0 0 |
| Philain Askin | 2 0 0 1 3 1 1 0 1 0 0 |
| Pleasant Carver | 1 0 0 1 1 0 1 0 0 0 0 |
| Harmonious Kimble | 0 0 1 0 2 0 0 1 0 0 0 |
| John Lahue | 0 0 1 0 2 0 0 1 1 0 0 |
| Jessey Lansley | 1 0 1 0 1 1 2 1 0 0 0 |
| Ezehiel Harlin | 0 1 0 0 0 0 1 0 0 0 0 |
| James Penley | 4 0 0 1 2 1 1 1 0 0 0 |
| Barnet Decker | 0 0 1 0 2 0 1 0 0 0 0 |
| Ally Smith | 0 1 0 0 0 0 0 0 1 0 2 |
| Galrich Smith | 0 1 1 0 2 0 1 0 0 0 1 |
| John Jeremiah | 0 1 0 1 0 1 0 1 1 0 1 |
| John Decker | 1 1 0 1 0 1 1 0 1 0 0 |
| Aaron Spurrier - | 0 1 0 1 0 0 1 0 1 0 0 |
| Elisha Spurrier | 0 0 0 1 2 0 0 0 0 0 0 |
| Thomas Carver | 1 2 1 1 0 0 1 0 1 0 0 |
| William Carver | 0 1 0 0 0 0 1 0 0 0 0 |
| John Shanks | 2 0 0 1 0 0 0 1 0 0 0 |
| Robert Zack | 0 0 1 0 0 0 1 0 0 0 0 |
| James Nelson | 1 0 1 0 4 0 0 0 1 0 0 |
| Daniel Byers | 0 0 1 0 0 1 0 0 1 0 0 |
| Thomas Byers | 0 0 1 0 0 0 1 0 0 0 0 |
| James Byers | 0 1 1 0 1 0 1 0 0 0 0 |
| Benjamin Burtle | 0 0 0 1 1 0 1 0 1 0 0 |
| William Corn | 0 1 0 0 0 0 1 0 0 0 0 |
| David Corn | 0 1 0 0 0 0 1 0 0 0 0 |
| Jonathon Aterton | 0 0 1 0 0 0 0 1 0 0 0 |
| Frederick Kiper | 0 0 1 0 2 0 0 1 0 0 0 |
| Jacob Kiper | 0 0 1 0 1 0 0 1 0 0 0 |
| John Burnet | 0 1 2 0 4 2 1 1 0 0 0 |
| John Young | 0 0 1 0 1 0 1 0 0 0 0 |
| Cornelius Westfall | 1 0 1 0 1 0 1 1 0 0 0 |
| Hopkins Mathis | 0 1 0 0 1 0 1 0 0 0 0 |

| Name | Census Data |
| --- | --- |
| Jacob Williams | 1 0 1 0 4 0 0 1 0 0 0 |
| James Newton | 0 0 1 0 2 2 0 0 2 0 0 |
| Jacob Hornback | 0 1 0 0 0 0 1 0 0 0 0 |
| Reubin Ash | 1 1 0 1 1 1 0 0 1 0 0 |
| David Quick | 0 0 1 0 1 0 1 0 0 0 0 |
| James Jamison | 0 0 0 1 1 1 3 0 1 0 0 |
| William Brown | 0 0 1 0 3 0 1 0 0 0 0 |
| William Hauks | 3 0 0 1 2 1 0 1 0 0 0 |
| Patrick Cain | 2 1 0 1 3 1 0 1 0 0 0 |
| Richard Stubville | 0 1 0 0 1 0 1 0 0 0 0 |
| Michael Artman | 3 0 1 0 4 0 1 1 0 0 0 |
| Barten Vincent | 1 0 1 0 1 0 0 1 0 0 0 |
| Henrietta Miles | 1 2 0 0 0 0 2 0 1 0 0 |
| Martin Scaggs | 0 1 0 0 0 0 1 0 0 0 0 |
| William Scaggs | 0 0 1 0 0 0 1 0 0 0 0 |
| Noah Herral | 0 0 1 0 1 2 1 1 0 0 0 |
| Alexander Briant | 0 0 1 0 1 0 0 1 0 0 0 |
| Jonathan Bozarth | 2 0 0 1 0 0 0 1 0 0 0 |
| John Bracher | 2 0 1 0 2 0 0 1 0 0 0 |
| Henry Brown | 0 0 1 0 1 0 1 0 0 0 0 |
| John Miller | 1 0 0 1 1 1 0 1 0 0 0 |
| John Carver | 0 1 0 1 0 0 0 1 0 0 0 |
| John Putt | 0 1 0 0 0 0 1 0 0 0 0 |
| Jay Woby | 0 1 0 0 1 0 1 0 0 0 0 |
| James Gosay | 0 0 1 0 1 0 1 0 0 0 0 |
| Hary Hardest | 2 2 0 1 1 1 1 0 1 0 0 |
| George Wilson | 0 0 1 0 1 0 1 0 0 0 0 |
| William English | 1 1 0 1 0 2 1 0 0 0 0 |
| William Johnson | 0 1 0 0 1 0 1 0 0 0 0 |
| Sally Kindle | 0 0 1 0 2 0 0 1 0 0 0 |
| William Goggen | 0 0 1 0 2 0 0 1 0 0 0 |
| C. W. Stutwille | 0 2 0 1 1 1 1 0 1 0 0 |
| Jonathan Goldsberry | 0 0 1 0 4 0 1 0 0 0 3 |
| Jacob Artman | 1 0 1 0 2 1 1 1 0 0 0 |
| Wm. Whitehorn | 0 0 1 0 2 0 0 1 0 0 0 |
| Elisha Duwit | 1 0 0 1 3 1 1 0 1 0 0 |
| Henry Scaggs | 0 1 0 1 0 2 0 0 1 0 0 |
| John Rhoades | 0 1 0 0 1 0 1 0 0 0 0 |
| Jonathan Harris | 1 1 1 0 4 1 1 1 0 0 0 |
| Jacob Saltsman | 1 2 1 0 0 0 1 1 0 0 0 |
| Abraham Dale | 2 1 0 1 1 1 1 0 1 0 0 |
| John Kelly, Jr. | 0 1 1 0 0 0 1 0 0 0 0 |

| Name | Census Data |
|---|---|
| Daniel Hazle | 0 1 1 0 4 0 1 0 0 0 0 |
| James Scaggs | 0 1 0 0 0 0 1 0 0 0 0 |
| John Kays | 2 2 1 1 3 0 1 1 0 0 6 |
| George Roland | 0 0 1 0 1 0 0 1 0 0 0 |
| Charles Merideth | 0 1 1 0 1 0 0 1 0 0 0 |
| Samuel Jamison | 0 0 1 0 0 0 0 1 0 0 0 |
| John Johnson | 0 0 1 0 0 0 0 1 1 0 0 |
| Joseph Day | 4 1 1 0 0 0 1 1 0 0 0 |
| John Ramley | 0 1 1 0 4 2 1 1 0 0 0 |
| William Gore | 0 1 0 0 0 0 1 0 0 0 0 |
| Jacob Rhoades | 0 4 0 1 3 0 0 1 0 0 1 |
| John Yates | 2 1 0 1 2 1 0 1 0 0 0 |
| John Fenwick | 0 1 0 1 1 0 1 1 1 0 0 |
| Frances Higdon | 2 0 1 0 1 0 1 1 0 0 1 |
| Moses Stone | 0 1 0 0 2 0 1 0 0 0 0 |
| Elijah Kelly | 0 1 0 0 2 0 1 0 0 0 0 |
| Thompson Rude | 0 1 0 0 2 0 1 0 0 0 0 |
| John Kelly | 0 0 0 1 0 0 0 0 1 0 6 |
| William Hall | 0 0 1 0 3 1 1 1 0 0 0 |
| John Smoot | 0 0 1 0 1 0 1 0 0 0 0 |
| John Peebles | 2 0 0 1 2 1 0 0 1 0 0 |
| Abner Peebles | 0 1 0 0 2 0 1 0 0 0 0 |
| Michael Atterberry | 0 0 0 1 0 1 0 0 1 0 0 |
| James Watkins | 0 0 1 0 1 0 1 0 0 0 0 |
| Melchezedick (?) Atterberry | 0 0 1 0 0 0 1 0 0 0 0 |
| Israel Atterberry | 2 0 1 0 3 0 0 1 0 0 0 |
| Jackman Smith | 2 0 1 0 2 0 0 1 0 0 1 |
| Thomas Smith | 0 0 0 1 0 0 1 0 1 0 0 |
| Ezekiel Downing | 3 1 0 1 0 0 1 0 1 0 0 |
| Joseph Logsdon | 0 0 1 0 2 0 0 1 0 0 0 |
| John Wilkeson | 0 0 1 0 0 0 1 0 0 0 0 |
| James Hoskins | 0 0 2 0 2 1 1 0 0 0 0 |
| Thomas Lee | 0 1 0 0 0 1 1 0 0 0 0 |
| James Butler | 0 0 1 0 0 0 1 0 0 0 0 |
| Abraham Riley | 0 0 1 0 2 0 1 0 0 0 0 |
| Irwin Morris | 0 1 0 0 0 0 1 0 0 0 0 |
| John Brady | 0 1 0 0 0 0 1 0 0 0 0 |
| Richard Davis | 0 0 1 0 3 0 1 0 0 0 0 |
| Elizabeth Brooks | 0 0 0 0 0 2 0 1 0 0 0 |
| Joseph Beaty | 0 0 0 1 0 2 1 2 0 0 0 |
| William Kays | 0 0 1 0 3 0 0 1 0 0 0 |
| Adam Beaty | 0 0 1 0 1 1 0 1 0 0 0 |

| Name | Census Data |
|---|---|
| James Harris | 1 2 0 1 2 1 1 0 1 0 0 |
| John Daniel | 0 1 0 0 0 0 1 0 0 0 0 |
| Mahu Harris | 1 2 0 1 2 1 2 0 0 0 0 |
| Winny Ogden | 1 1 0 0 0 0 1 0 1 0 0 |
| Peter Storm | 0 1 1 0 4 1 1 1 0 0 0 |
| Jacob Lemons | 1 0 1 0 2 1 0 1 0 0 0 |
| Benjamin Bott | 2 1 1 0 1 0 0 1 0 0 0 |
| Anny Hopkins | 0 0 0 0 2 0 0 1 0 0 0 |
| Joseph Dawees | 1 2 0 1 0 1 0 0 0 0 0 |
| Michael Ramer | 0 0 1 0 2 1 0 0 1 0 0 |
| Michael Bracher | 0 1 0 0 0 0 1 0 0 0 0 |
| William Jones | 0 1 0 1 0 1 0 0 1 0 0 |
| William Anderson | 0 0 1 0 1 1 0 0 1 0 0 |
| Joseph Campbell | 0 2 0 1 4 1 3 1 1 0 0 |
| John Campbell | 0 0 1 0 0 0 1 0 0 0 0 |
| John Watson | 0 1 0 0 2 0 0 1 0 0 0 |
| James English | 0 1 0 0 2 0 1 0 0 0 0 |
| John Nichols | 2 1 0 0 1 0 0 2 0 0 0 |
| Volentine Nichols | 1 1 0 1 0 2 2 0 1 0 0 |
| John Smith | 1 2 0 1 0 1 0 1 1 0 0 |
| John Morris | 0 1 0 1 0 0 1 0 1 0 0 |
| Benjamin Morris | 0 1 0 0 0 0 1 0 0 0 0 |
| Elijah Hendrix | 1 1 0 1 0 1 0 1 1 0 0 |
| Joseph Miller | 0 1 0 0 1 0 1 0 0 0 0 |
| Thomas Elder | 0 1 0 0 1 1 1 1 0 0 0 |
| Patrick English | 0 1 0 0 4 0 1 0 0 0 0 |
| David Miller | 3 1 0 1 0 1 0 0 1 0 0 |
| John Miller | 0 1 0 0 2 0 1 0 0 0 0 |
| David Miller | 0 1 0 0 0 0 1 0 0 0 0 |
| Robert Slaning | 0 1 0 0 1 0 1 0 0 0 0 |
| Samuel Miller | 3 3 0 1 2 0 0 0 1 0 0 |
| Christey Miller | 0 1 0 0 0 0 1 0 0 0 0 |
| Adam Hartman | 0 0 1 0 2 0 1 0 0 0 0 |
| Vincent Dunn | 1 0 0 1 2 2 1 1 0 0 2 |
| Abrm. Vanmatre | 0 1 0 0 1 0 1 0 0 0 0 |
| Hezekiah Porter | 0 1 0 0 2 1 0 1 0 0 0 |
| Jacob Coonrad | 3 2 1 0 2 0 0 1 0 0 0 |
| Thomas Smith | 0 0 0 1 1 1 0 1 0 0 0 |
| Richard Collard | 2 0 1 0 4 1 0 1 0 0 0 |
| Nathan Atterberry | 0 1 0 0 1 0 0 1 0 0 0 |
| Edward Lee | 0 1 0 1 2 2 0 0 1 0 4 |
| Abrm. Neighbours | 0 0 1 0 0 2 0 1 0 0 0 |

| Name | Census Data |
|---|---|
| James Burtle | 0 0 1 0 1 0 1 1 0 0 0 |
| Isaiah Atterberry | 1 0 1 0 1 1 1 1 0 0 0 |
| James Atterberry | 2 3 0 1 1 1 1 0 1 0 0 |
| Charles Atterberry | 1 2 3 1 1 3 1 0 0 0 0 |
| John Fenley | 0 1 0 0 0 0 1 0 0 0 0 |
| William Denny | 1 0 0 1 3 2 0 1 0 0 0 |
| Daniel Ashcraft | 1 0 1 0 2 1 0 1 0 0 0 |
| William Burtle | 0 0 1 0 0 0 1 0 0 0 0 |
| Philip Dale | 0 1 0 0 1 0 1 0 0 0 0 |
| Thomas Rose | 3 0 0 1 3 0 1 0 0 0 0 |
| William Beatty | 0 0 1 0 3 0 1 0 0 0 0 |
| David McClure | 1 2 0 1 3 1 0 0 1 0 0 |
| John Artman | 0 1 0 1 0 1 0 1 1 0 0 |
| John Walters | 3 0 1 0 0 1 1 1 0 0 0 |
| Ichabod Hauners | 1 2 0 1 0 1 3 0 1 0 0 |
| William Stone | 1 3 1 0 1 1 0 1 0 0 0 |
| John Snider | 2 1 0 1 2 0 0 1 0 0 0 |
| Christan Weedman | 2 0 1 0 0 1 1 1 0 0 0 |
| John Craig | 0 0 1 0 2 0 0 1 0 0 0 |

Union County, Kentucky, Old Highland Cemetery, Near Uniontown.

| Name | Birth | Death |
|---|---|---|
| Nancy C. Buckman  (Age: 50Y 11M 16D) | | Sep. 17, 1889 |
| Martha M. Barron, wife of | | |
| John O. Barron (Age: About 26Y) | | Dec., 1856 |
| Mary Jay Abell | Apr. 17, 1825 | Nov. 15, 1906 |
| Zodol Abel | Feb. 9, 1822 | Oct. 21, 1854 |
| Anna Maria Abell | Feb. 14, 1827 | Oct. 14, 1888 |
| Peter Abell | Aug. 20, 1820 | Jun. 26, 1903 |
| Samuel Abell | Jul. 8, 1782 | Oct. 15, 1861 |
| Hull Higginson | --- | Mar. 9, 1801 |
| Sibbie Higginson | Jul. 29, 1809 | Feb. 4, 1870 |
| Geprge T. Higginson | Mar. 27, `836 | Sep. 1, 1864 |
| Sue Higginson Duke | Sep. 20, 1839 | Mar. 4, 1921 |
| Waller Clements | Jan. 5, 1805 | Jul. 3, 1881 |
| Martha Clements | Aug. 15, 1814 | Feb. 19, 1901 |
| William T. Congrove (Age: 22Y 7M 28D) | | May 15, 1853 |
| Thomas Coon | Oct. 24, 1822 | Mar. 4, 1896 |
| Samuel Cooper | Nov. 26, 1821 | Nov. 18, 1861 |
| John R. Cooper | Apr. 20, 1829 | Jun. 16, 1856 |
| Hollis Culver | Sep. 16, 1797 | Aug. 20, 1855 |
| Hanna Culver | May 7, 1806 | Mar. 12, 1877 |

| Name | Birth | Death |
|---|---|---|
| B. N. Culver | May 11, 1833 | Jan. 16, 1903 |
| Elizabeth Culver, wife of | | |
| Ben Culver | Jan. 25, 1835 | Sep. 24, 1900 |
| Johnson Harris | Oct. 5, 1827 | May 21, 1863 |
| Catherine Harris | Dec. 22, 1826 | Nov. 11, 1908 |
| Addison Harris | Apr. 12, 1813 | Dec. 30, 1891 |
| Mary E. Griggs | Oct. 25, 1838 | Oct. 10, 1908 |
| Roland A. Griggs | Feb. 2, 1839 | Feb. 9, 1915 |
| M. T. Griggs | Nov. 15, 1828 | Sep. 14, 1878 |
| Mary Griggs, wife of Rolen Griggs and mother | | |
| of J. N. Griggs | Mar. 28, 1810 | Jan. 10, 1888 |
| Minor Griggs | Jun. 13, 1798 | Nov. 2, 1872 |
| Elias Livesay | Jan. 25, 1824 | Jul. 12, 1862 |
| John Davis | Aug. 28, 1798 | Jun. 6, 865 |
| Abner Davis | Mar. 4, 1792 | Apr. 15, 1875 |
| Amanda F. Dayberry, wife of | | |
| John Dayberry | Mar. 30, 1816 | Mar. 4, 1892 |
| Mary J. Hewitt | Jan. 31, 1833 | Sep. 20, 1857 |
| P. P. Marschal | Feb. 23, 1830 | Jan. 10, 1863 |
| Maggie Medley | Jul. 10, 1838 | May 5, 1866 |
| Isaac Wilcox | Apr. 16, 1813 | Nov. 1, 1864 |
| Ella J. Hibbs, wife of | | |
| E. H. Hibbs | Jan. 29, 1832 | Mar. 11, 1879 |
| M. Kingsbury | 1811 | Jul. 29, 1861 |
| Ellis Yeager | Jan. 3, 1820 | Jul. 12, 1871 |
| Sarah J. Yeager | Jan 3, 1820 | Jul. 27, 1856 |
| Judith R and olph, wife of | | |
| W. O. Randolph | Jan. 4, 1795 | Oct. 14, 1859 |
| John B. Lambert | May 11, 1822 | Apr. 27, 1885 |
| Mary Latta, wife of | | |
| Haywood Latta | Dec. 25, 1815 | Apr. 12, 1895 |
| Hiram McElroy | Aug. 28, 1800 | Feb. 7, 1877 |
| Mary McElroy | May 23, 1809 | Dec. 14, 186- |
| George Phipps | Sep. 7, 1794 | Jun. 7, 1869 |
| Margaret Phipps | Oct. 29, 1799 | Dec. 3, 1879 |
| Samuel W. Willett, Sr. | Sep. 8, 1796 | Nov. 29, 1867 |
| Elder William Morrison | May 25, 1795 | Aug. 30, 1858 |
| Elizabeth G. Morrison | Oct. 29, 1797 | Nov. 15, 1884 |
| L. U. Peters | Apr. 2, 1816 | Jan. 31, 1878 |
| Ann Peters | Aug. 6, 1815 | Mar. 31, 1865 |
| Mary A. Schlight, wife of | | |
| C. Schlight | Aug. 2, 1837 | Feb. 6, 1891 |

| Name | Birth | Death |
|------|-------|-------|
| James Irwin White | Dec. 29, 1815 | Nov. 15, 1853 |
| William Scott White | Apr. 6, 1818 | Aug. 6, 1819 |
| Weden A. Wilson | Sep. 11, 1797 | --- |
| John H. Wright, (B. VA) | May 12, 1812 | Feb. 7, 18971 |

Kentucky Connections:1850 Mortality Schedule for Morgan County, Indiana.
Metilda Calahan: (A) 50Y, (BP) KY, (D) May
Nancy Curtis: (A) 21Y, (BP) KY, (D) May
Rebecca Epperson: (A) 61Y, (BP) KY, (D) December.
Ellen K. Glasscock: (A) 15Y, (BP) KY, (D) January.
Jimison Kilgore: (A) 67Y, (ST) Married, (BP) KY, (D) November.
William Park: (A) 55Y, (ST) Married, (BP) KY, (D) August.
Archibald Wheeler: (A) 17Y, (BP) KY, (D) December.

Kentucky Connections: Heads of Household on the 1870 Census, Morgan County, Indiana.
Wickley Able: (A) 41 Y, (B) 1829 ca, (BP) KY, (TWP) Adams, (P) 312
Wm. Ackers: (A) 59 Y, (B) 1811 ca, (BP) KY, (TWP) Monroe, (P) 481
David Adams: (A) 39 Y, (B) 1831 ca, (BP) KY, (TWP) Jackson, (P) 437
Henry Adams: (A) 66 Y, (B) 1804 ca, (BP) KY, (TWP) Jackson, (P) 423
Hugh Adams: (A) 62 Y, (B) 1808 ca, (BP) KY, (TWP) Jackson, (P) 423
Jacob Adams, Sr.: (A) 57 Y, (B) 1813 ca, (BP) KY, (TWP) Jackson, (P) 429
Peter Adams: (A) 41 Y, (B) 1829 ca, (BP) KY, (TWP) Jackson, (P) 441
Jacob Adkins: (A) 52 Y, (B) 1818 ca, (BP) KY, (TWP) Washington, (P) 508
Elijah Allison: (A) 62 Y, (B) 1808 ca, (BP) KY, (TWP) Gregg, (P) 411
Joseph W. H. Allison: (A) 38 Y, (B) 1832 ca, (BP) KY, (TWP) Monroe, (P) 473
Andrew Anderson: (A) 37 Y, (B) 1833 ca, (BP) KY, (TWP) Adams, (P) 315
Ellender Anderson: (A) 64 Y, (B) 1806 ca, (BP) KY, (TWP) Jackson, (P) 422
Joseph W. Asbury: (A) 47 Y, (B) 1823 ca, (BP) KY, (TWP) Brown, (P) 352
Andrew Asher: (A) 37 Y, (B) 1833 ca, (BP) KY, (TWP) Washington, (P) 521
Dillon Asher: (A) 36 Y, (B) 1834 ca, (BP) KY, (TWP) Washington, (P)

514

Easter Asher: (A) 53 Y, (B) 1817 ca, (BP) KY, (TWP) Washington, (P) 536

James Asher: (A) 42 Y, (B) 1828 ca, (BP) KY, (TWP) Washington, (P) 529

Benjamin Bailey: (A) 47 Y, (B) 1823 ca, (BP) KY, (TWP) Green, (P) 393

Delilah Baker: (A) 62 Y, (B) 1808 ca, (BP) KY, (TWP) Washington, (P) 503

George Baker: (A) 56 Y, (B) 1814 ca, (BP) KY, (TWP) Washington, (P) 507

Henry Baker: (A) 42 Y, (B) 1828 ca, (BP) KY, (TWP) Jefferson, (P) 455

Isaac Baker: (A) 40 Y, (B) 1830 ca, (BP) KY, (TWP) Jefferson, (P) 454

IsaacC. Baker: (A) 42 Y, (B) 1828 ca, (BP) KY, (TWP) Ray, (P) 492

JohnL. Baker: (A) 34 Y, (B) 1836 ca, (BP) KY, (TWP) Jackson, (P) 441

Littleton H. Baker: (A) 51 Y, (B) 1819 ca, (BP) KY, (TWP) Madison, (P) 460

Thomas Baker: (A) 37 Y, (B) 1833 ca, (BP) KY, (TWP) Washington, (P) 523

Chaney Bales: (A) 47 Y, (B) 1823 ca, (BP) KY, (TWP) Washington, (P) 508

James Bales: (A) 57 Y, (B) 1813 ca, (BP) KY, (TWP) Washington, (P) 505

John F. Ballenger: (A) 36 Y, (B) 1834 ca, (BP) KY, (TWP) Washington, P) 509

Sarah Barnard: (A) 46 Y, (B) 1824 ca, (BP) KY, (TWP) Washington, (P) 534

Wm. Barton: (A) 38 Y, (B) 1832 ca, (BP) KY, (TWP) Ray, (P) 493

John Beecheam: (A) 36 Y, (B) 1834 ca, (BP) KY, (TWP) Jackson, (P) 439

Franklin Benge: (A) 89 Y, (B) 1781 ca, (BP) KY, (TWP) Jefferson, (P) 456

Allen Bethurem: (A) 31 Y, (B) 1839 ca, (BP) KY, (TWP) Ray, (P) 498

George Blake: (A) 42 Y, (B) 1828 ca, (BP) KY, (TWP) Ashland, (P) 333

Balam Bolen: (A) 40 Y, (B) 1830 ca, (BP) KY, (TWP) Washington, (P) 502

Elijah Bourn: (A) 63 Y, (B) 1807 ca, (BP) KY, (TWP) Ray, (P) 496

Daniel Branham: (A) 66 Y, (B) 1804 ca, (BP) KY, (TWP) Washington, (P) 535

Gideon Brasier: (A) 55 Y, (B) 1815 ca, (BP) KY, (TWP) Adams, (P) 325

Wesley Brasier: (A) 55 Y, (B) 1815 ca, (BP) KY, (TWP) Ray, (P) 498

Elizabeth Brees: (A) 60 Y, (B) 1810 ca, (BP) KY, (TWP) Harrison, (P) 416

Joshua Brewer: (A) 36 Y, (B) 1834 ca, (BP) KY, (TWP) Adams, (P) 321

Mary Briton: (A) 42 Y, (B) 1828 ca, (BP) KY, (TWP) Clay, (P) 371
Nancy Briton: (A) 47 Y, (B) 1823 ca, (BP) KY, (TWP) Clay, (P) 371
Mary J. Britton: (A) 42 Y, (B) 1828 ca, (BP) KY, (TWP) Madison, (P) 469
Jacob Brown: (A) 36 Y, (B) 1834 ca, (BP) KY, (TWP) Gregg, (P) 412
James W. Brown: (A) 57 Y, (B) 1813 ca, (BP) KY, (TWP) Monroe, (P) 479
John Brown: (A) 67 Y, (B) 1803 ca, (BP) KY, (TWP) Ashland, (P) 334
Lucy Brown: (A) 36 Y, (B) 1834 ca, (BP) KY, (TWP) Gregg, (P) 413
Rice Brown: (A) 51 Y, (B) 1819 ca, (BP) KY, (TWP) Gregg, (P) 411
Thomas Brown: (A) 48 Y, (B) 1822 ca, (BP) KY, (TWP) Gregg, (P) 410
Thomas Brown: (A) 34 Y, (B) 1836 ca, (BP) KY, (TWP) Green, (P) 383
Wm. Bryant: (A) 47 Y, (B) 1823 ca, (BP) KY, (TWP) Jefferson, (P) 455
Jehu Buckner: (A) 74 Y, (B) 1796 ca, (BP) KY, (TWP) Washington, (P) 502
George Bunch: (A) 57 Y, (B) 1813 ca, (BP) KY, (TWP) Clay, (P) 379
William Bunnell: (A) 49 Y, (B) 1821 ca, (BP) KY, (TWP) Brown, (P) 348
George Burns: (A) 39 Y, (B) 1831 ca, (BP) KY, (TWP) Washington, (P) 507
John Burns: (A) 32 Y, (B) 1838 ca, (BP) KY, (TWP) Washington, (P) 507
Wm. Burns: (A) 46 Y, (B) 1824 ca, (BP) KY, (TWP) Washington, (P) 508
Sarah Burton: (A) 54 Y, (B) 1816 ca, (BP) KY, (TWP) Baker, (P) 342
Saluda Buskirk: (A) 52 Y, (B) 1818 ca, (BP) KY, (TWP) Baker, (P) 343
Am and a Butterfield: (A) 52 Y, (B) 1818 ca, (BP) KY, (TWP) Clay, (P) 373
Elizabeth Byers: (A) 79 Y, (B) 1791 ca, (BP) KY, (TWP) Green, (P) 384
Daniel Byron: (A) 31 Y, (B) 1839 ca, (BP) KY, (TWP) Ray, (P) 492
Samuel Cahill: (A) 57 Y, (B) 1813 ca, (BP) KY, (TWP) Washington, (P) 527
Wm. Cain: (A) 51 Y, (B) 1819 ca, (BP) KY, (TWP) Green, (P) 391
Ballard Callahan: (A) 50 Y, (B) 1820 ca, (BP) KY, (TWP) Ashland, (P) 335
George Canatsey: (A) 48 Y, (B) 1822 ca, (BP) KY, (TWP) Jackson, (P) 433
Cely Carpenter: (A) 54 Y, (B) 1816 ca, (BP) KY, (TWP) Ashland, (P) 336
Fielding G. Carpenter: (A) 50 Y, (B) 1820 ca, (BP) KY, (TWP) Madison, (P) 466
Madison W. Carpenter: (A) 52 Y, (B) 1818 ca, (BP) KY, (TWP) Madison, (P) 462

Mary A. Carpenter: (A) 41 Y, (B) 1829 ca, (BP) KY, (TWP) Brown, (P) 346

Wyatt Carpenter: (A) 60 Y, (B) 1810 ca, (BP) KY, (TWP) Jefferson, (P) 446

Samuel Carrell: (A) 55 Y, (B) 1815 ca, (BP) KY, (TWP) Green, (P) 398

James A. Carter: (A) 43 Y, (B) 1827 ca, (BP) KY, (TWP) Madison, (P) 460

Melinda Carter: (A) 50 Y, (B) 1820 ca, (BP) KY, (TWP) Washington, (P) 531

Sylvina Clark: (A) 54 Y, (B) 1816 ca, (BP) KY, (TWP) Adams, (P) 313

John M. Collett: (A) 51 Y, (B) 1819 ca, (BP) KY, (TWP) Jackson, (P) 431

Joel Collier: (A) 43 Y, (B) 1827 ca, (BP) KY, (TWP) Baker, (P) 341

John Collyer: (A) 48 Y, (B) 1822 ca, (BP) KY, (TWP) Ray, (P) 492

John Coonfield: (A) 74 Y, (B) 1796 ca, (BP) KY, (TWP) Jackson, (P) 427

Robert Corns: (A) 43 Y, (B) 1827 ca, (BP) KY, (TWP) Adams, (P) 310

Harrison Costin: (A) 55 Y, (B) 1815 ca, (BP) KY, (TWP) Ray, (P) 495

Lewis Costin: (A) 61 Y, (B) 1809 ca, (BP) KY, (TWP) Ashland, (P) 333

Lewis Costin: (A) 60 Y, (B) 1810 ca, (BP) KY, (TWP) Ashland, (P) 331

Mary Costin: (A) 56 Y, (B) 1814 ca, (BP) KY, (TWP) Adams, (P) 322

Lucinda Cox: (A) 50 Y, (B) 1820 ca, (BP) KY, (TWP) Clay, (P) 375

Mary Cox: (A) 54 Y, (B) 1816 ca, (BP) KY, (TWP) Clay, (P) 374

Hiram Craig: (A) 71 Y, (B) 1799 ca, (BP) KY, (TWP) Washington, (P) 537

John Crank: (A) 60 Y, (B) 1810 ca, (BP) KY, (TWP) Washington, (P) 524

Wm. Crum: (A) 52 Y, (B) 1818 ca, (BP) KY, (TWP) Gregg, (P) 410

Hugh Cunningham: (A) 50 Y, (B) 1820 ca, (BP) KY, (TWP) Washington, (P) 509

Wm. Cunningham: (A) 58 Y, (B) 1812 ca, (BP) KY, (TWP) Jefferson, (P) 449

Jonathan Dark: (A) 42 Y, (B) 1828 ca, (BP) KY, (TWP) Jefferson, (P) 451

Joseph Davee: (A) 61 Y, (B) 1809 ca, (BP) KY, (TWP) Green, (P) 396

Jeremiah Davis: (A) 52 Y, (B) 1818 ca, (BP) KY, (TWP) Ashland, (P) 332

Thomas Davis: (A) 61 Y, (B) 1809 ca, (BP) KY, (TWP) Washington, (P) 530

Martha Dawson: (A) 65 Y, (B) 1805 ca, (BP) KY, (TWP) Gregg, (P) 401

Samuel Dawson: (A) 40 Y, (B) 1830 ca, (BP) KY, (TWP) Gregg, (P) 401

James Demoss: (A) 66 Y, (B) 1804 ca, (BP) KY, (TWP) Monroe, (P) 475

Benoni Denny: (A) 64 Y, (B) 1806 ca, (BP) KY, (TWP) Baker, (P) 340

Edward Dickenson: (A) 35 Y, (B) 1835 ca, (BP) KY, (TWP) Brown, (P) 352

John H. Dodson: (A) 35 Y, (B) 1835 ca, (BP) KY, (TWP) Jackson, (P) 440

Thomas Doherty: (A) 58 Y, (B) 1812 ca, (BP) KY, (TWP) Washington, (P) 519

Wm. Dohoney: (A) 51 Y, (B) 1819 ca, (BP) KY, (TWP) Harrison, (P) 415

Jacob Donaldson: (A) 45 Y, (B) 1825 ca, (BP) KY, (TWP) Adams, (P) 316

Joseph Donaldson: (A) 48 Y, (B) 1822 ca, (BP) KY, (TWP) Adams, (P) 316

Aleana Douglas: (A) 33 Y, (B) 1837 ca, (BP) KY, (TWP) Monroe, (P) 489

Ann Drakins: (A) 86 Y, (B) 1784 ca, (BP) KY, (TWP) Washington, (P) 537

William Dunagan: (A) 42 Y, (B) 1828 ca, (BP) KY, (TWP) Ashland, (P) 333

Hiram Dunnagan: (A) 71 Y, (B) 1799 ca, (BP) KY, (TWP) Ashland, (P) 336

Thomas Dunnagan: (A) 47 Y, (B) 1823 ca, (BP) KY, (TWP) Ashland, (P) 336

John Dunnigan: (A) 39 Y, (B) 1831 ca, (BP) KY, (TWP) Ashland, (P) 328

Thomas Eastham: (A) 38 Y, (B) 1832 ca, (BP) KY, (TWP) Ray, (P) 492

John Edwards: (A) 42 Y, (B) 1828 ca, (BP) KY, (TWP) Gregg, (P) 409

Elisha Eggers: (A) 60 Y, (B) 1810 ca, (BP) KY, (TWP) Jefferson, (P) 449

David Elkins: (A) 56 Y, (B) 1814 ca, (BP) KY, (TWP) Green, (P) 398

Henry Elkins: (A) 50 Y, (B) 1820 ca, (BP) KY, (TWP) Green, (P) 388

Joseph Elkins: (A) 53 Y, (B) 1817 ca, (BP) KY, (TWP) Green, (P) 399

John Elliott: (A) 40 Y, (B) 1830 ca, (BP) KY, (TWP) Washington, (P) 530

Jacob Ellmore: (A) 38 Y, (B) 1832 ca, (BP) KY, (TWP) Adams, (P) 311

Anderson Ennis: (A) 41 Y, (B) 1829 ca, (BP) KY, (TWP) Green, (P) 398

Perlina Ennis: (A) 53 Y, (B) 1817 ca, (BP) KY, (TWP) Green, (P) 385

Lewis Faris: (A) 55 Y, (B) 1815 ca, (BP) KY, (TWP) Adams, (P) 319

Samuel Farley: (A) 54 Y, (B) 1816 ca, (BP) KY, (TWP) Adams, (P) 321

Catherine Farr: (A) 88 Y, (B) 1782 ca, (BP) KY, (TWP) Ray, (P) 495

Jefferson Farr: (A) 57 Y, (B) 1813 ca, (BP) KY, (TWP) Baker, (P) 340

Samuel Farr: (A) 36 Y, (B) 1834 ca, (BP) KY, (TWP) Washington, (P) 515

Samuel Farr and : (A) 52 Y, (B) 1818 ca, (BP) KY, (TWP) Jackson, (P) 425

Thomas Felkins: (A) 45 Y, (B) 1825 ca, (BP) KY, (TWP) Adams, (P) 312

William Fiddler: (A) 31 Y, (B) 1839 ca, (BP) KY, (TWP) Ashland, (P) 331
Edward Fishback: (A) 54 Y, (B) 1816 ca, (BP) KY, (TWP) Gregg, (P) 414
James Flowers: (A) 60 Y, (B) 1810 ca, (BP) KY, (TWP) Jefferson, (P) 452
Araminta Ford: (A) 54 Y, (B) 1816 ca, (BP) KY, (TWP) Ray, (P) 497
Reuben Foster: (A) 37 Y, (B) 1833 ca, (BP) KY, (TWP) Jefferson, (P) 448
Enoch Foxworthy: (A) 45 Y, (B) 1825 ca, (BP) KY, (TWP) Ashland, (P) 326
Sarah Franklin: (A) 58 Y, (B) 1812 ca, (BP) KY, (TWP) Green, (P) 391
Wm. Frye: (A) 59 Y, (B) 1811 ca, (BP) KY, (TWP) Ray, (P) 500
John Furgerson: (A) 56 Y, (B) 1814 ca, (BP) KY, (TWP) Clay, (P) 372
Frank Garison: (A) 54 Y, (B) 1816 ca, (BP) KY, (TWP) Gregg, (P) 412
Brad Garrison: (A) 47 Y, (B) 1823 ca, (BP) KY, (TWP) Gregg, (P) 411
Wm. Garrison: (A) 49 Y, (B) 1821 ca, (BP) KY, (TWP) Jefferson, (P) 443
Samuel Gash: (A) 41 Y, (B) 1829 ca, (BP) KY, (TWP) Adams, (P) 310
Monroe Gentry: (A) 48 Y, (B) 1822 ca, (BP) KY, (TWP) Adams, (P) 317
John Gibbs: (A) 47 Y, (B) 1823 ca, (BP) KY, (TWP) Washington, (P) 513
Oliver Gibbs: (A) 45 Y, (B) 1825 ca, (BP) KY, (TWP) Washington, (P) 529
Jane Gilhan: (A) 50 Y, (B) 1820 ca, (BP) KY, (TWP) Adams, (P) 322
George Gillaspy: (A) 72 Y, (B) 1798 ca, (BP) KY, (TWP) Washington, (P) 528
Milton Glasco: (A) 42 Y, (B) 1828 ca, (BP) KY, (TWP) Adams, (P) 317
Samuel Goldsmith: (A) 47 Y, (B) 1823 ca, (BP) KY, (TWP) Jefferson, (P) 450
Dabney Gooch: (A) 60 Y, (B) 1810 ca, (BP) KY, (TWP) Clay, (P) 375
Sylvanius C. Goodpaster: (A) 38 Y, (B) 1832 ca, (BP) KY, (TWP) Madison, (P) 465
Cynthia Goodpasture: (A) 46 Y, (B) 1824 ca, (BP) KY, (TWP) Madison, (P) 465
Mary Gose: (A) 66 Y, (B) 1804 ca, (BP) KY, (TWP) Washington, (P) 505
John Gosney: (A) 39 Y, (B) 1831 ca, (BP) KY, (TWP) Gregg, (P) 413
Mary Gray: (A) 52 Y, (B) 1818 ca, (BP) KY, (TWP) Adams, (P) 320
Priscilla Gray: (A) 42 Y, (B) 1828 ca, (BP) KY, (TWP) Ashland, (P) 332
Joshua Green: (A) 57 Y, (B) 1813 ca, (BP) KY, (TWP) Gregg, (P) 402
Thomas Green: (A) 37 Y, (B) 1833 ca, (BP) KY, (TWP) Clay, (P) 370
James M. Greer: (A) 43 Y, (B) 1827 ca, (BP) KY, (TWP) Green, (P) 387
John Greer: (A) 43 Y, (B) 1827 ca, (BP) KY, (TWP) Green, (P) 391

Thomas Gresham: (A) 75 Y, (B) 1795 ca, (BP) KY, (TWP) Monroe, (P) 472

John W. Gross: (A) 54 Y, (B) 1816 ca, (BP) KY, (TWP) Jackson, (P) 423

William E. Gross: (A) 45 Y, (B) 1825 ca, (BP) KY, (TWP) Jackson, (P) 430

Berry Gum: (A) 49 Y, (B) 1821 ca, (BP) KY, (TWP) Adams, (P) 319

Rebecca Guy: (A) 64 Y, (B) 1806 ca, (BP) KY, (TWP) Ray, (P) 498

James Hamilton: (A) 55 Y, (B) 1815 ca, (BP) KY, (TWP) Jackson, (P) 436

John Hamilton: (A) 49 Y, (B) 1821 ca, (BP) KY, (TWP) Jackson, (P) 435

Wm. Hamilton: (A) 56 Y, (B) 1814 ca, (BP) KY, (TWP) Jackson, (P) 436

George Hammack: (A) 63 Y, (B) 1807 ca, (BP) KY, (TWP) Clay, (P) 377

Martha Hancock: (A) 72 Y, (B) 1798 ca, (BP) KY, (TWP) Ashland, (P) 337

William Hancock: (A) 45 Y, (B) 1825 ca, (BP) KY, (TWP) Ashland, (P) 336

Uriah H and : (A) 45 Y, (B) 1825 ca, (BP) KY, (TWP) Jefferson, (P) 452

Absalom Hanes: (A) 55 Y, (B) 1815 ca, (BP) KY, (TWP) Clay, (P) 374

John Hanna: (A) 35 Y, (B) 1835 ca, (BP) KY, (TWP) Washington, (P) 514

Elias Harden: (A) 49 Y, (B) 1821 ca, (BP) KY, (TWP) Washington, (P) 503

Benjamin Hardin: (A) 51 Y, (B) 1819 ca, (BP) KY, (TWP) Clay, (P) 370

James Hardy: (A) 36 Y, (B) 1834 ca, (BP) KY, (TWP) Ray, (P) 493

Samuel W. Harrah: (A) 38 Y, (B) 1832 ca, (BP) KY, (TWP) Madison, (P) 460

Thomas C. Harrah: (A) 75 Y, (B) 1795 ca, (BP) KY, (TWP) Madison, (P) 461

Wm. Harrah: (A) 41 Y, (B) 1829 ca, (BP) KY, (TWP) Madison, (P) 461

Fred A. Harrison: (A) 41 Y, (B) 1829 ca, (BP) KY, (TWP) Jefferson, (P) 444

Oscar Harrison: (A) 35 Y, (B) 1835 ca, (BP) KY, (TWP) Jefferson, (P) 447

Virginius Harrison: (A) 38 Y, (B) 1832 ca, (BP) KY, (TWP) Jefferson, (P) 444

Araminta Hawk: (A) 66 Y, (B) 1804 ca, (BP) KY, (TWP) Brown, (P) 350

George Hayden: (A) 53 Y, (B) 1817 ca, (BP) KY, (TWP) Adams, (P) 320

Samuel Hazellett: (A) 80 Y, (B) 1790 ca, (BP) KY, (TWP) Adams, (P) 318

James Helton: (A) 45 Y, (B) 1825 ca, (BP) KY, (TWP) Washington, (P) 516

James B. Helton: (A) 42 Y, (B) 1828 ca, (BP) KY, (TWP) Jackson, (P) 438

Elijah Henderson: (A) 69 Y, (B) 1801 ca, (BP) KY, (TWP) Clay, (P) 372
Talton Hendron: (A) 44 Y, (B) 1826 ca, (BP) KY, (TWP) Adams, (P) 322
James L. Hensley: (A) 46 Y, (B) 1824 ca, (BP) KY, (TWP) Clay, (P) 368
Allen Hicklin: (A) 67 Y, (B) 1803 ca, (BP) KY, (TWP) Madison, (P) 464
Logan Hicks: (A) 50 Y, (B) 1820 ca, (BP) KY, (TWP) Washington, (P) 510
Washington Hicks: (A) 78 Y, (B) 1792 ca, (BP) KY, (TWP) Washington, (P) 509
John Higgins: (A) 78 Y, (B) 1792 ca, (BP) KY, (TWP) Jefferson, (P) 443
Warren Hill: (A) 56 Y, (B) 1814 ca, (BP) KY, (TWP) Ashland, (P) 330
Lewis H. Hiser: (A) 35 Y, (B) 1835 ca, (BP) KY, (TWP) Madison, (P) 467
Milton Hite: (A) 55 Y, (B) 1815 ca, (BP) KY, (TWP) Washington, (P) 535
Robert Hite: (A) 59 Y, (B) 1811 ca, (BP) KY, (TWP) Gregg, (P) 403
Wm. Hite: (A) 32 Y, (B) 1838 ca, (BP) KY, (TWP) Gregg, (P) 402
Arrena Hix: (A) 43 Y, (B) 1827 ca, (BP) KY, (TWP) Jackson, (P) 442
John Hix: (A) 36 Y, (B) 1834 ca, (BP) KY, (TWP) Gregg, (P) 404
Rebecca Hobbs: (A) 64 Y, (B) 1806 ca, (BP) KY, (TWP) Jackson, (P) 439
John Hoglan: (A) 50 Y, (B) 1820 ca, (BP) KY, (TWP) Green, (P) 393
Charles Holman: (A) 50 Y, (B) 1820 ca, (BP) KY, (TWP) Washington, (P) 533
Mary Holsclaw: (A) 73 Y, (B) 1797 ca, (BP) KY, (TWP) Jefferson, (P) 456
Liza Hour: (A) 59 Y, (B) 1811 ca, (BP) KY, (TWP) Jackson, (P) 434
Henry Howard: (A) 48 Y, (B) 1822 ca, (BP) KY, (TWP) Jefferson, (P) 452
Wm. Howard: (A) 32 Y, (B) 1838 ca, (BP) KY, (TWP) Harrison, (P) 418
David Howell: (A) 52 Y, (B) 1818 ca, (BP) KY, (TWP) Jackson, (P) 426
Wm. Howell: (A) 52 Y, (B) 1818 ca, (BP) KY, (TWP) Jackson, (P) 425
Peleg Hubble: (A) 39 Y, (B) 1831 ca, (BP) KY, (TWP) Adams, (P) 313
Sarah Hubble: (A) 63 Y, (B) 1807 ca, (BP) KY, (TWP) Adams, (P) 318
John Hudson: (A) 50 Y, (B) 1820 ca, (BP) KY, (TWP) Washington, (P) 515
Wm. Hughes: (A) 65 Y, (B) 1805 ca, (BP) KY, (TWP) Washington, (P) 539
Oliver Hurley: (A) 33 Y, (B) 1837 ca, (BP) KY, (TWP) Jackson, (P) 431
Eliza Hurt: (A) 48 Y, (B) 1822 ca, (BP) KY, (TWP) Adams, (P) 311
Ephraim James: (A) 35 Y, (B) 1835 ca, (BP) KY, (TWP) Washington, (P) 503
John James: (A) 48 Y, (B) 1822 ca, (BP) KY, (TWP) Washington, (P) 504

George M. Johnson: (A) 35 Y, (B) 1835 ca, (BP) KY, (TWP) Brown, (P) 353

Holman Johnson: (A) 52 Y, (B) 1818 ca, (BP) KY, (TWP) Brown, (P) 350

Wm. T. Johnson: (A) 32 Y, (B) 1838 ca, (BP) KY, (TWP) Madison, (P) 468

Eli Jones: (A) 61 Y, (B) 1809 ca, (BP) KY, (TWP) Washington, (P) 509

Elizabeth Jones: (A) 44 Y, (B) 1826 ca, (BP) KY, (TWP) Jefferson, (P) 448

John Jordan: (A) 39 Y, (B) 1831 ca, (BP) KY, (TWP) Monroe, (P) 487

George Kays: (A) 56 Y, (B) 1814 ca, (BP) KY, (TWP) Clay, (P) 373

Mason Kays: (A) 50 Y, (B) 1820 ca, (BP) KY, (TWP) Clay, (P) 371

James Kemp: (A) 54 Y, (B) 1816 ca, (BP) KY, (TWP) Jackson, (P) 440

John Kemp: (A) 54 Y, (B) 1816 ca, (BP) KY, (TWP) Jackson, (P) 434

Luke Kennedy: (A) 65 Y, (B) 1805 ca, (BP) KY, (TWP) Jefferson, (P) 449

Joseph Kent: (A) 46 Y, (B) 1824 ca, (BP) KY, (TWP) Washington, (P) 519

Samuel Kephart: (A) 71 Y, (B) 1799 ca, (BP) KY, (TWP) Jackson, (P) 423

George King: (A) 38 Y, (B) 1832 ca, (BP) KY, (TWP) Clay, (P) 369

Wm. King: (A) 54 Y, (B) 1816 ca, (BP) KY, (TWP) Clay, (P) 367

James Kipphart: (A) 48 Y, (B) 1822 ca, (BP) KY, (TWP) Jackson, (P) 422

John Kirby: (A) 42 Y, (B) 1828 ca, (BP) KY, (TWP) Jefferson, (P) 450

Susan Kirk: (A) 45 Y, (B) 1825 ca, (BP) KY, (TWP) Jefferson, (P) 449

Susannah Kirk: (A) 63 Y, (B) 1807 ca, (BP) KY, (TWP) Jefferson, (P) 448

Martha Kirkendoll: (A) 44 Y, (B) 1826 ca, (BP) KY, (TWP) Clay, (P) 379

Jacob Kiser: (A) 55 Y, (B) 1815 ca, (BP) KY, (TWP) Clay, (P) 380

John L. Knox: (A) 49 Y, (B) 1821 ca, (BP) KY, (TWP) Brown, (P) 355

Nancy C. Koons: (A) 67 Y, (B) 1803 ca, (BP) KY, (TWP) Green, (P) 387

Isaac Lafever: (A) 64 Y, (B) 1806 ca, (BP) KY, (TWP) Baker, (P) 343

George Laisfield: (A) 58 Y, (B) 1812 ca, (BP) KY, (TWP) Clay, (P) 375

Berry Lambert: (A) 51 Y, (B) 1819 ca, (BP) KY, (TWP) Washington, (P) 520

George W. Lambert: (A) 55 Y, (B) 1815 ca, (BP) KY, (TWP) Jackson, (P) 435

Mathias Lambert: (A) 62 Y, (B) 1808 ca, (BP) KY, (TWP) Jackson, (P) 434

David H. Lasley: (A) 55 Y, (B) 1815 ca, (BP) KY, (TWP) Madison, (P) 462

Ruth A. Lear: (A) 70 Y, (B) 1800 ca, (BP) KY, (TWP) Madison, (P) 469

James M. Leathers: (A) 56 Y, (B) 1814 ca, (BP) KY, (TWP) Brown, (P) 359

John Leathers: (A) 64 Y, (B) 1806 ca, (BP) KY, (TWP) Madison, (P) 457

Nancy Leathers: (A) 65 Y, (B) 1805 ca, (BP) KY, (TWP) Madison, (P) 467

Abraham Long: (A) 55 Y, (B) 1815 ca, (BP) KY, (TWP) Jefferson, (P) 447

Andrew Long: (A) 31 Y, (B) 1839 ca, (BP) KY, (TWP) Washington, (P) 503

John Long: (A) 73 Y, (B) 1797 ca, (BP) KY, (TWP) Brown, (P) 353

Nancy Long: (A) 34 Y, (B) 1836 ca, (BP) KY, (TWP) Washington, (P) 507

Nancy Long: (A) 33 Y, (B) 1837 ca, (BP) KY, (TWP) Brown, (P) 355

Wm. K. Long: (A) 48 Y, (B) 1822 ca, (BP) KY, (TWP) Monroe, (P) 483

Jacob Lopossa: (A) 38 Y, (B) 1832 ca, (BP) KY, (TWP) Adams, (P) 311

Joseph Lopossa: (A) 33 Y, (B) 1837 ca, (BP) KY, (TWP) Adams, (P) 314

Harriet Losh: (A) 53 Y, (B) 1817 ca, (BP) KY, (TWP) Clay, (P) 368

Thomas J. Males: (A) 56 Y, (B) 1814 ca, (BP) KY, (TWP) Brown, (P) 351

Charles Mallory: (A) 69 Y, (B) 1801 ca, (BP) KY, (TWP) Jefferson, (P) 456

Killian Mann: (A) 37 Y, (B) 1833 ca, (BP) KY, (TWP) Washington, (P) 520

Decker Marshall: (A) 42 Y, (B) 1828 ca, (BP) KY, (TWP) Baker, (P) 341

Frank Martin: (A) 38 Y, (B) 1832 ca, (BP) KY, (TWP) Monroe, (P) 487

Isabella Martin: (A) 71 Y, (B) 1799 ca, (BP) KY, (TWP) Brown, (P) 358

Perry Martin: (A) 50 Y, (B) 1820 ca, (BP) KY, (TWP) Ray, (P) 498

John Maxwell: (A) 65 Y, (B) 1805 ca, (BP) KY, (TWP) Clay, (P) 376

Sarah Maxwell: (A) 48 Y, (B) 1822 ca, (BP) KY, (TWP) Washington, (P) 506

Arthur Mccauhey: (A) 44 Y, (B) 1826 ca, (BP) KY, (TWP) Madison, (P) 467

John McClary: (A) 62 Y, (B) 1808 ca, (BP) KY, (TWP) Washington, (P) 513

Wesley McCleland: (A) 34 Y, (B) 1836 ca, (BP) KY, (TWP) Adams, (P) 312

Enoch McDaniel: (A) 58 Y, (B) 1812 ca, (BP) KY, (TWP) Washington, (P) 506

John McDaniel: (A) 33 Y, (B) 1837 ca, (BP) KY, (TWP) Baker, (P) 340

Henry H. McFarlin: (A) 45 Y, (B) 1825 ca, (BP) KY, (TWP) Jackson, (P) 442

John McGinnis: (A) 52 Y, (B) 1818 ca, (BP) KY, (TWP) Adams, (P) 314

Samuel McGinnis: (A) 47 Y, (B) 1823 ca, (BP) KY, (TWP) Ashland, (P)

331
George McKinley: (A) 68 Y, (B) 1802 ca, (BP) KY, (TWP) Clay, (P) 380
Casadore McNab: (A) 60 Y, (B) 1810 ca, (BP) KY, (TWP) Madison, (P)
463
Rebecca McNab: (A) 63 Y, (B) 1807 ca, (BP) KY, (TWP) Madison, (P)
461
Thomas McNab: (A) 60 Y, (B) 1810 ca, (BP) KY, (TWP) Madison, (P)
461
James Measles: (A) 49 Y, (B) 1821 ca, (BP) KY, (TWP) Adams, (P)  318
Lucinda Miles: (A) 39 Y, (B) 1831 ca, (BP) KY, (TWP) Washington, (P)
541
Clarinda Mills: (A) 42 Y, (B) 1828 ca, (BP) KY, (TWP) Washington, (P)
502
Wm. Mills: (A) 32 Y, (B) 1838 ca, (BP) KY, (TWP) Washington, (P)  525
James Mitchell: (A) 60 Y, (B) 1810 ca, (BP) KY, (TWP) Washington, (P)
501
Benjamin Moody: (A) 39 Y, (B) 1831 ca, (BP) KY, (TWP) Clay, (P)  371
Anna Moore: (A) 66 Y, (B) 1804 ca, (BP) KY, (TWP) Washington, (P)
504
David Moore: (A) 47 Y, (B) 1823 ca, (BP) KY, (TWP) Jackson, (P)  425
John L. Moore: (A) 50 Y, (B) 1820 ca, (BP) KY, (TWP) Brown, (P)  357
Samuel Moore: (A) 39 Y, (B) 1831 ca, (BP) KY, (TWP) Jackson, (P)  425
Jackson Morrison: (A) 34 Y, (B) 1836 ca, (BP) KY, (TWP) Jefferson, (P)
451
Thomas Murphy: (A) 52 Y, (B) 1818 ca, (BP) KY, (TWP) Ashland, (P)
337
Wilson Murphy: (A) 38 Y, (B) 1832 ca, (BP) KY, (TWP) Ashland, (P)
333
Jane Neal: (A) 45 Y, (B) 1825 ca, (BP) KY, (TWP) Washington, (P)  507
James Newton: (A) 64 Y, (B) 1806 ca, (BP) KY, (TWP) Ray, (P)  492
Thomas Nichols: (A) 64 Y, (B) 1806 ca, (BP) KY, (TWP) Monroe, (P)
474
Andrew Nix: (A) 38 Y, (B) 1832 ca, (BP) KY, (TWP) Ray, (P)  493
Tempy Norman: (A) 65 Y, (B) 1805 ca, (BP) KY, (TWP) Jackson, (P)
441
Hiram Normand : (A) 52 Y, (B) 1818 ca, (BP) KY, (TWP) Jackson, (P)
438
Clement Nutter: (A) 49 Y, (B) 1821 ca, (BP) KY, (TWP) Washington, (P)
512
John Nutter: (A) 52 Y, (B) 1818 ca, (BP) KY, (TWP) Washington, (P)
526
Henry D. Oakley: (A) 38 Y, (B) 1832 ca, (BP) KY, (TWP) Madison, (P)
465

John F. Oakley: (A) 54 Y, (B) 1816 ca, (BP) KY, (TWP) Madison, (P) 468

Nancy Oakly: (A) 60 Y, (B) 1810 ca, (BP) KY, (TWP) Madison, (P) 463

Ira Ogles: (A) 47 Y, (B) 1823 ca, (BP) KY, (TWP) Adams, (P) 315

Ezra A. Olleman: (A) 41 Y, (B) 1829 ca, (BP) KY, (TWP) Madison, (P) 470

Willis Oneal: (A) 43 Y, (B) 1827 ca, (BP) KY, (TWP) Jefferson, (P) 453

Martha Owens: (A) 43 Y, (B) 1827 ca, (BP) KY, (TWP) Washington, (P) 507

Benjamin P. Park: (A) 42 Y, (B) 1828 ca, (BP) KY, (TWP) Madison, (P) 464

Hennettie Park: (A) 70 Y, (B) 1800 ca, (BP) KY, (TWP) Madison, (P) 464

John T. Park: (A) 31 Y, (B) 1839 ca, (BP) KY, (TWP) Madison, (P) 464

John Parker: (A) 44 Y, (B) 1826 ca, (BP) KY, (TWP) Washington, (P) 525

Martha J. Parker: (A) 45 Y, (B) 1825 ca, (BP) KY, (TWP) Brown, (P) 350

John Parkhurst: (A) 71 Y, (B) 1799 ca, (BP) KY, (TWP) Jackson, (P) 431

Lucinda Parks: (A) 56 Y, (B) 1814 ca, (BP) KY, (TWP) Washington, (P) 537

Luann Passmore: (A) 48 Y, (B) 1822 ca, (BP) KY, (TWP) Madison, (P) 457

Jane Patent: (A) 48 Y, (B) 1822 ca, (BP) KY, (TWP) Adams, (P) 315

Elizabeth Payton: (A) 54 Y, (B) 1816 ca, (BP) KY, (TWP) Ray, (P) 494

Dixon Pennington: (A) 72 Y, (B) 1798 ca, (BP) KY, (TWP) Brown, (P) 358

Benjamin Perkins: (A) 34 Y, (B) 1836 ca, (BP) KY, (TWP) Jackson, (P) 433

Leroy R. Peyton: (A) 50 Y, (B) 1820 ca, (BP) KY, (TWP) Baker, (P) 341

Jeremiah Poe: (A) 35 Y, (B) 1835 ca, (BP) KY, (TWP) Brown, (P) 355

Elisha Poole: (A) 52 Y, (B) 1818 ca, (BP) KY, (TWP) Jefferson, (P) 447

George Poole: (A) 31 Y, (B) 1839 ca, (BP) KY, (TWP) Washington, (P) 506

John Pottorff: (A) 48 Y, (B) 1822 ca, (BP) KY, (TWP) Ashland, (P) 336

Robert Pottorff: (A) 36 Y, (B) 1834 ca, (BP) KY, (TWP) Ashland, (P) 331

Thomas Pottorff: (A) 36 Y, (B) 1834 ca, (BP) KY, (TWP) Ashland, (P) 335

William Pottorff: (A) 53 Y, (B) 1817 ca, (BP) KY, (TWP) Ashland, (P) 328

Ransdale Poulter: (A) 69 Y, (B) 1801 ca, (BP) KY, (TWP) Brown, (P) 354

William Poulter: (A) 33 Y, (B) 1837 ca, (BP) KY, (TWP) Brown, (P) 347

Elizabeth Prosser: (A) 47 Y, (B) 1823 ca, (BP) KY, (TWP) Jackson, (P) 429

Nancy Provence: (A) 54 Y, (B) 1816 ca, (BP) KY, (TWP) Clay, (P) 372

David Pruett: (A) 42 Y, (B) 1828 ca, (BP) KY, (TWP) Jackson, (P) 436

John Pruett: (A) 41 Y, (B) 1829 ca, (BP) KY, (TWP) Monroe, (P) 481

Benjamine Pruitt: (A) 35 Y, (B) 1835 ca, (BP) KY, (TWP) Adams, (P) 317

Daniel Pruitt: (A) 42 Y, (B) 1828 ca, (BP) KY, (TWP) Adams, (P) 317

Eli Pruitt: (A) 50 Y, (B) 1820 ca, (BP) KY, (TWP) Adams, (P) 310

George Pursall: (A) 51 Y, (B) 1819 ca, (BP) KY, (TWP) Madison, (P) 458

John Radcliff: (A) 53 Y, (B) 1817 ca, (BP) KY, (TWP) Green, (P) 383

William Radford: (A) 32 Y, (B) 1838 ca, (BP) KY, (TWP) Green, (P) 384

John W. Ragsdell: (A) 58 Y, (B) 1812 ca, (BP) KY, (TWP) Jackson, (P) 430

William B. Ramsey: (A) 52 Y, (B) 1818 ca, (BP) KY, (TWP) Jackson, (P) 428

Wesley R and olph: (A) 53 Y, (B) 1817 ca, (BP) KY, (TWP) Madison, (P) 458

Robert Rankin: (A) 45 Y, (B) 1825 ca, (BP) KY, (TWP) Gregg, (P) 413

Samuel Rankin: (A) 45 Y, (B) 1825 ca, (BP) KY, (TWP) Gregg, (P) 411

Thomas Rankin: (A) 42 Y, (B) 1828 ca, (BP) KY, (TWP) Gregg, (P) 412

John Ray: (A) 40 Y, (B) 1830 ca, (BP) KY, (TWP) Washington, (P) 501

Jackson Record: (A) 55 Y, (B) 1815 ca, (BP) KY, (TWP) Clay, (P) 379

Naaman Reed: (A) 57 Y, (B) 1813 ca, (BP) KY, (TWP) Washington, (P) 507

Mahala Reese: (A) 43 Y, (B) 1827 ca, (BP) KY, (TWP) Madison, (P) 464

John Reeves: (A) 79 Y, (B) 1791 ca, (BP) KY, (TWP) Jefferson, (P) 454

Newton Reid: (A) 36 Y, (B) 1834 ca, (BP) KY, (TWP) Ashland, (P) 334

William Reid: (A) 68 Y, (B) 1802 ca, (BP) KY, (TWP) Ashland, (P) 333

George Reynolds: (A) 40 Y, (B) 1830 ca, (BP) KY, (TWP) Washington, (P) 503

Mary A. Reynor: (A) 50 Y, (B) 1820 ca, (BP) KY, (TWP) Jackson, (P) 39

Kenner Risinger: (A) 57 Y, (B) 1813 ca, (BP) KY, (TWP) Ashland, (P) 36

Rachel Roberts: (A) 54 Y, (B) 1816 ca, (BP) KY, (TWP) Green, (P) 389

Coleman Robertson: (A) 34 Y, (B) 1836 ca, (BP) KY, (TWP) Madison, (P) 458

Gabriel Robinson: (A) 42 Y, (B) 1828 ca, (BP) KY, (TWP) Ray, (P) 493

Joseph Robinson: (A) 35 Y, (B) 1835 ca, (BP) KY, (TWP) Ray, (P) 492

Thomas Robinson: (A) 40 Y, (B) 1830 ca, (BP) KY, (TWP) Washington, (P) 502

Thomas Rude: (A) 48 Y, (B) 1822 ca, (BP) KY, (TWP) Jackson, (P) 432
Silas Russell: (A) 58 Y, (B) 1812 ca, (BP) KY, (TWP) Ashland, (P) 334
Graham Ryan: (A) 39 Y, (B) 1831 ca, (BP) KY, (TWP) Ashland, (P) 330
James Ryan: (A) 32 Y, (B) 1838 ca, (BP) KY, (TWP) Adams, (P) 316
William Ryan: (A) 33 Y, (B) 1837 ca, (BP) KY, (TWP) Ashland, (P) 331
Sarah Sanders: (A) 53 Y, (B) 1817 ca, (BP) KY, (TWP) Green, (P) 390
Harvey Satterwhite: (A) 38 Y, (B) 1832 ca, (BP) KY, (TWP) Washington,
    (P) 538
Owen Satterwhite: (A) 37 Y, (B) 1833 ca, (BP) KY, (TWP) Jackson, (P)
    422
Charles Scaggs: (A) 45 Y, (B) 1825 ca, (BP) KY, (TWP) Jackson, (P) 441
John Scaggs: (A) 69 Y, (B) 1801 ca, (BP) KY, (TWP) Green, (P) 385
Mark Scaggs: (A) 31 Y, (B) 1839 ca, (BP) KY, (TWP) Jackson, (P) 441
Thomas Schrimsher: (A) 69 Y, (B) 1801 ca, (BP) KY, (TWP) Gregg, (P)
    413
Valentine Scison: (A) 37 Y, (B) 1833 ca, (BP) KY, (TWP) Madison, (P)
    463
Harden Scott: (A) 55 Y, (B) 1815 ca, (BP) KY, (TWP) Adams, (P) 313
John Scott: (A) 32 Y, (B) 1838 ca, (BP) KY, (TWP) Gregg, (P) 411
Joseph Scott: (A) 48 Y, (B) 1822 ca, (BP) KY, (TWP) Ashland, (P) 337
Grandison Scrogin: (A) 55 Y, (B) 1815 ca, (BP) KY, (TWP) Green, (P)
    385
Robert Scrogin: (A) 60 Y, (B) 1810 ca, (BP) KY, (TWP) Green, (P) 385
Sarah A. Scrogin: (A) 43 Y, (B) 1827 ca, (BP) KY, (TWP) Green, (P) 385
Allen Seaton: (A) 62 Y, (B) 1808 ca, (BP) KY, (TWP) Gregg, (P) 413
John Seaton: (A) 39 Y, (B) 1831 ca, (BP) KY, (TWP) Gregg, (P) 411
Peter Selch: (A) 36 Y, (B) 1834 ca, (BP) KY, (TWP) Gregg, (P) 409
Archibald Sexson: (A) 69 Y, (B) 1801 ca, (BP) KY, (TWP) Jefferson, (P)
    448
Adam Shake: (A) 49 Y, (B) 1821 ca, (BP) KY, (TWP) Adams, (P) 310
Alexander Shake: (A) 35 Y, (B) 1835 ca, (BP) KY, (TWP) Adams, (P)
    310
George Shake: (A) 52 Y, (B) 1818 ca, (BP) KY, (TWP) Gregg, (P) 410
Jacob Shake: (A) 58 Y, (B) 1812 ca, (BP) KY, (TWP) Adams, (P) 310
Harrison J. Shelton: (A) 58 Y, (B) 1812 ca, (BP) KY, (TWP) Monroe, (P)
    473
Joseph Shelton: (A) 42 Y, (B) 1828 ca, (BP) KY, (TWP) Washington, (P)
    529
Samuel Shepherd: (A) 38 Y, (B) 1832 ca, (BP) KY, (TWP) Brown, (P)
    347
Wm. Shirley: (A) 33 Y, (B) 1837 ca, (BP) KY, (TWP) Washington, (P)
    533
John Simpson: (A) 34 Y, (B) 1836 ca, (BP) KY, (TWP) Washington, (P)

530

Ellison Sligar: (A) 48 Y, (B) 1822 ca, (BP) KY, (TWP) Adams, (P) 324
Thomas Sliger: (A) 56 Y, (B) 1814 ca, (BP) KY, (TWP) Adams, (P) 315
John Sloan: (A) 36 Y, (B) 1834 ca, (BP) KY, (TWP) Washington, (P) 532
Allen Smith: (A) 54 Y, (B) 1816 ca, (BP) KY, (TWP) Gregg, (P) 404
Daniel Smith: (A) 72 Y, (B) 1798 ca, (BP) KY, (TWP) Gregg, (P) 412
Elijah Smith: (A) 37 Y, (B) 1833 ca, (BP) KY, (TWP) Gregg, (P) 412
Samuel Smith: (A) 35 Y, (B) 1835 ca, (BP) KY, (TWP) Green, (P) 388
John J. Smithy: (A) 54 Y, (B) 1816 ca, (BP) KY, (TWP) Harrison, (P)
418
Cook Southard: (A) 44 Y, (B) 1826 ca, (BP) KY, (TWP) Jefferson, (P)
446
Henry Spain: (A) 45 Y, (B) 1825 ca, (BP) KY, (TWP) Ashland, (P) 329
Stephen D. Spain: (A) 70 Y, (B) 1800 ca, (BP) KY, (TWP) Ashland, (P)
334
Frederick Spangler: (A) 78 Y, (B) 1792 ca, (BP) KY, (TWP) Clay, (P)
378
Thomas A. Spark: (A) 46 Y, (B) 1824 ca, (BP) KY, (TWP) Jackson, (P)
432
Thomas Spaulding: (A) 37 Y, (B) 1833 ca, (BP) KY, (TWP) Brown, (P)
363
Rachel St. Clair: (A) 73 Y, (B) 1797 ca, (BP) KY, (TWP) Jackson, (P)
425
Lucinda Steel: (A) 46 Y, (B) 1824 ca, (BP) KY, (TWP) Madison, (P) 467
Wm. Stephenson: (A) 33 Y, (B) 1837 ca, (BP) KY, (TWP) Green, (P) 394
Alexander Steward: (A) 42 Y, (B) 1828 ca, (BP) KY, (TWP) Washington,
(P) 523
Cephas Stine: (A) 40 Y, (B) 1830 ca, (BP) KY, (TWP) Washington, (P)
522
Mary Stockwell: (A) 55 Y, (B) 1815 ca, (BP) KY, (TWP) Washington, (P)
527
Eli Stone: (A) 38 Y, (B) 1832 ca, (BP) KY, (TWP) Madison, (P) 462
Isabella Stone: (A) 69 Y, (B) 1801 ca, (BP) KY, (TWP) Madison, (P) 457
James Stone: (A) 48 Y, (B) 1822 ca, (BP) KY, (TWP) Madison, (P) 464
Milley Stone: (A) 49 Y, (B) 1821 ca, (BP) KY, (TWP) Madison, (P) 464
David Stotts: (A) 58 Y, (B) 1812 ca, (BP) KY, (TWP) Jackson, (P) 427
Nancy Strader: (A) 56 Y, (B) 1814 ca, (BP) KY, (TWP) Clay, (P) 368
Richard Stringer: (A) 37 Y, (B) 1833 ca, (BP) KY, (TWP) Adams, (P)
317
Ellen Sturgeon: (A) 50 Y, (B) 1820 ca, (BP) KY, (TWP) Ashland, (P) 337
Granville Summers: (A) 51 Y, (B) 1819 ca, (BP) KY, (TWP) Adams, (P)
315
Lewis Summers: (A) 35 Y, (B) 1835 ca, (BP) KY, (TWP) Ashland, (P)

330

Martillus Summers: (A) 60 Y, (B) 1810 ca, (BP) KY, (TWP) Brown, (P) 365

Jacob Surber: (A) 58 Y, (B) 1812 ca, (BP) KY, (TWP) Adams, (P) 323

Henry T. Swearingin: (A) 52 Y, (B) 1818 ca, (BP) KY, (TWP) Madison, (P) 466

Austin Sweet: (A) 38 Y, (B) 1832 ca, (BP) KY, (TWP) Washington, (P) 525

Dudley Sweet: (A) 41 Y, (B) 1829 ca, (BP) KY, (TWP) Washington, (P) 526

Enoch Tabor: (A) 63 Y, (B) 1807 ca, (BP) KY, (TWP) Washington, (P) 518

Wm. Tacket: (A) 50 Y, (B) 1820 ca, (BP) KY, (TWP) Ray, (P) 499

Andrew J Tarleton: (A) 44 Y, (B) 1826 ca, (BP) KY, (TWP) Harrison, (P) 416

Robert H. Tarlton: (A) 48 Y, (B) 1822 ca, (BP) KY, (TWP) Washington, (P) 501

Catherine Taylor: (A) 64 Y, (B) 1806 ca, (BP) KY, (TWP) Green, (P) 393

David Taylor: (A) 40 Y, (B) 1830 ca, (BP) KY, (TWP) Adams, (P) 321

John Thacker: (A) 40 Y, (B) 1830 ca, (BP) KY, (TWP) Washington, (P) 511

Wm. Thacker: (A) 42 Y, (B) 1828 ca, (BP) KY, (TWP) Washington, (P) 512

Isaac Thomas: (A) 65 Y, (B) 1805 ca, (BP) KY, (TWP) Washington, (P) 536

John Thomas: (A) 54 Y, (B) 1816 ca, (BP) KY, (TWP) Washington, (P) 521

John Thompson: (A) 51 Y, (B) 1819 ca, (BP) KY, (TWP) Green, (P) 399

Sally Thompson: (A) 67 Y, (B) 1803 ca, (BP) KY, (TWP) Ashland, (P) 328

Benjamin Thornburgh: (A) 72 Y, (B) 1798 ca, (BP) KY, (TWP) Brown, (P) 363

Hulan Toney: (A) 55 Y, (B) 1815 ca, (BP) KY, (TWP) Green, (P) 391

Elijah Trusty: (A) 43 Y, (B) 1827 ca, (BP) KY, (TWP) Harrison, (P) 418

Samuel Tucker: (A) 54 Y, (B) 1816 ca, (BP) KY, (TWP) Washington, (P) 504

Blumer Tudor: (A) 59 Y, (B) 1811 ca, (BP) KY, (TWP) Monroe, (P) 481

Wm. Tull: (A) 63 Y, (B) 1807 ca, (BP) KY, (TWP) Harrison, (P) 418

John L. Turner: (A) 54 Y, (B) 1816 ca, (BP) KY, (TWP) Monroe, (P) 478

Samuel V and egriff: (A) 53 Y, (B) 1817 ca, (BP) KY, (TWP) Jackson, (P) 424

Elijah V and egrifft: (A) 45 Y, (B) 1825 ca, (BP) KY, (TWP) Jackson, (P) 439

Joshua Wagaman: (A) 60 Y, (B) 1810 ca, (BP) KY, (TWP) Green, (P) 399

James Walker: (A) 41 Y, (B) 1829 ca, (BP) KY, (TWP) Jackson, (P) 429

William Wall: (A) 74 Y, (B) 1796 ca, (BP) KY, (TWP) Clay, (P) 379

Richard Walters: (A) 65 Y, (B) 1805 ca, (BP) KY, (TWP) Adams, (P) 315

Leonard Ward: (A) 42 Y, (B) 1828 ca, (BP) KY, (TWP) Clay, (P) 380

Mary Ware: (A) 38 Y, (B) 1832 ca, (BP) KY, (TWP) Clay, (P) 369

Bright Warmoth: (A) 53 Y, (B) 1817 ca, (BP) KY, (TWP) Adams, (P) 319

Green Warmoth: (A) 54 Y, (B) 1816 ca, (BP) KY, (TWP) Adams, (P) 319

Wm. Warmoth: (A) 47 Y, (B) 1823 ca, (BP) KY, (TWP) Adams, (P) 311

George Warner: (A) 44 Y, (B) 1826 ca, (BP) KY, (TWP) Washington, (P) 535

George Wellman: (A) 49 Y, (B) 1821 ca, (BP) KY, (TWP) Gregg, (P) 413

Jeremiah L. Wellman: (A) 38 Y, (B) 1832 ca, (BP) KY, (TWP) Monroe, (P) 479

Madison Welman: (A) 51 Y, (B) 1819 ca, (BP) KY, (TWP) Gregg, (P) 402

Calvin Wesmoland: (A) 41 Y, (B) 1829 ca, (BP) KY, (TWP) Gregg, (P) 410

Jesse Wharton: (A) 59 Y, (B) 1811 ca, (BP) KY, (TWP) Green, (P) 390

Allen Wheeler: (A) 70 Y, (B) 1800 ca, (BP) KY, (TWP) Adams, (P) 313

Henry Wheeler: (A) 34 Y, (B) 1836 ca, (BP) KY, (TWP) Ashland, (P) 326

Wm. Wheeler: (A) 40 Y, (B) 1830 ca, (BP) KY, (TWP) Jefferson, (P) 452

James Whitaker: (A) 50 Y, (B) 1820 ca, (BP) KY, (TWP) Jackson, (P) 435

James Whitaker: (A) 50 Y, (B) 1820 ca, (BP) KY, (TWP) Ray, (P) 497

Joshua Whitaker: (A) 38 Y, (B) 1832 ca, (BP) KY, (TWP) Jackson, (P) 433

Levi Whitaker: (A) 66 Y, (B) 1804 ca, (BP) KY, (TWP) Ray, (P) 497

Levi Whitaker: (A) 51 Y, (B) 1819 ca, (BP) KY, (TWP) Adams, (P) 310

Joseph White: (A) 36 Y, (B) 1834 ca, (BP) KY, (TWP) Ray, (P) 496

Samuel White: (A) 57 Y, (B) 1813 ca, (BP) KY, (TWP) Washington, (P) 513

John Whitson: (A) 51 Y, (B) 1819 ca, (BP) KY, (TWP) Ashland, (P) 331

Charles Whittaker: (A) 56 Y, (B) 1814 ca, (BP) KY, (TWP) Jackson, (P) 435

Sarah Wible: (A) 56 Y, (B) 1814 ca, (BP) KY, (TWP) Ashland, (P) 330

Aquilla Wigginton: (A) 50 Y, (B) 1820 ca, (BP) KY, (TWP) Washington, (P) 532

Aaron Wiley: (A) 46 Y, (B) 1824 ca, (BP) KY, (TWP) Harrison, (P) 417

Aaron Wilhite: (A) 46 Y, (B) 1824 ca, (BP) KY, (TWP) Gregg, (P) 411

Aaron D. Wilhite: (A) 49 Y, (B) 1821 ca, (BP) KY, (TWP) Monroe, (P) 480

Michael Wilhite: (A) 44 Y, (B) 1826 ca, (BP) KY, (TWP) Gregg, (P) 412

Thomas Wilhite: (A) 38 Y, (B) 1832 ca, (BP) KY, (TWP) Gregg, (P) 412

Henry Willens: (A) 56 Y, (B) 1814 ca, (BP) KY, (TWP) Washington, (P) 503

Edward Willhite: (A) 45 Y, (B) 1825 ca, (BP) KY, (TWP) Gregg, (P) 401

Elijah Willhite: (A) 44 Y, (B) 1826 ca, (BP) KY, (TWP) Gregg, (P) 402

Joshua Willhite: (A) 35 Y, (B) 1835 ca, (BP) KY, (TWP) Gregg, (P) 410

Elizabeth Williams: (A) 78 Y, (B) 1792 ca, (BP) KY, (TWP) Washington, (P) 533

John Williams: (A) 68 Y, (B) 1802 ca, (BP) KY, (TWP) Ray, (P) 497

Owen G. Williams: (A) 57 Y, (B) 1813 ca, (BP) KY, (TWP) Monroe, (P) 474

Wm. Williams: (A) 36 Y, (B) 1834 ca, (BP) KY, (TWP) Gregg, (P) 406

Lettitia Wilson: (A) 68 Y, (B) 1802 ca, (BP) KY, (TWP) Washington, (P) 502

Mary Wilson: (A) 51 Y, (B) 1819 ca, (BP) KY, (TWP) Washington, (P) 534

Thomas Wilson: (A) 71 Y, (B) 1799 ca, (BP) KY, (TWP) Ray, (P) 493

James Winchester: (A) 43 Y, (B) 1827 ca, (BP) KY, (TWP) Jackson, (P) 423

Clelland Woodard: (A) 44 Y, (B) 1826 ca, (BP) KY, (TWP) Madison, (P) 467

Elisabeth Woodard: (A) 75 Y, (B) 1795 ca, (BP) KY, (TWP) Clay, (P) 368

Jefferson Wooden: (A) 49 Y, (B) 1821 ca, (BP) KY, (TWP) Gregg, (P) 411

Joshua Wooden: (A) 47 Y, (B) 1823 ca, (BP) KY, (TWP) Adams, (P) 322

Nancy Worth: (A) 72 Y, (B) 1798 ca, (BP) KY, (TWP) Madison, (P) 466

Wm. Wyatt: (A) 47 Y, (B) 1823 ca, (BP) KY, (TWP) Clay, (P) 375

Walend Yager: (A) 56 Y, (B) 1814 ca, (BP) KY, (TWP) Gregg, (P) 401

Geo. Yount: (A) 42 Y, (B) 1828 ca, (BP) KY, (TWP) Washington, (P) 522

Jacob Yount: (A) 66 Y, (B) 1804 ca, (BP) KY, (TWP) Green, (P) 385

Edy Youse: (A) 40 Y, (B) 1830 ca, (BP) KY, (TWP) Jackson, (P) 435

John Zarring: (A) 52 Y, (B) 1818 ca, (BP) KY, (TWP) Green, (P) 393

Henry Zike: (A) 44 Y, (B) 1826 ca, (BP) KY, (TWP) Green, (P) 383

John Zike: (A) 40 Y, (B) 1830 ca, (BP) KY, (TWP) Green, (P) 384

Daviess County, Kentucky, Ayer Family Cemetery, Near Utica,Hwy 140.

| Name | Birth | Death |
|------|-------|-------|
| Jacob C. Talbott | Jul. 2, 1802 | Aug. 5, 1862 |

| Name | Birth | Death |
|---|---|---|
| Ann Talbott (Age: 27Y) | | Mar. 25, 1835 |
| Hester Talbott (Age: 72Y 2M) | | Nov. 20, 1849 |
| Ann Johnson (Age: 59Y) | | Jun. 17, 1836 |
| Jane Caroline Johnson | Apr. 16, 1808 | Mar. 4, 1841 |
| Pascal Johnson | Jun. 13, 1792 | Sep. 12, 1853 |
| Elvira Duke (Age: 51Y) | | Jan. 15, 1861 |
| William Brown (Age: 44Y) | | Jul. 26, 1863 |
| Andrew J. Ayer | Jan. 10, 1813 | May 27, 1866 |
| Dr. Alexander Ayer | Jan. 16, 1805 | Jun. 20, 1876 |
| Ester D. Ayer | Apr. 29, 1806 | Nov. 8, 1884 |
| Mary J. Ayer | Nov. 15, 1829 | May 8, 1838 |
| Mary J. Ayer | Aug. 21, 1834 | Jul. 2, 1873 |

## Bath County, Kentucky, Gossett Hill Cemetery, Near Sharpsburg

| Name | Birth | Death |
|---|---|---|
| Jacob Gossett | Sep. 6, 1770 | Oct. 30, 1852 |
| Rev. Mathias Gossett | May 6, 1798 | Dec. 23, 1874 |
| Rebecca Gossett | Aug. 9, 1790 | Feb. 8, 1862 |
| Gideon J. Holt | Sep. 12, 1800 | Oct. 28, 1843 |
| Elizabeth Judy | Jan. 20, 1760 | Jan. 24, 1844 |

## Webster County, Kentucky, Onton Old Methodist Church Cemetery.

| Name | Birth | Death |
|---|---|---|
| Margery Branson | Feb. 13, 1807 | Oct. 13, 1865 |
| Bales Branson | Jun. 9, 1801 | Dec. 12, 18?? |
| Frank Branson | May 29, 1833 | Feb. 22, 192? |
| Pernecia Beal (Age: 74Y) | | Jan. 15, 1876 |
| Jesse Ashby | Mar. 24, 179? | Mar. 15, 1884 |
| J. B. Ashby | De. 10, 183? | Nov. 6, 1909 |
| Sarah F. Ashby | Jun. 29, 1832 | Oct. 6, 1895 |
| Nancy Ashby, wife of | | |
| Peter Ashby | 1796 | 1873 |
| Martha Smith | Nov. 10, 1825 | Jul. 26, 1870 |
| Elisha B. Smith | Mar. 30, 1819 | Mar. 20, 1872 |
| Orman Sellers | May 29, 1824 | Jun. 20, 1872 |
| Western A. Sellers | Apr. 2, 1822 | Mar. 17, 1861 |
| Ephriam H. Branson | May 19, 1817 | Oct. 12, 1885 |
| Cythnia Howard | Jul. 5, 1828 | Jul. 14, 1909 |
| A. D. Howard | Feb. 15, 1828 | Sep. 12, 1915 |

<u>Grant County, Kentucky, Marriage Bond Book 1, 1820-1839.</u>

John Abbott and Elizabeth Lacy, (MD) Nov. 10, 1833, (P) 23

S. C. Abernathy and Sarah Oldrum, (BOND) Jul. 23, 1836, (P) 28

Henry Ackman and Rebeccah Ackman, (BOND) Aug. 22, 1827, (P) 10

James Alexander and Abigail Hutcherson, (BOND) May 2, 1831, (P) 18

Zebulon T. Allphin and Sidney Jenkins, (BOND) Feb. 7, 1833, (P) 20

Zebulan Alphin and Polley Brown, (BOND) Aug. 2, 1827, (P) 9

James Anderson and Indiana Tongate, (BOND) Dec. 31, 1835, (P) 26

James Anderson and Louisa Seechrest, (BOND) Dec. 11, 1838, (P) 33

Thomas Anderson and Salley Myers, (BOND) Oct. 12, 1826, (P) 9

John C. Arnold and Sarah Ann Gavit, (BOND) Nov. 21, 1839, (P) 39

Wm. Arnold, Jr. and Charity Banks, (BOND) Jul. 26, 1824, (P) 4

Jacob Asby and Delila Henry, (BOND) Aug. 3, 1825, (P) 4

Henry Ashcraft and Salley Hix, (BOND) Nov. 9, 1828, (P) 14

Jediah Ashcraft and Polly Morris, (BOND) Apr. 2, 1833, (P) 20

Job L. Ashcraft and Susannah Clark, (BOND) Dec. 12, 1822, (P) 2

William Ashcraft and Eleanor Clark, (BOND) Feb. 2, 1828, (P) 11

Jonathan Atherstone and Ann Webster, (BOND) May 27, 1822, (P) 2

James Bailey and Polley Chandler, (BOND) May 31, 1828, (P) 11

James Bailey and Polly Rains, (BOND) Mar. 22, 1836, (P) 28

Andrew Baird and Sophia Gaugh, (BOND) Feb. 6, 1836, (P) 26

Lynn Banks and Nancy Wheeler, (BOND) Sep. 23, 1832, (P) 21

Willis Banks and Rebeccah E. Thomas, (BOND) Mar. 10, 1830, (P) 15

Peyton Barclay and Bennett Gregory, (BOND) Jul. 20, 1826, (P) 8

Reuben Barker and Berthia Daniel, (BOND) Nov. 7, 1833, (P) 23

Simeon L. Barker and Louisa Mackay, (BOND) Aug. 21, 1839, (P) 35

James Barnes and Nancy Milton, (BOND) Dec. 4, 1839, (P) 36

John Barnett and Polley Howe, (BOND) Jan. 8, 1830, (P) 15

William H. Barnett and Polly F. Nicholson, (BOND) Apr. 23, 1835, (P) 25

Edward B. Bartlett and Ann T. Landess, (BOND) May 31, 1834, (P) 23

Henry Baxter and Sabry Pernell, (BOND) Apr. 9, 1838, (P) 31

Coleman Beach and Elizabeth McCulloch, (BOND) Dec. 9, 1824, (P) 5

James Beach and Betsy Custard, (BOND) Jan. 7, 1822, (P) 1

James Beach and Elizabeth Speagle, (BOND) Apr. 13, 1834, (P) 23

Jesse Beard and Margaret J. Casey, (BOND) Aug. 12, 1838, (P) 32

Addison Beech and Mary Franks, (BOND) Jan. 8, 1835, (P) 24

James Belew and Mary Collins, (BOND) Jun. 27, 1822, (P) 2

Elijah Belletter and Marilla Childres, (BOND) Jan. 24, 1833, (P) 22

Samuel Belletter and Betsy Marksberry, (BOND) Nov. 3, 1823, (P) 3

Charles Bennett and Martha Childres, (BOND) Oct. 13, 1836, (P) 29

John Bennett and America Nailor, (BOND) Sep. 18, 1832, (P) 19

John Beverly and Mary Sipple, (BOND) Mar. 9, 1823, (P) 3

Amos Bingham and Polley Wilson, (BOND) Nov. 2, 1822, (P) 3

Amos Bingham and Peggy Deck, (BOND) Sep. 28, 1826, (P) 12

John Bingham and Betsy Coots, (BOND) Sep. 1, 1822, (P) 3

Reuben Bingham and Pollyan Scott, (BOND) Nov. 9, 1829, (P) 15

Samuel Bingham and Salley Johnson, (BOND) Jul. 24, 1828, (P) 12

Christopher Botts and Sarah Barker, (BOND) Jul. 19, 1829, (P) 14

William Brand and Nancy Morgan, (BOND) Dec. 19, 1821, (P) 1

Charles Bratton and Elizabeth Summers, (BOND) Jul. 31, 1832, (P) 22

H. C. Bratton and Harriett Woodyard, (BOND) Mar. 6, 1832, (P) 22

John Brooks and Elizabeth Beverly, (BOND) May 4, 1826, (P) 8

Robert Brooks and Rebekah Points, (BOND) Nov. 22, 1826, (P) 9

William Brooks and Melinda Huffman, (BOND) Jun. 1, 1824, (P) 3

William Broows and Elizabeth Edmondson, (BOND) Feb. 24,

1831, (P) 17

Ephraim Brown and Betsy Hix, (BOND) Apr. 3, 1836, (P) 28

Harvey Brown and Elizabeth Mcclure, (BOND) Sep. 3, 1834, (P) 23

John Brown and Sarah Points, (BOND) Sep. 20, 1821, (P) 1

Mason Brown and Matilda Cunningham, (BOND) Mar. 31, 1830, (P) 16

William Brown and Mahaley Gaugh, (BOND) Mar. 26, 1829, (P) 14

Wm. H. Brown and Sorelda A. Hilton, (BOND) Dec. 12, 1839, (P) 36

George G. Brumback and Sally Corbin, (BOND) Oct. 9, 1832, (P) 21

Silas Brumback and Lucinda Johnson, (BOND) Apr. 13, 1832, (P) 19

D. C. Buckland and Am and a W. Evans, (BOND) Sep. 5, 1839, (P) 35

James Burnes and Malinda Gravit, (BOND) Mar. 15, 1838, (P) 31

George Burns and Polley Richardson, (BOND) Jul. 15, 1825, (P) 4

Rossell Burress and Esther Edmonson, (BOND) Feb. 9, 1829, (P) 15

Rossell Burrows and Esther Edmonson, (BOND) Feb. 9, 1829, (P) 13

William Burrows and Elizabeth Edmonson, (BOND) Feb. 24, 1831, (P) 15

George Buskirk and Lucy Clark, (BOND) Oct. 28, 1834, (P) 26

John Buskirk and Eliza Woodyard, (BOND) Jun. 14, 1827, (P) 10

Jonas Buskirk and Elizabeth Tongate, (BOND) Feb. 1, 1827, (P) 9

Michael Buskirk and Ancy Carben, (BOND) Mar. 4, 1828, (P) 10

Joseph Caldwell and Elizabeth Jump, (BOND) Jul. 30, 1835, (P) 27

George Carlton and Amanda Tull, (BOND) Sep. 19, 1832, (P) 19

Wm. H. Carter and Emaline Skirvin, (BOND) Mar. 28, 1838, (P) 31

Henry Case and Nancy Williamson, (BOND) Jul. 1, 1827, (P) 10

Joseph Casey and Emaline Ammerman, (BOND) Oct. 31, 1837, (P) 31

Harmon Childers and Nancy Childers, (BOND) Dec. 4, 1836, (P) 30

Abram Childres and Betsy Clark, (BOND) May 4, 1827, (P) 11

James Childres and Elizabeth Tongate, (BOND) Jul. 22, 1823, (P) 3

James P. Childres and Susannah Huffman, (BOND) Apr. 14, 1825, (P) 5

John Childres and Jane Pierce, (BOND) Jun. 25, 1822, (P) 2

Joshua Childres and Polley Harmon, (BOND) Aug. 12, 1827, (P) 11

Reuben Childres and Polley Huffman, (BOND) Mar. 25, 1824, (P) 4

Robert Childres and Nancy Coleman, (BOND) Jun. 27, 1822, (P) 2

Thomas C. Childres and Lucinda Thornhill, (BOND) Mar. 3, 1833, (P) 20

Wesly Childres and Lucy Childres, (BOND) Sep. 28, 1833, (P) 22

James Chipman and Polley Kinman, (BOND) Jul. 18, 1833, (P) 22

John Chipman and Mary Edwards, (BOND) Dec. 15, 1836, (P) 30

James Clark and Cassander Powers, (BOND) Oct. 26, 1834, (P) 25

James Clark and Sarah Ashcraft, (BOND) Feb. 19, 1839, (P) 38

John T. Clark and Nancy Theobald, (BOND) Mar. 19, 1836, (P) 27

Thomas L. Clark and Elvia M. Davis, (BOND) Sep. 12, 1839, (P) 35

Eli Clarke and Mary Elizabeth Draper, (BOND) Nov. 17, 1836, (P) 30

Milton Clifton and Debby Wilson, (BOND) Feb. 10, 1829, (P) 13

Wyatt Clifton and Polly Wilson, (BOND) Mar. 9, 1830, (P) 15

William Cobb and Elizabeth Cox, (BOND) Jul. 15, 1822, (P) 2

William Cobb and Nelly Simpson, (BOND) Jul. 28, 1836, (P) 28

Clayton Coleman and Mary Curry, (BOND) Apr. 1, 1822, (P) 2

James Coleman and Susannah Thornhill, (BOND) Apr. 25, 1826, (P) 6

Jesse Coleman and Salley Ann Steers, (BOND) Feb. 12, 1833, (P) 20

William Coleman and Sarah Myers, (BOND) Sep. 1, 1822, (P) 2

William L. Coleman and Amelia Ann McCoy, (BOND) Jan. 29, 1836, (P) 28

Pendleton Collier and Helen Brumback, (BOND) May 20, 1822, (P) 2

Hosea Collins and Sarah Wheeler, (BOND) Dec. 23, 1829, (P) 14

James Collins and Margaret Smith, (BOND) Feb. 16, 1829, (P) 15

James Collins and Elizabeth Burns, (BOND) Aug. 3, 1835, (P) 26

James Collins and Angeline Smith, (BOND) Oct. 1, 1837, (P) 32

James C. Collins and Margaret Smith, (BOND) Feb. 16, 1829, (P) 13

James W. Collins and Cordelia E. Carlile, (BOND) Oct. 11, 1837, (P) 30

John A. Collins and Juliann Clarke, (BOND) Sep. 21, 1837, (P) 30

John C. Collins and Eliza Jane Buskirk, (BOND) Jul. 14, 1836, (P) 28

William C. Collins and Fanny Burrows, (BOND) Jan. 18, 1827, (P) 10

William H. Collins and Sarah Ann Cooper, (BOND) Jul. 28, 1839, (P) 38

Wm. H. Conner and Paulina Nicholson, (BOND) Feb. 2, 1832, (P) 22

William Conover and Mary Ann Arnold, (BOND) May 22, 1829, (P) 15

Sandford Conrad and Anne Theobald, (BOND) Sep. 6, 1836, (P) 28

Luther Conrey and Julian Odey, (BOND) Dec. 11, 1828, (P) 16

Abraham Conyers and Elizabeth Harmon, (BOND) Jan. 6, 1828, (P) 14

Jesse Conyers and Nancy Childres, (BOND) Jan. 24, 1822, (P) 2

Berrywick Cook and Phebe Kinman, (BOND) Sep. 15, 1836, (P) 28

Mathew Cook and Sarah Barton, (BOND) Feb. 28, 1824, (P) 12

William Cook and Eberliza Kinman, (BOND) Nov. 10, 1836, (P) 29

John Cooper and Ruth Owens, (BOND) Dec. 15, 1821, (P) 2

James Corbin and Mary Lake, (BOND) Dec. 16, 1830, (P) 17

Patrick Courtney and Cynthia McMirron, (BOND) Feb. 4, 1829, (P) 13

Nathan Cox and Polley Morgan, (BOND) Sep. 3, 1831, (P) 18

Wm. Craig and Mary Conover, (BOND) Sep. 21, 1831, (P) 18

Benjamin Crook and Nancy McGlasson, (BOND) Nov. 12, 1824, (P) 4

Robert Crook and Nancy Anderson, (BOND) Nov. 6, 1825, (P) 6

Thomas G. P. Cunningham and Comfort Nichols, (BOND) Dec.
30, 1830, (P) 17

Thos. Cunningham and Nancy Franks, (BOND) Feb. 3, 1825, (P)
4

Nathan Dale and Emily Gatewood, (BOND) Aug. 24, 1831, (P)
17

James Dane and Lethy Robinson, (BOND) Nov. 7, 1826, (P) 7

Robert Daniel and Patsy Brown, (BOND) Jul. 18, 1826, (P) 7

Travis T. Daniel and Isabella Carr, (BOND) Nov. 18, 1834, (P)
25

Joseph Daugherty and Elizabeth C. Collins, (BOND) Jan. 20,
1831, (P) 18

Joseph Daugherty and Elizabeth Ashcraft, (BOND) Jan. 1, 1837,
(P) 30

Henry Day and Betsy Ann Williams, (BOND) Dec. 22, 1839, (P)
35

William Dehart and Rachel Ann Holliday, (BOND) Sep. 21,
1825, (P) 5

John W. Dejarnett and Margaret Williams, (BOND) Oct. 19,
1838, (P) 34

Wilson Dewees and Polley Winings, (BOND) Sep. 2, 1821, (P) 2

J. P. Dickerson and Maria E. Peak, (BOND) Nov. 10, 1836, (P)
29

James D. Dillan and Betsy Masterson, (BOND) Mar. 25, 1829,
(P) 14

Reuben Doty and Mary Hickerson, (BOND) Mar. 1, 1821, (P) 1

Robert Drinkard and Adelia Robinson, (BOND) Sep. 25, 1834,
(P) 23

Roberson J. Dyas and Mary Jane Henderson, (BOND) Nov. 2,
1837, (P) 31

Charles Edwards and Rachel Marksberry, (BOND) Jan. 24, 1825,
(P) 5

Jerael Ellis and Sarah Morris, (BOND) Dec. 19, 1830, (P) 16

William Ellis and Nancy Smith, (BOND) Nov. 25, 1830, (P) 16

Robert Elliston and Polley Tull, (BOND) Dec. 23, 1828, (P) 12

Caleb Evans and Salley Smith, (BOND) May 10, 1832, (P) 22

John Evans and Catharine Gaugh, (BOND) Feb. 10, 1825, (P) 5

John H. Evans and Jane J. Green, (BOND) Oct. 25, 1838, (P) 34

William Evans and Phebe Kinchloe, (BOND) Dec. 17, 1829, (P)
15

Taylor Ewing and Elleanor Fugate, (BOND) Mar. 6, 1829, (P) 13

James Faulkner and Elizabeth Chipman, (BOND) Sep. 9, 1830,
(P) 15

Joshua Faulkner and Nancy Sipple, (BOND) Jan. 26, 1833, (P) 20

Thomas Faulkner and Elizabeth Laflin, (BOND) Dec. 5, 1824, (P) 5

William Faulkner and Nancy Simpson, (BOND) Dec. 25, 1823, (P) 3

John W. Findley and Polley Ann Robinson, (BOND) May 24, 1827, (P) 9

John Ford, Sr. and Susannah New, (BOND) Aug. 24, 1826, (P) 7

Thomas Foster and Elizabeth Carlton, (BOND) Oct. 16, 1827, (P) 12

James Franks and Franky Cowgill, (BOND) Jun. 13, 1824, (P) 3

William Franks and Martha Hutchison, (BOND) Jan. 31, 1839, (P) 33

Edward Fugate and Mahala Ashcraft, (BOND) Jul. 3, 1833, (P) 21

Henry Fugate and Nancy Gregory, (BOND) Jul. 30, 1835, (P) 27

John C. Gale and Mary Jump, (BOND) Dec. 22, 1835, (P) 27

Peter Gasney and Julia Ann Barker, (BOND) Apr. 3, 1828, (P) 10

Frances Gaugh and Mary Evans, (BOND) Mar. 23, 1826, (P) 11

William T. Gooch and Theodocia Hampton, (BOND) Jun. 9, 1836, (P) 28

Samuel Gossett and Eliza Faulkner, (BOND) May 19, 1834, (P) 24

George S. Gravit and Nancy Franks, (BOND) Apr. 5, 1838, (P) 32

Benjamin F. Green and Sarah More, (BOND) Sep. 2, 1838, (P) 34

Nathaniel Green and Nancy Collins, (BOND) Jan. 24, 1825, (P) 5

John Greenlee and Hester Layton, (BOND) Apr. 2, 1833, (P) 20

Nathaniel R. Gregg and Susan J. Daniel, (BOND) Jul. 29, 1837, (P) 30

Jacob Gross and Keziah Agee, (BOND) Feb. 5, 1832, (P) 22

Zach. Hagan and Elizabeth Doty, (BOND) Dec. 4, 1828, (P) 10

Elijah Hammond and Elizabeth Winans, (BOND) Sep. 6, 1826, (P) 8

Benjamin Harmon and Betsy Williams, (BOND) Dec. 23, 1830, (P) 17

Davies H. Harmon and Salley Mitts, (BOND) Aug. 23, 1827, (P) 11

John Harmon and Elizabeth Norton, (BOND) Sep. 1, 1824, (P) 4

Hosea Harris and Margarett Landrum, (BOND) Jan. 11, 1837, (P) 31

Daniel Harrison and Jane Williams, (BOND) Mar. 23, 1823, (P) 2

Henry Harrison and Polley Zinn, (BOND) Aug. 5, 1827, (P) 10

John Harrison and Elizabeth Childres, (BOND) Sep. 13, 1822, (P) 2

John Harrison and Elvina Tongate, (BOND) Apr. 3, 1825, (P) 5

Wm. H. Harrison and Nancy Ann Faulkner, (BOND) Sep. 9, 1833, (P) 22

Philip Hawkins and Sinah Arnold, (BOND) Mar. 30, 1836, (P) 29

Alfred Hays and Martha Pierce, (BOND) Jan. 8, 1832, (P) 19

Vaun Hays and Margaret Fuller, (BOND) Jul. 17, 1832, (P) 22

James Hazelwood and Elizabeth Buskirk, (BOND) Dec. 18, 1834, (P) 25

William Hazlewood and Salley Zinn, (BOND) Nov. 10, 1830, (P) 16

Charles D. Henderson and Josephine Wilson, (BOND) Dec. 21, 1835, (P) 27

Jones Henderson and Malinda Bryant, (BOND) May 2, 1831, (P) 18

Nathaniel Henderson and P. A. Evans, (BOND) Feb. 28, 1834, (P) 24

David Hensly and Leanner W. Draper, (BOND) Aug. 9, 1838, (P) 31

James Hill and Milly Hutchison, (BOND) Mar. 24, 1825, (P) 4

Jordan Hill and Denecia Hawkins, (BOND) Jan. 27, 1825, (P) 5

John Hix and Elizabeth Morris, (BOND) Aug. 14, 1827, (P) 11

Thos. Hix and Susan Robinson, (BOND) Mar. 31, 1839, (P) 38

William Hix and Catherine Jump, (BOND) Feb. 5, 1835, (P) 24

John F. Hixman and Elizabeth Deck, (BOND) Jun. 3, 1827, (P) 7

William Hogan and Polley Board, (BOND) Mar. 11, 1825, (P) 7

Lawson Hopper and Mary Ann Williamson, (BOND) Nov. 5, 1834, (P) 24

Justis Horton and Effy Lawless, (BOND) May 20, 1824, (P) 3

Leonard D. Howard and Roda Arnold, (BOND) Jul. 24, 1834, (P) 24

Joseph Haran and Nancy Vinnes, (BOND) Mar. 31, 1825, (P) 4

Henry Humphries and Rebecca Wallice, (BOND) Dec. 24, 1829, (P) 16

James Hutcheson and Katharine Piner, (BOND) May 2, 1831, (P) 18

John Hutchison and Lydia Ann Pendleton, (BOND) May 17,
    1838, (P) 33
Wm. M. Hutchison and Martha A. Ellis, (BOND) Jan. 8, 1839,
    (P) 33
James Hutton and Elizabeth Baker, (BOND) Jun. 30, 1835, (P)
    26
Isaac Ingram and Lavina Faulkner, (BOND) Nov. 27, 1823, (P) 3
John Ingram and Elizabeth Faulkner, (BOND) Aug. 3, 1820, (P)
    1
Peter Ireland and Elizabeth Hogan, (BOND) Jan. 20, 1835, (P)
    26
Scott James and Elizabeth Antle, (BOND) Nov. 11, 1839, (P) 36
Adams Jewett and Elizabeth Renneker, (BOND) Apr. 12, 1838,
    (P) 31
Elijah John and Nancy Webster, (BOND) Mar. 10, 1836, (P) 27
James Johnson and Sally Williams, (BOND) Jul. 19, 1825, (P) 4
William L. Johnson and Frances Boulten, (BOND) Sep. 11,
    1834, (P) 25
John Jones and Clarissa Stewart, (BOND) Jul. 19, 1825, (P) 4
Joseph Jones and Polley Ellison, (BOND) Jun. 8, 1820, (P) 1
Vardamen Jones and Eliza Ann Kidwell, (BOND) Dec. 4, 1833,
    (P) 23
William Jones and Polley Lambert, (BOND) Dec. 2, 1826, (P) 12
William Jones and Priscilla Sipple, (BOND) Feb. 16, 1831, (P)
    16
Abram Jump and Nancy Beach, (BOND) Jan. 7, 1822, (P) 1
James Jump and Patsey McCullock, (BOND) Aug. 18, 1828, (P)
    12
Joseph F. Jump and Elizabeth Jane Caldwell, (BOND) Sep. 25,
    1834, (P) 23
Robert Jump and Paulina Tucker, (BOND) Dec. 31, 1835, (P) 26
William Jump and Cordelia Beverly, (BOND) Aug. 26, 1834, (P)
    24
William Jump and Peggy Webster, (BOND) Mar. 21, 1839, (P)
    34
John Kinman and Anny Jump, (BOND) Feb. 22, 1838, (P) 31
Thomas Kinman and Jane Points, (BOND) Dec. 21, 1826, (P) 8
John Lail and Peggy Mccullough, (BOND) Nov. 20, 1825, (P) 6
Boswell Landrum and Salley Frakes, (BOND) Jan. 9, 1835, (P) 5
George Landrum and Sally Childres, (BOND) May 24, 1828, (P)
    10
John Landrum and Margaret Marshall, (BOND) Feb. 5, 1824, (P)
    3

Richard Landrum and Elizabeth Frakes, (BOND) Sep. 16, 1820, (P) 1

Lewis Lawless and Effy Stewart, (BOND) Jan. 28, 1821, (P) 1

Ezra Leech and Minerva Robinson, (BOND) Mar. 11, 1832, (P) 18

Thomas G. Leonard and Jane Points, (BOND) Feb. 17, 1827, (P) 9

David Lillard, Jr. and Salley Cox, (BOND) Sep. 10, 1829, (P) 13

James Lillard and Patsey Cox, (BOND) Sep. 6, 1827, (P) 11

Joseph Lillard and Elizabeth Campbell, (BOND) Jan. 17, 1826, (P) 6

Wm. H. Lillard and Ann Jones, (BOND) Dec. 27, 1836, (P) 30

James H. Lingenfelter and Nancy Case, (BOND) Jan. 15, 1837, (P) 29

Isaac Littell and Easther Baird, (BOND) Feb. 14, 1832, (P) 22

Abel Longworthy and Haney Simpson, (BOND) Apr. 15, 1821, (P) 1

John Lucas and Nancy Tomlinson, (BOND) Mar. 10, 1835, (P) 26

Richard Lucas and Elizabeth Burns, (BOND) Jul. 25, 1832, (P) 22

Squire Lucas and Mary Childres, (BOND) Jul. 11, 1833, (P) 21

James Mann and Elizabeth Mildham, (BOND) Mar. 30, 1837, (P) 30

Arash Marksberry and Patsy McCarty, (BOND) Sep. 4, 1837, (P) 30

Arasha Marksberry and Margaret Divine, (BOND) May 22, 1828, (P) 11

Henry Marksberry and Pamelia Morris, (BOND) Sep. 25, 1833, (P) 21

Hensley Marksberry and Peggy C. Jump, (BOND) Mar. 21, 1836, (P) 27

William Marksberry and Sarah Jump, (BOND) Mar. 26, 1829, (P) 14

Willis Marksberry and Milly Younger, (BOND) Aug. 13, 1834, (P) 25

Thomas Massey and Elizabeth Loyd, (BOND) Feb. 12, 1827, (P) 9

John C. Masterson and Polley Wilson, (BOND) Jul. 29, 1823, (P) 3

Thomas McBee and Helena Tull, (BOND) Jan. 17, 1836, (P) 26

Walter McBee and Sarah Cannon, (BOND) Jan. 17, 1839, (P) 34

John McClure and Jane McClure, (BOND) Jan. 26, 1837, (P) 29

Wm. J. McCoy and Dorinda Marksbury, (BOND) Apr. 2, 1833, (P) 20

Hugh McEarly and Catharine Lail, (BOND) Oct. 21, 1827, (P) 12

Angus McGhee and Salley Speigle, (BOND) Jul. 15, 1832, (P) 19

John McGibney and Mary Rowland, (BOND) Jul. 26, 1826, (P) 11

Thomas J. McGinness and Mary Ann Glascock, (BOND) Oct. 27, 1836, (P) 30

William McGinnis and Priscilla Wilson, (BOND) Aug. 5, 1828, (P) 14

Ezekiah McGlasson and Caroline Noe, (BOND) Aug. 26, 1838, (P) 34

Alexander McHatton and Elizabeth Marks, (BOND) Dec. 24, 1826, (P) 12

Wm. McIntyre and Louisa Gossett, (BOND) Nov. 16, 1831, (P) 18

Adam McKenzie and Martha Radcliffe, (BOND) Nov. 10, 1836, (P) 29

William P. McKinsey and Eliza Jane Sechrest, (BOND) Dec. 19, 1839, (P) 35

Thomas McMillen and Margaret Shively, (BOND) Aug. 31, 1820, (P) 1

David McNeil and Eliza Burnes, (BOND) Aug. 28, 1836, (P) 28

Spencer R. Melton and Elizabeth Skirvin, (BOND) Oct. 1, 1829, (P) 14

Ebenezer Mildham and Elizabeth Gibson, (BOND) ???. ??, 1836, (P) 27

Samuel Miller and Mary Jane Armstrong, (BOND) Sep. 21, 1837, (P) 30

Vincent Miller and Betsy Grimsley, (BOND) Sep. 18, 1830, (P) 16

William H. Miller and Nancy Clifton, (BOND) Mar. 2, 1824, (P) 3

Robert Million and Elizabeth Anness, (BOND) Mar. 11, 1824, (P) 3

William F. Mitchell and Ann H. Bennett, (BOND) Nov. 1, 1838, (P) 32

William Montgomery and Henrietta McBee, (BOND) Aug. 18, 1830, (P) 17

Jefferson Moore and Anne Dunn, (BOND) Jan. 5, 1830, (P) 17

Elijah Morgan and Jane Simpson, (BOND) Dec. 22, 1824, (P) 4

John H. Morris and Amanda Markesberry, (BOND) May 10,

1838, (P) 32

Francis Myers and Leevisy Dewees, (BOND) May 29, 1823, (P) 2

Jacob Myers and Elizabeth Layton, (BOND) Apr. 2, 1833, (P) 20

Sandford Myers and Martha Ann Buskirk, (BOND) Dec. 24, 1833, (P) 25

Thomas L. Nailor and America Robinson, (BOND) Jul. 10, 1828, (P) 12

Westley Nathan and Jemima Harison, (BOND) Sep. 20, 1821, (P) 2

Mathew Neal and Helena Collier, (BOND) Mar. 8, 1831, (P) 19

John Nichols and Anne Lowe, (BOND) Jan. 14, 1836, (P) 26

John Nichols and Mary Ann Lowe, (BOND) Jan. 1, 1836, (P) 28

Solomon Nichols and Martha Glascock, (BOND) Dec. 7, 1837, (P) 31

Robert F. Nicholson and Sally Landrum, (BOND) Jan. 29, 1838, (P) 32

Samuel Noe and Permelia Collins, (BOND) Dec. 27, 1829, (P) 15

Archibald Norton and Nancy Mitts, (BOND) Jun. 27, 1824, (P) 3

Hiram Norton and Lydia Ashcraft, (BOND) Jul. 15, 1831, (P) 16

James Norton and Sarah Mitts, (BOND) Nov. 21, 1834, (P) 25

Charles Oder and Caroline U. Beverly, (BOND) Aug. 26, 1838, (P) 32

George W. O'Neal and Harriett Williams, (BOND) Dec. 22, 1839, (P) 36

James H. O'Neal and Arena Webster, (BOND) Feb. 8, 1838, (P) 33

Richard Osborn and Lucinda Jump, (BOND) Oct. 17, 1839, (P) 35

Wesley Osborn and Hatty Ann Jump, (BOND) Oct. 31, 1839, (P) 36

Richardson Osbourne and Margaret Jump, (BOND) Mar. 20, 1834, (P) 28

Richard A. Osburn and Salley Woodruff, (BOND) Apr. 14, 1826, (P) 8

John Owens and Salley Cooper, (BOND) Dec. 9, 1822, (P) 2

Rasbery Owens and Grizzelda L. Brown, (BOND) Jul. 1, 1825, (P) 4

William Owens and Melinda Hawkins, (BOND) Jun. 4, 1824, (P) 3

William Rawson and Fanny Clark, (BOND) ???. ??, 1836, (P) 27

David Pains and Polly Younger, (BOND) Apr. 2, 1833, (P) 20

Woodson Parish and Polley Marksberry, (BOND) Jun. 16, 1822,

(P) 2

William H. Parrant and America Henson, (BOND) Sep. 1, 1836, (P) 28

Hambleton Pernell and Polly Stewart, (BOND) Dec. 9, 1837, (P) 31

John Pernell and Margaret Cortney, (BOND) Jul. 31, 1839, (P) 36

William H. Pernell and Mary Webster, (BOND) Feb. 18, 1839, (P) 34

George C. Perry and Clarissa Seely, (BOND) Mar. 20, 1826, (P) 8

Elijah Pettitt and Elizabeth Secrest, (BOND) Mar. 16, 1826, (P) 6

James Pierce and Nancy Frakes, (BOND) Apr. 3, 1828, (P) 10

Urial Piercefield and C. Collins, (BOND) Sep. 13, 1839, (P) 37

John Piers and Nancy Wilson, (BOND) Mar. 22, 1831, (P) 17

Benjamin Pierson and Mary Speigle, (BOND) Mar. 21, 1822, (P) 1

Samuel Plunkett and Margaret Myers, (BOND) Feb. 13, 1832, (P) 18

Wm. Plunkett and Barbara Jump, (BOND) Jun. 25, 1832, (P) 22

Edwd. Points and Elizabeth Lee, (BOND) Apr. 17, 1825, (P) 4

Frances Points and Elizabeth Beach, (BOND) Jul. 9, 1829, (P) 13

John Points and Salley Moore, (BOND) Nov. 4, 1824, (P) 5

William Points and Margaret Franks, (BOND) Oct. 8, 1838, (P) 33

William Points and Margaret Franks, (BOND) Oct. 8, 1838, (P) 34

Robert B. Porter and Martha Shaver, (BOND) Dec. 16, 1830, (P) 17

Wesly Porter and Elizabeth Smith, (BOND) May 20, 1826, (P) 8

Larken F. Potter and America Firl, (BOND) Jan. 10, 1839, (P) 33

John Readnower and Polly Furgerson, (BOND) Jul. 23, 1837, (P) 29

Thomas Redman and Mary Tucker, (BOND) Jun. 15, 1822, (P) 2

Thomas Redman and Catherine Ann Wilson, (BOND) Feb. 26, 1834, (P) 24

Nathan Reed and Salley Adams, (BOND) Dec. 30, 1821, (P) 1

William Reed and Anne Adams, (BOND) Jan. 24, 1822, (P) 1

Wm. S. Reed and Sarah Hix, (BOND) Mar. 19, 1837, (P) 30

William Rich and Jane Jump, (BOND) Jan. 10, 1827, (P) 8

Hiram G. Richardson and Sarah Ann Williams, (BOND) Feb. 10, 1835, (P) 25

Jesse Richardson and Margaret Montague, (BOND) Mar. 11,

1832, (P) 19

Wiley Richardson and Eliza Jane Lee, (BOND) Dec. 17, 1835, (P) 27

William Richey and Sally Wilson, (BOND) Nov. 8, 1838, (P) 34

John Riffle and Elizabeth Ashcraft, (BOND) Oct. 17, 1822, (P) 3

Richard Robards and Margaret Gossett, (BOND) Jul. 28, 1836, (P) 29

Jesse Roberson and Susan Hix, (BOND) Jul. 27, 1837, (P) 29

Elijah Roberts and Lucinda Schuyler, (BOND) Sep. ??, 1836, (P) 29

Dudley Robinson and Mary Ann Robinson, (BOND) Aug. 8, 1824, (P) 4

James H. Robinson and Eliza Seely, (BOND) Nov. 25, 1827, (P) 10

John L. Robinson and Liticia O. Mitchell, (BOND) Sep. 13, 1838, (P) 32

Charles G. Rose and Harriett Peak, (BOND) Apr. 6, 1837, (P) 29

James H. Rose and Elender J. Cullin, (BOND) Feb. 1, 1838, (P) 33

Josiah Rossell and Eliza Brasure, (BOND) Jan. 30, 1834, (P) 23

N. B. D. Rossell and Matilda Hone, (BOND) Oct. 19, 1831, (P) 18

Eden S and ford and Elizabeth Mildham, (BOND) Feb. 15, 1835, (P) 26

William Sayers and Jemima Jane Theobald, (BOND) Nov. 15, 1838, (P) 35

Peter Schindler and Catharine Furgerson, (BOND) Apr. 21, 1839, (P) 36

William Sechrest and Salley Ann Jones, (BOND) Dec. 8, 1829, (P) 16

Charles Sechrist and Catharine Sechrist, (BOND) Jan. 26, 1829, (P)15

Elliott Sewards and Amanda McCarty, (BOND) Dec. 4, 1836, (P) 30

Perry T. Sewards and Patsy Ann McLinn, (BOND) Aug. 8, 1839, (P) 35

Watson Sharp and Matilda Scott, (BOND) Feb. 20, 1825, (P) 6

Jacob Shively and Salley Thompson, (BOND) Jul. 4, 1822, (P) 2

Samuel P. Simms and Lucy McLinn, (BOND) May 29, 1835, (P) 27

James Simpson and Polly Ann Jump, (BOND) Feb. 5, 1835, (P) 25

John Simpson and Mary Mitchum, (BOND) Jan. 10, 1839, (P) 35

Johnson Simpson and Delilah Marksberry, (BOND) Feb. 5, 1825, (P) 5

Lorenzo D. Simpson and Polly Williams, (BOND) Jan. 14, 1834, (P) 25

Samuel F. Simpson and Mary Ann Grant, (BOND) Nov. 9, 1832, (P) 21

William Simpson and Milly Rennicker, (BOND) Apr. 26, 1838, (P) 33

John Sipple and Polley Littell, (BOND) Jun. 25, 1826, (P) 8

John Sipple and Ann L. Williams, (BOND) Mar. 28, 1833, (P) 21

Wm. H. Sipple and Nancy Ashcraft, (BOND) Jul. 3, 1833, (P) 21

Enoch Skirvin and Delilah Huffman, (BOND) Aug. 27, 1827, (P) 44

John Skirvin and Polley Ann Bingham, (BOND) Sep. 25, 1833, (P) 22

Nathan Skirvin and Mariah Bambgardner, (BOND) Jun. 3, 1828, (P) 13

Wm. Skirvin and Sarah Roland, (BOND) Jul. 11, 1832, (P) 22

Joseph Smallwood and Casey Tongate, (BOND) Apr. 7, 1833, (P) 20

Joseph Smallwood and Elizabeth Hopper, (BOND) Oct. 14, 1835, (P) 27

Archibald Smith and Elizabeth Petty, (BOND) Jan. 25, 1825, (P) 5

Hubbard B. Smith and Nancy Stansiffer, (BOND) Feb. 8, 1826, (P) 7

James Smith and Mary Franks, (BOND) Apr. 9, 1835, (P) 26

Jesse E. Smith and Rosey Ann Beard, (BOND) Nov. 5, 1837, (P)31

Patterson Smith and Mary Simpson, (BOND) Sep. 18, 1837, (P) 31

Thompson Smith and Margaret Hazelwood, (BOND) Jun. 27, 1833, (P) 21

George Speagle and Mahaly Boyd, (BOND) May 2, 1831, (P) 18

Edward Spencer and Lucy Moore, (BOND) Jul. 31, 1827, (P) 9

William Spencer and Elizabeth Elliston, (BOND) Oct. 23, 1836, (P) 29

Albert Steele and Emily Hampton, (BOND) Jan. 31, 1838, (P) 31

John Steers and Jane Frakes, (BOND) Jan. 9, 1834, (P) 24

Lewis Stephens and Sarah A. Draper, (BOND) Jul. 28, 1839, (P) 35

Thomas Stephenson and Nancy Richardson, (BOND) Jun. 7, 1829, (P) 15

William Stephenson and Elizabeth Tell, (BOND) Dec. 6, 1829,
(P) 12
Feilden Stevens and Nancy Stevens, (BOND) Sep. 12, 1833, (P)
23
Elisha Stewart and Sarah Beverly, (BOND) Nov. 13, 1828, (P)
13
Isaac Stewart and Nancy Beverly, (BOND) Aug. 25, 1831, (P) 17
Purnell Stewart and Ariana Matilda Masterson, (BOND) Nov. 5,
1832, (P) 19
Samuel Stewart and Elizabeth Hiler, (BOND) Jan. 12, 1834, (P)
22
Shelton Stewart and Nancy Parnell, (BOND) Jan. 29, 1831, (P)
17
John Strode and Cagey Woodyard, (BOND) May 15, 1828, (P)
11
Edward Stroud and Harriet Vanlandingham, (BOND) Sep. 15,
1825, (P) 5
Elijah Sturgeon and Lucy McCullock, (BOND) Aug. 16, 1821,
(P) 1
Daniel Sweigart and Manor (?) Marksberry, (BOND) Jun. 8,
1828, (P) 11
James Taylor and Rebeckah Zinn, (BOND) Jan. 11, 1821, (P) 1
James A. Taylor and Sarah M. Westlake, (BOND) Apr. 12, 1838,
(P) 32
Thomas P. Taylor and Sealah Holbrook, (BOND) May 14, 1828,
(P) 12
William Templeton and Polley Childres, (BOND) Aug. 18, 1822,
(P) 3
James Theobald and Mary Dickerson, (BOND) Jan. 14, 1837, (P)
30
Nathaniel J. Theobald and Margaret A. J. Theobald, (BOND)
Sep. 30, 1835, (P) 23
Hezekiah Thomas and Polley Theobald, (BOND) Aug. 9, 1821,
(P) 1
John Thomas and Eleanor Jones, (BOND) Aug. 8, 1822, (P) 3
John Thomas and Merinda Childres, (BOND) Jan. 8, 1824, (P) 4
Thomas Thomas, Jr. and Joana C. Masterson, (BOND) Feb. 6,
1828, (P) 14
William P. Thomas and Jane Lockhart, (BOND) Jan. 16, 1831,
(P) 19
William P. Thomas and Mahala Brown, (BOND) Nov. 4, 1838,
(P) 38
John Thompson and Elizabeth Childres, (BOND) Oct. 28, 1826,

(P) 8

Asa Tomlin and Eliza Jane Franks, (BOND) Mar. 21, 1839, (P) 34

Gibson Tongate and Eliza McCarty, (BOND) Aug. 20, 1834, (P) 25

John Tongate and Sarah Ann Mcbee, (BOND) Dec. 31, 1837, (P) 31

Samuel Tongate and Peggy Marksberry, (BOND) Jul. 19, 1825, (P) 4

Wm. Tongate and Nancy Doyle, (BOND) Jul. 9, 1833, (P) 21

Westly Tully and Cass and ra Arnold, (BOND) Mar. 10, 1822, (P) 2

Alexander Turner and Susannah Stewart, (BOND) Jan. 10, 1832, (P) 19

Richard Vallandingham and Kizziah Stewart, (BOND) Dec. 27, 1838, (P) 32

Griffin Vaughan and Salley Lee, (BOND) Feb. 6, 1823, (P) 3

John Walden and Rachel Crook, (BOND) Apr. 29, 1830, (P) 19

Adam R. Walker and Judith Collins, (BOND) Feb. 28, 1839, (P) 34

Allen Waller and Melissa Gurley, (BOND) Jun. 1, 1826, (P) 7

Thomas Waller and Mariam Coppage, (BOND) Jun. 29, 1823, (P) 3

John Warnick and Margaret Ann Nicholson, (BOND) Dec. 11, 1838, (P) 38

Albert Wash and Nancy Butter, (BOND) Jan. 11, 1839, (P) 35

Joseph Watson and Ann E. Wallace, (BOND) Jul. 21, 1839, (P) 35

Alfred Webster and Matilda Broows, (BOND) Dec. 3, 1835, (P) 27

Bivin Webster and Polley Burns, (BOND) Jun. 16, 1822, (P) 1

John Webster and Malinda Underwood, (BOND) Aug. 17, 1820, (P) 1

John Webster and Polley Kinchloe, (BOND) Sep. 18, 1828, (P) 12

Nicholas Webster and Amanda Bates, (BOND) May 2, 1831, (P) 18

S and ford Webster and Catharine A. Webster, (BOND) Nov. 3, 1834, (P) 26

Wiley Webster and Lydia Hawkins, (BOND) Jun. 25, 1837, (P) 31

William Webster and Virginia Beech, (BOND) Aug. 1, 1824, (P) 1

William Webster and Sally Webster, (BOND) Oct. 25, 1832, (P) 24

John Wetham and Elizabeth Hutchison, (BOND) Dec. 5, 1821, (P) 1

Aquilla Wheeler and Bethelem Woodyard, (BOND) Nov. 2, 1823, (P) 3

Emery Wheeler and Salley Banks, (BOND) Dec. 25, 1827, (P) 14

Alexander T. Wilhoit and Sarah Gossett, (BOND) Mar. 19, 1839, (P) 34

Alfred Williams and Salley Theobald, (BOND) May 6, 1835, (P) 27

Cyrus Williams and Sally Younger, (BOND) Apr. 2, 1833, (P) 20

David Williams and Susannah Hutchison, (BOND) Jan. 16, 1839, (P) 33

David L. Williams and Harriet M. Day, (BOND) Oct. 3, 1839, (P) 35

Eli Williams and Nancy Harrison, (BOND) Feb. 14, 1822, (P) 2

Hiatt J. Williams and Henrietta Gouge, (BOND) Nov. 8, 1831, (P) 19

Jeremiah Williams and Susannah Crook, (BOND) Jan. 30, 1830, (P) 17

John Williams and Nancy Hix, (BOND) Jan. 5, 1832, (P) 18

Kavanaugh Williams and Louisiana Gouge, (BOND) Feb. 20, 1830,(P) 19

Thomas Williams and Polley Huffman, (BOND) Nov. 10, 1826, (P) 9

William Williams and Mary Jones, (BOND) Oct. 1, 1836, (P) 28

William L. Williams and Jemima Norton, (BOND) Mar. 26, 1829, (P) 13

Winder D. Williams and Rebecca How, (BOND) Jun. 11, 1838, (P) 32

Austin Willis and Sophia Marksberry, (BOND) Aug. 18, 1836, (P) 28

David Wilson and Nancy Brumback, (BOND) Aug. 16, 1821, (P) 1

James Wilson and Sarah Oder, (BOND) Apr. 8, 1839, (P) 34

James Wilson and Permelia Webster, (BOND) Mar. 20, 1839, (P) 34

James Madison Wilson and Zerilda Marksberry, (BOND) May 25, 1829, (P) 13

Jameson Wilson and Eleanor Thornhill, (BOND) Apr. 2, 1833, (P)20

Robert E. Wilson and Mary Collins, (BOND) May 7, 1837, (P)

30

Samuel Wilson and Sidney Mcmillen, (BOND) Aug. 9, 1821, (P)
1

Samuel Wilson and Sarah Simpson, (BOND) Nov. 8, 1838, (P)
38

William Wilson and Elizabeth Jump, (BOND) Jun. 28, 1831, (P)
19

William A. Wilson and Elizabeth Williamson, (BOND) Dec. 27, 1830, (P) 17

James Winans and Sarah Howe, (BOND) Apr. 19, 1829, (P) 14

Henry Winkle and Mary Ann Beach, (BOND) Jun. 28, 1834, (P)
24

John Winkle and Ebelina Sowders, (BOND) Jul. 17, 1828, (P) 13

Thomas Wood and Harriett Johnson, (BOND) Dec. 30, 1836, (P)
29

Barney Woodyard and Dorinda Marksberry, (BOND) Oct. 21, 1824,(P) 4

Henry Woodyard and Bridella Black, (BOND) Aug. 31, 1834, (P)
24

Strother Woodyard and Polley Coleman, (BOND) Dec. 10, 1825, (P) 6

Edward Wyatt and Elizabeth Courtney, (BOND) Oct. 17, 1835, (P) 28

Charles Younger and Margaret Laflin, (BOND) Dec. 9, 1839, (P)
37

John B. Younger and Lucinda Heflin, (BOND) Nov. 11, 1838, (P)
32

William Zinn and Elizabeth Hazlewood, (BOND) Mar. 21, 1830, (P) 16

Cathalina Garnhart, St. Fernand to de las Barrancas to Jose Deville Degoutin, Commandant of St. Fernando de las Barrancas, Feb. 24, 1797

Cathalina Garnhart declares that she is the daughter of Miguel Garnhart, of Kentucky, who arrived here on the 3rd of the present month, and having lost some papers, were forced to remain while getting others. On the day after their arrival, she was proposed to by Second Lieutenant Francisco Borras of this fort and after a short courtship she agreed to marry him. On the 6th of the present month they met, each with two witnesses, Thomas Baker and wife for her and Miguel Solivella, a warehouse watchman and Berndo Molina, Commander of a ship, assisted as interpreter by Juan Glas. Borras took her hand and declared her to be his wife, giving her a gold coin in place of the ring usually given. Having objected to the form of marriage, Borras assured her it was valid. She has

148

been informed a short time ago that this ceremony is not valid and was done with the purpose of deceiving her because of her ignorance. She begs to be taken under Degoutin's protection.

Father John Brady, May 16, 1796, Performing Unlawful Marriage
Proceedings carried out against Father Juan Brady for having married Pedro Cervantes and Maria Roger without banns, and Roberto Jonsons and Maria Souvage without previous proceedings, there being suspicion of his having been married in Kentoque.

Benedict Joseph Flaget, Bishop of Bardstown, Kentucky to Father Brutey, Baltimore, Maryland, Oct. 28, 1811
Sends thanks to Madame Berquin who told him of the death of Mrs. Duffant and who has promised rosaries for him, to Madame Fournier, Madame Leroy, Madame Lacombe, Madame Miran, and Dumoulin. Also Mesdames St. Martin, De Levite, and Mademoiselle Constance. He asks to be remembered to Mesdames Orrourck and Latallaye, Madam Granpre and her brother, Madame Amiote and Madame de Volumbrun. Mr. Xoupy is a little negligent in not writing, and that goes for Didier. He asks that Bruté embrace Nagot and the others. He greets the seminarists beginning with Mr. Cloriviere. He greets the families of Elder, Jourdain, Walsh, Sinott, etc. Father Badin joins him in greeting all the guests and Mr. Godefroy.

Father I. A. Reynolds, Bardstown, Kentucky to Father John Timon, Perryville, Missouri, Jun. 22, 1831
After the letter of December 12, Reynolds wrote to Father McMahon who visits Danville, requesting McMahon to give some information relative to the son of Mr. Brown, Timon's late convert. Young Brown is residing in the Deaf and Dumb Asylum of Danville, in good health and improving rapidly. The institution is entirely under Presbyterian control; the principal is the Reverend John R. Carr. McMahon begs that the boy's father and Timon interest themselves concerning the youth's religion. The Bishop remembers Brown and family and has been delighted on hearing of his conversion. Timon's greetings are reciprocated by Father Clark, the Mother Superior and Sisters of Nazareth and all his acquaintances. Reynolds wishes to be remembered to Bishop Rosati and Mr. Rapier.

Mrs. Balfour and her sister, Miss Long, converts, have moved from Baltimore to Atlas, Illinois. Reynolds hopes some clergyman will from time to time visit Atlas. Mrs. Balfour and family are particular friends of Flaget. Could not Timon visit them himself.

Miscellaneous Vital Kentucky Records.

A. D. Collins: (CO) Fulton, (D) May 14, 1914, (A) 81Y, (B) 1833ca.

Aron Hite: (CO) Trigg, (D) Aug. 24, 1923, (A) 100Y, (B) 1823ca.

George Woodford Crain: (CO) Hart, (B) Mar. 15, 1827, (D) Dec. 2, 1902.

William H. Senour: (CO) Boone, (D) Jan. 11, 1920, (A) 87Y, (B) 1833ca.

Elijah Arnold: (CO) Owen, (D) May 28, 1912, (A) 80Y, (B) 1832ca.

A. J. Skillman: (CO) Bourbon, (D) Jul. 27, 1921, (A) 86Y, (B) 1835ca

Katy Wilhoit: (CO) Henry, (B) Oct. 23, 1807.

Porter S. Campbell: (CO) Logan, (D) May 10, 1911, (A) 82Y, (B) 1829ca.

Amanda Adams: (CO) Marion, (D) Jul. 15, 1924, (A) 85Y, (B) 1839ca.

Martha W. Smith: (CO) Taylor, (D) Jun. 15, 1915, (A) 82Y, (B) 1833ca.

A. B. Tapp: (CO) Jefferson, (D) Dec, 10, 1911, (A) 72Y, (B) 1839ca.

Christophe T. Ellis: (CO) Barren, (D) Aug. 23, 1913, (A) 78Y, (B) 1835ca.

Amanda Adams: (CO) Clark, (D) Dec. 18, 1914, (A) 79Y, (B) 1835ca.

Jane Anderson: (CO) Perry, (B) Mar. 18, 1832, (D) Jul. 19, 1920, (DP) Breathitt.

Allen W. Ellis: (CO)Warren, (D) Aug. 7, 1920, (A) 84Y (B) 1836ca.

W. J. Bagby: (CO) Henderson, (B) Jul. 10, 1837, (D) Jun. 1, 1911, (PRTS) Jessie Bagby, (CMTS) Buried at Fernwood Cemetery.

Bryant Senour: (CO) Kenton, (D) Feb. 8, 1917, (A) 78Y, (B) 1839ca.

Jane A. Senour: (CO) Kenton, (D) Aug. 15, 1914, (A) 78Y, (B) 1836ca.

Margaret McCune: (B) May 20, 1776, (D) Mar. 24, 1857, (DP) Cythiana, Harrison Co., Ky.

Elijah S. Armstrong: (CO) Boyle, (D) Aug. 26, 1922, (A) 88Y (B) 1834ca.

David Faulker: (CO) Bourbon, (B) Sep. 2, 1789, (D) Jul. 19, 1849, (PD) Barren Co.

Calvin Adkins: (B) 1822ca., (CMTS) Corp, CO. H, 2nd TN Vol. Inf., Enrolled at Somerset, KY on Jan. 1, 1862, Discharged at Murfreesboro, TN with chronic disability.

Martha A. Smith (CO) Owen, (D) Nov. 21, 1924, (A) 88Y, (B) 1836ca.

Betsey Smith: (B) Mar. 2, 1795, (BP) Bourbon Co., KY, (D) Jun. 30, 1855, (DP) Louisiana, MO.

Margaret B. Reading: (B) Nov. 11, 1797, (D) May 18, 1860, (DP) Pike Co., MO.

William Reading: (B) Oct. 9, 1792, (BP) Bourbon Co., KY, (D) Sep. 2, 1868, (DP) Pike Co., MO.

George T. Porter: (CO) Jefferson, (D) Nov. 3, 1914, (A) 82Y, (B) 1832ca.

James C. Young: (B) 1826ca, (CMTS) Pvt. CO. F, 2nd TN Vol. Inf., Enrolled at Camp Dick Robinson, KY on Sep. 23, 1861, Mustered in at Wilcat, KY on Oct. 26, 1861. Captured Oct. 20, 1862, Imprisoned at Richmond and later at Andersonville on Feb. 18, 1864. He died at Andersonville on Apr. 20, 1864.

Am and a Adams: (CO) Pulaski, (D) Nov. 10, 1912, (A) 73Y, (B) 1831ca.

Isabella Bishop: (CO) Kenton, (D) Aug. 25, 1917, (A) 83Y, (B) 1834ca.

Elijah Engle: (CO) Henry, (B) Apr. 23, 1823.

Capt. James M. Melton: (B)1833ca. (CMTS) Enrolled in Co. B, 2nd TN Vol. Inf. at Montgomery, TN; Mustered in at Camp Dick Robinson, KY on Aug. 20, 1861, Promoted to major on Apr. 1, 1862 and Lt. Col. On Oct. 18, 1862.

Allen Markham: (CO) Russell, (D) Jan. 7, 1914, (A) 85Y, (B) 1829ca.

Elizabeth Orman: (CO) Boyles, (D) Nov. 20, 1920, (A) 83Y, (B) 1837ca.

Eleazor Gore: (CO) Trigg, (D) Feb. 14, 1830.

A. T. Ellis: (CO) Simpson, (D) Feb. 19, 1912, (A) 81Y, (B) 1831ca.

John Quincy Adams: (CO) Perry, (B) Apr. 17, 1831.

Jacob Dye: (B) May 17, 1774, (BP) NJ, (D) Jan. 15, 1822, (DP) Mason Co., KY.

Ara A. Goodloe: (CO) Daviess, (D) Dec. 27, 1914, (A) 82Y, (B) 1832ca.

Euphemia A. Foley: (CO) Kentucky, (B) May 6, 1831, (D) Nov. 18, 1912, (PD) Mount Zion, Macon Co., IL.

Sarah Cartwright: (CO) Greenup, (B) Jun. 12, 1832.

John Shawhan: (B) Oct. 23, 1771, (BP) Hampshire Co., VA, (D) Apr. 5, 1845, (DP) Bourbon Co., KY.

Kentucky Connections: 1882 Doniphan County, Kansas Plat Book

H. N. Beauchamp: (B) 1815, (BP) Breckenridge County, Ky, (ARVD) 1854; (RES) Section 33, Township 4, Range 20, (PO) Doniphan; (OC) farmer.

Andrew Dutton: (B) 1830, (BP) Pulaski County, Ky., (ARVD) 1865; (RES) Section 34, Township 1, Range 19, (PO) Iowa Point; (OC) Farming and Stock-Raising.

W. H. Dutton: (B) 1829, (BP) Pulaski County, Ky., (ARVD) 1861, (RES) Section 35, Township 1, Range 19, (PO) Iowa Point, (OC) Farming.

T. J. Drummond: (B) 1821, (BP) Lincoln County, Ky., (ARVD) 1864, (RES) Section 28, Township 4, Range 21, (PO) Doniphan, (OC) Farmer and Fruit-Grower; Mason and Cistern-Builder, (CMTS) He has lived in Chariton, Platte and Holt Counties, Mo.; in Brown County, KS. He is the father of ten children, five sons and five daughters. All living but one son.

W. H. Fenley: (B) 1823, (BP) Shelby County, Ky., (ARVD) 1867, (RES) On Section 22, Township 2, Range 19, (PO) Highland; (OC) Farmer and Stock-Raiser; (CMTS) Was in the First Kentucky Infantry, known as the "Louisville Legion," During The Mexican War ; was in the Battle Of Monterey September 21-24, 1846; a stanch Democrat.

E. Gee: (B) 1805, (BP) Garrett County, Ky., (ARVD)1863, (RES) Highland, (OC) Farmer; (CMTS) He was a slave 58 years in Kentucky and Missouri.

John Harding: (B) 1834, (BP) Taylor County, Ky., (ARVD) 1854, (RES) Section 34, Town 4, Range 20; (PO) Doniphan, (OC) Farming.

William M. Hamner: (B) 1818, (BP) Hardin County, Ky., (ARVD) 1854, (RES) Section 18, Township 3, Range 21, (PO) Troy, (OC) Farmer and Stock-Raiser.

Price E. Isles: (B) 1838, (BP) Campbell County, Ky.; (ARVD) 1857; (RES) Section 13, Township 2, Range 20; (PO) Troy; (OC) Farmer.

Nancy Lancaster: (B) 1810, (BP) Marion County, Ky., (ARVD) 1854; (RES) Section 36, Town 4, Range 19, (PO) Eden; (OC) Farming, (CMTS) Mr. Lancaster was born in Maryland in 1805 and died in 1881; There are four sons and four daughters living; one son and one daughter have died.

Daniel Landis: (B) 1836, (BP) Allen County, Ky, (ARVD) 1855; (RES) Section 8, Town 4, Range 21; (PO) Brenner; (OC) Farmer and Breeder of Poland-China Hogs.

David Lee: (B) 1808, (BP) Warren County, Ky., (ARVD) 1855;

(RES) Section 23, Town 3, Range 20, (PO) Troy; (OC) Farmer and Stock-Raiser.

T. F. Loyd: (B) 1825, (BP) Fleming County, Ky., (ARVD) 1866, (RES) Section 8, Town 4, Range 20, (PO) East Norway, (OC) Farming and Stock-Raising, (CMTS) During the late War belonged to Ohio Squirrel Hunters.

W. H. Nesbit: (B) 1830, (BP) Nicholas County, Ky., (ARVD)1858; (RES) Doniphan; (OC) Dealer in Drugs, Groceries and Hardware.

J. G. Sparks: (B) 1826, (BP) Greenup County, Ky., (ARVD) 1864, (RES) Section 32, Town 2, Range 20, (PO) Highland Station, (OC) Farmer and Stock-Raiser.

X. K. Stout: (B)1824, (BP) Hardin County, Ky., (ARVD) 1855, (RES) Section 17, Town 3, Range 21; (PO) Troy; (OC) Farmer, Attorney At Law and Loan Agent.

S. S. Swim: (B) 1830, (BP) Fleming County, Ky., (ARVD) 1868, (RES) Section 10, Township 3, Range 19, (PO) Severance, (OC) Farmer; (CMTS) Enlisted in Thirtieth Iowa Volunteer Infantry; Served three Years; was with Gen. Sherman; served as sergeant.

W. G. Tate: (B) 1827, (BP) Clark County, Ky.; (ARVD) 1854; (RES) Section 3, Township 5, Range 21;(PO) Doniphan; (OC) Farmer and Stock-Raiser.

R. Tracy: (B) 1832, (BP) Garrett County, Ky.; (ARVD)1855; (RES) Iowa Point; (OC) Groceries, Hardware, Meat Market.

Kentucky Connections: 1860 Census, Clay Co., Texas.

| Name | Age | Page | |
|---|---|---|---|
| Mary E. Green | 25 | | 798-80B |
| John Johnson | 62 | | 801-81B |

Union County, Kentucky, Old Bethel Cemetery, Off Hwy 109.

| Name | Birth | Death |
|---|---|---|
| Henry W. Collins | Jan. 31, 1839 | Jul. 1, 1851 |
| William W. Collins | Aug. 10, 1832 | Jun. 5, 1847 |
| Joshua W. Collins | Jun. 11, 1817 | Dec. 2, 1878 |
| Edward E. Collins | Dec. 23, 1830 | Jun. 29, 1852 |
| Mary Collins | Sep. 8, 1823 | Oct. 16, 1859 |
| Philip Collins | Nov. 30, 1822 | --- |
| Amanda F. Collins | Nov. 20, 1828 | Jan. 13, 1882 |
| Serina Cusic | 1816 | 1900 |
| John Cusic | Oct. 9, 1822 | Nov. 15, 1891 |
| Charles Johns | May 31, 1811 | Sep. 26, 1878 |
| Charles W. Hammock | Feb. 25, 1834 | Sep. 21, 1859 |
| Henry P. Francis | 1831 | 1915 |

| Name | Birth | Death |
|---|---|---|
| Thomas Francis | Jan. 14, 1836 | Sep. 20, 1879 |
| Elizabeth Francis | Jan. 12, 1835 | Apr. 20, 1877 |
| Mary Ann Scott | Jan. 3, 1811 | --- |
| Nancy Johns | Apr. 18, 1829 | Nov. 29, 1876 |
| J. G. Dodge | Feb. 1, 1816 | Oct. 13, 1896 |
| Eveline Dodge | Dec. 1, 1819 | --- |
| Julian Dodge | Dec. 22, 1816 | Jun. 14, 1850 |
| Robert G. McIntire | Apr. 15, 1818 | Nov. 1, 1875 |
| Martha Price | Feb. 11, 1830 | Oct. 5, 1854 |
| Lewis Omer | Jan. 26, 1817 | Sep. 6, 1888 |
| Mary Sprague | Apr. 30, 1814 | Jan. 2, 1849 |

Revolutionary Pensioners, Pension List of the United States, 1813, Residing in Kentucky, Jun. 1, 1813.

| Name | Rank | Amt |
|---|---|---|
| William Little | Private | 60 |
| Robert Barron | Private | 60 |
| Oliver Bennett | Private | 60 |
| Henry Shaw | Private | 30 |
| Squire Boone | Private | 36 |
| Quintin Moore | Private | 20 |
| George Fennell | Private | 30 |
| James Warson | Private | 40 |
| James Berry | Private | 20 |
| Isaac Burnham | Private | 48 |
| John Shanks | Private | 40 |
| Andrew Allison | Private | 36 |
| John Brown | Sergeant | 30 |
| William Nieves | Private | 30 |
| Thomas Hickman | Private | 24 |
| John Jacobs | Private | 60 |
| Robert Patterson | Colonel | 300 |
| Virgil Poe | Private | 30 |
| Joseph Shaw | Private | 24 |
| Joseph Todd | Private | 24 |

Grant County, Kentucky, Marriage Bond Book 2, 1832-1838
John Abbott and Elizabeth Lacy, (BOND) Nov. 9, 1833, (BDMAN) Jesse Conyers, (P) 21
S. C. Abernathy and Sarah Oldrum, (BOND) Jul. 23, 1836, (BDMAN) Bryan Ingels, (P) 61

Zebulon T. Allphin and Sidian Jenkins, (BOND) Feb. 3, 1833, (BDMAN) Roberts Philips, (P) 11

James Anderson and Indiana Tungate, (BOND) Dec. 31, 1835, (BDMAN) John Tungate, (P) 51

Charles T. Anness and Pamelia A. Kidwell, (BOND) Mar. 6, 1838, (BDMAN) Philip A. Anness, (P) 93

William T. Anness and Julien Groves, (BOND) Feb. 10, 1838, (BDMAN) John N. Anness, (P) 92

James Bailey and Polley Raines, (BOND) Feb. 20, 1836, (BDMAN) John Coulson, (P) 57

Lynn Banks and Nancy Wheeler, (BOND) Sep. 22, 1832, (BDMAN) George F. Wheeler, (P) 6

Reuben Barker and Berthian Daniel, (BOND) Nov. 6, 1833, (BDMAN) Robert M. Daniel, (P) 21

William Barnett and Polly F. Nicholson, (BOND) Apr. 20, 1835, (BDMAN) Robt. F. Nicholson, (P) 42

Edward B. Bartlett and Ann T. Sanders, (BOND) May 31, 1834, (BDMAN) A. Jonas, (P) 29

Henry Baxter and Saberry Purnell, (BOND) Mar. 29, 1838, (BDMAN) Reuben Bingham, (P) 94

James Beach and Elizabeth Spiegal, (BOND) Apr. 12, 1834, (BDMAN) Lawson Hopper, (P) 28

Andrew Beard and Sophia Margaret Gaugh, (BOND) Mar. 3, 1836, (BDMAN) Philip Gough, (P) 54

Elisha Beard and Mary Points, (BOND) Nov. 22, 1836, (BDMAN) William Points, (P) 70

Jesse Beard and Margaret J. Casey, (BOND) Aug. 7, 1838, (BDMAN) Archibald Casey, (P) 98

Addison Beech and Mary Beech, (BOND) Jan. 5, 1835, (BDMAN) Wm. Franks, (P) 38

Thomas Beekers and Mary Ann Beard, (BOND) May 21, 1832, (BDMAN) H. B. Smith, (P) 1

Chesley Bennett and Martha Childres, (BOND) Oct. 12, 1836, (BDMAN) D. P. Mcneill, (P) 66

John Bennett and America Naylor, (BOND) Sep. 17, 1832, (BDMAN) Littleton Robinson, (P) 5

Elijah Billetter and Marilla Childers, (BOND) Jan. 24, 1833, (BDMAN) Wesley Shilcers, (P) 10

Charles Bratton and Eliza Sammers, (BOND) Jul. 31, 1832, (BDMAN) Jesse Woodyard, (P) 4

Ephraim Brown and Thomas Hix, (BOND) Apr. 2, 1836, (BDMAN) Thomas Hix, (P) 58

Harvey Brown and Elizabeth Mcclure, (BOND) Sep. 2, 1834, (BDMAN) Thomas G. Mcclure, (P) 32

Henry L. Brown and Mary Daniel, (BOND) Nov. 21, 1832, (BDMAN) Hubbard B. Smith, (P) 9

George G. Brumback and Sally Corbin, (BOND) Oct. 20, 1832, (BDMAN) Bailey W. Kendall, (P) 7

James Burnes and Malinday Gravit, (BOND) Mar. 12, 1838, (BDMAN) Samuel F. Simpson, (P) 93

George Buskirk and Louisa Clark, (BOND) Oct. 28, 1834, (BDMAN) Wm. M. Ashcraft, (P) 35

John Butner and Isabel Ellis, (BOND) Oct. 14, 1836, (BDMAN) William Woodyard, (P) 67

Joseph M. Caldwell and Elizabeth Jump, (BOND) Jul. 30, 1835, (BDMAN) William M. Jump, (P) 44

William Harrison Carter and Emaline Skirvin, (BOND) Mar. 27, 1838, (BDMAN) Joel Skirvin, (P) 94

Joseph Casey and Emeline Ammerman, (BOND) Oct. 27, 1837, (BDMAN) Robert J. Dyas, (P) 86

Harmon Childers and Nancy Childers, (BOND) Dec. 24, 1836, (BDMAN) Joshua Childers, (P) 72

Westley Childers and Lucy Childers, (BOND) Sep. 7, 1833, (BDMAN) Squire Childers, (P) 18

Thomas C. Childers and Lucinda Thornhill, (BOND) Mar. 2, 1833, (BDMAN) Wm. M. Jump, (P) 12

James Chipman and Polly Kinman, (BOND) Jul. 15, 1833, (BDMAN) Samuel Kinman, (P) 17

John Chipman and Mary Edwards, (BOND) Dec. 12, 1836, (BDMAN) Jesse Edwards, (P) 71

Eli Clark and Mary Elizabeth Draper, (BOND) Nov. 26, 1836, (BDMAN) Martin Draper, (P) 73

Jameson Clark and Cass and er Powers, (BOND) Oct. 24, 1834, (BDMAN) Robert E. Wilson, (P) 34

John T. Clark and Nancy Theobald, (BOND) Mar. 18, 1836, (BDMAN) S and ford A. Theobald, (P) 56

William Cobb and Nelly Simpson, (BOND) Jul. 26, 1836, (BDMAN) Anderson Simpson, (P) 61

Jesse Coleman and Sally Ann Stears, (BOND) Feb. 11, 1833, (BDMAN) William Stears, (P) 11

William A. Coleman and Amelia Ann Mccoy, (BOND) Jan. 29, 1836, (BDMAN) Reuben L. Coleman, (P) 53

James Collins and Elizabeth Burns, (BOND) Aug. 1, 1835, (BDMAN) Wm. Richie, (P) 45

James Collins and Anjeline Smith, (BOND) Sep. 29, 1837, (BDMAN) Willis Smith, (P) 85

James W. Collins and Cordelia E. Carlisle, (BOND) Oct. 9, 1837, (BDMAN) J. J. Grant, (P) 85

John Collins and July Ann Clark, (BOND) Sep. 18, 1837, (BDMAN) John Clark, (P) 83

John C. Collins and Eliza Jane Buskirk, (BOND) Jul. 14, 1836, (BDMAN) William Smith, (P) 60

George Colton and Miranda Tull, (BOND) Sep. 17, 1832, (BDMAN) Andrew Tull, (P) 5

S and ford Conrad and Anne Theobald, (BOND) Sep. 6, 1836, (BDMAN) Moses Theobald, (P) 64

Berrywick Cook and Phebe Kinman, (BOND) Sep. 12, 1836, (BDMAN) James Ashcraft, (P) 64

William Cook and Edalina Kinman, (BOND) Nov. 9, 1836, (BDMAN) Abram Jonas, (P) 69

Johnston Cunningham and Mary Cunningham, (BOND) Nov. 3, 1835, (BDMAN) Thomas G. P. Cunningham, (P) 48

Charles Daniel and Nancy M. Venable, (BOND) Oct. 5, 1836, (BDMAN) Jas. Daniel, (P) 65

Travis T. Daniel and Isabella Carr, (BOND) Nov. 14, 1834, (BDMAN) Ebenezer Mildham, (P) 36

Joseph H. Daugherty and Elizabeth Ashcraft, (BOND) Dec. 26, 1836, (BDMAN) James Ashcraft, (P) 73

Anthony DeBrulear and Sarah Ann Ellis, (BOND) Sep. 19, 1835, (BDMAN) Rawson Plunkett, (P) 45

John W. Dejarnett and Margaret Williams, (BOND) Oct. 8, 1838, (BDMAN) James Daugherty, (P) 101

Israel P. Dickson and Mariah E. Peak, (BOND) Nov. 6, 1836, (BDMAN) Joel Peak, (P) 68

William C. Dickson and Permelia Loye, (BOND) Nov. 23, 1836, (BDMAN) Thos. W. Massey, (P) 70

R. B. Drinkard and Adelia F. Robinson, (BOND) Sep. 23, 1834, (BDMAN) John L. Robinson, (P) 34

Robert J. Dyas and Mary Jane Henderson, (BOND) Oct. 27, 1837, (BDMAN) Joseph Casey, (P) 86

Amos B. Evans and Mary Mccullough, (BOND) Dec. 26, 1836, (BDMAN) Willy Richarson, (P) 74

John W. Evans and Jane G. Green, (BOND) Oct. 23, 1838, (BDMAN) John W. Green, (P) 101

Joshua Faulkner and Nancy Sipple, (BOND) Jan. 24, 1833, (BDMAN) Hubbard B. Smith, (P) 10

Thomas Foster and Sarah Courtney, (BOND) Feb. 15, 1834, (BDMAN) William Carlton, (P) 27

Benjamin F. Fugate and Mariah Seecrest, (BOND) May 5, 1836, (BDMAN) Charles Secrest, (P) 58

Edward Fugate and Mahahalah Ashcraft, (BOND) Jul. 1, 1833, (BDMAN) Moses Scott, (P) 15

Henry Fugate and Nancy Gregory, (BOND) Jul. 28, 1835, (BDMAN) Jesse Gregory, (P) 44

John C. Gale and Mary Jump, (BOND) Dec. 21, 1835, (BDMAN) John Jump, (P) 50

Samuel Gossett and Eliza Faulkner, (BOND) May 17, 1834, (BDMAN) Moses Theobald, (P) 28

William T. Gouge and Theodicia Hampton, (BOND) Jun. 6, 1836, (BDMAN) Enoch Jones, (P) 59

George S. Gravit and Nancy Franks, (BOND) Apr. 3, 1838, (BDMAN) Asa Vall and ingham, (P) 95

Benjamin F. Green and Sarah Moore, (BOND) Aug. 28, 1838, (BDMAN) Wm. Hendrix, (P) 100

Nathaniell R. Gregg and Susan J. Daniel, (BOND) Jul. 29, 1837, (BDMAN) Henry L. Brown, (P) 81

Hosea Harris, Jr. and Sally Chipman, (BOND) May 14, 1832, (BDMAN) Hosea Harris, Sr. (P) 1

Hosea Harris, Sr. and Margaret Landrum, (BOND) Jan. 17, 1837, (BDMAN) Hosea Harris, Jr., (P) 75

Wm. H. Harrison and Nancy Ann Faulkner, (BOND) Sep. 18, 1835, (BDMAN) Richard Faulkner, (P) 19

Philip Hawkins and Sinai Arnold, (BOND) Mar. 16, 1836, (BDMAN) Caleb Arnold, (P) 55

Hawn Hays and Margaret Fuller, (BOND) Jul. 17, 1832, (BDMAN) Wm. Gilding, (P) 3

James Hazelwood and Elizabeth Buskirk, (BOND) Dec. 17, 1834, (BDMAN) Hiram Zinn, (P) 37

Charles B. Henderson and Josephine Wilson, (BOND) Dec. 21, 1835, (BDMAN) Wm. A. Wilson, (P) 50

John Henderson and Eliza Ann Elstner, (BOND) Oct. 8, 1835, (BDMAN) Alvin Kyes, (P) 46

Nathaniel Henderson and Polley Ann Evans, (BOND) Feb. 23, 1834, (BDMAN) H. B. Smith, (P) 27

David Hensley and Leanner W. Draper, (BOND) Aug. 1, 1838, (BDMAN) M. Draper, (P) 99

William Herron and Susannah Spegal, (BOND) Oct. 8, 1836, (BDMAN) Martin Spegal, (P) 66

William Hix and Catherarine Jump, (BOND) Feb. 3, 1835, (BDMAN) Joseph Jump, (P) 39

Lawson Hopper and Mary Ann Williamson, (BOND) Nov. 5, 1834, (BDMAN) Wm. Brooks, (P) 36

Leonard D. Howard and Rhoda Arnold, (BOND) Jul. 22, 1834, (BDMAN) Caleb Arnold, (P) 30

John Hutchinson and Lydia Ann Pendleton, (BOND) May 17, 1838, (BDMAN) John W. Marcus, (P) 96

James Hutton and Elizabeth Baker, (BOND) Jun. 29, 1835, (BDMAN) George S. Gravitt, (P) 43

Peter Ireland and Elizabeth Hogan, (BOND) Jan. 20, 1835, (BDMAN) Overton P. Hogan, (P) 38

Elijah John and Nancy Webster, (BOND) Mar. 8, 1836, (BDMAN) James Webster, (P) 55

William Lewis Johnson and Francis Boulten, (BOND) Sep. 11, 1834, (BDMAN) Thomas Redman, (P) 33

Verdamin Jones and Eliza Ann Tidwell, (BOND) Nov. 30, 1833, (BDMAN) Leonard Thidwell, (P) 22

Joseph F. Jump and Elizabeth Jane Caldwell, (BOND) Sep. 21, 1834, (BDMAN) Thos. Caldwell, (P) 33

Robert Jump and Polina Tucker, (BOND) Dec. 29, 1835, (BDMAN) Wyatt Clifton, (P) 51

William M. Jump and Cordelia Beverly, (BOND) Aug. 23, 1834, (BDMAN) John Brooks, (P) 32

Alfred Kendall and Mariatta Gouge, (BOND) Dec. 19, 1835, (BDMAN) William T. Gouge, (P) 49

John Kinman and Anny Jump, (BOND) Feb. 21, 1838, (BDMAN) Thomas Clark, (P) 92

Wm. H. Lillard and A. Jones, (BOND) Dec. 10, 1836, (BDMAN) A. Jones, (P) 72

James H. Lingenfelter and Nancy Case, (BOND) Jan. 18, 1837, (BDMAN) Wm. A. Wilson, (P) 76

James M. Littell and Sarah Sipple, (BOND) Nov. 18, 1833, (BDMAN) John Sipple, (P) 22

Jeremiah Lowe and Mary Collins, (BOND) Nov. 13, 1837, (BDMAN) John Nichols, (P) 87

Reynolds Loyd and Dyannah Jane Daniels, (BOND) May 25, 1838, (BDMAN) Travis T. Daniel, (P) 97

John Lucas and Nancy Thomas, (BOND) Mar. 10, 1835, (BDMAN) Wesley Roby, (P) 41

Richard Lucas and Elizabeth Burnes, (BOND) Jul. 25, 1832, (BDMAN) John Lawless, (P) 4

Squire Lucas and Mary Childers, (BOND) Jul. 10, 1833, (BDMAN) Wm. H. Childers, (P) 16

James Mann and Elizabeth Mildham, (BOND) Mar. 27, 1837, (BDMAN) John Mildham, (P) 77

Henry Marksberry and Pamelia Morris, (BOND) Sep. 21, 1833, (BDMAN) John Morris, (P) 19

Hensley Marksberry and Peggy C. Jump, (BOND) Mar. 28, 1836, (BDMAN) John Jump, (P) 57

Willis Marksberry and Milly Younger, (BOND) Aug. 13, 1834, (BDMAN) Peter Younger, (P) 31

William Marshal and Helener Peeveles?, (BOND) Nov. 3, 1838, (BDMAN) George W. Eeles, (P) 103

Arasha Maxberry and Patsy Mccarty, (BOND) Sep. 4, 1837, (BDMAN) Squire Lucas, (P) 83

Thomas McBee and Arrena Tull, (BOND) Jan. 9, 1836, (BDMAN) William Tull, (P) 52

John McClure and Jane McClure, (BOND) Jan. 26, 1837, (BDMAN) James E. Mcclure, (P) 76

Nathaniel McClure and Louisa Childres, (BOND) Aug. 31, 1836, (BDMAN) John H. Dehart, (P) 63

William J. McCoy and Dorinda Marksbury, (BOND) Dec. 20, 1832, (BDMAN) Ephraim T. McCoy, (P) 9

Angus McGhee and Salley Speigal, (BOND) Jul. 14, 1832, (BDMAN) George Speigal, (P) 3

Thomas S. J. McGinnis and Mary Ann Glasscock, (BOND) Oct. 26, 1836, (BDMAN) Robert E. Wilson, (P) 68

Ezekiah H. McGlasson and Caroline Noe, (BOND) Aug. 25, 1838, (BDMAN) James T. Noe, (P) 100

Addam McKinsey and Martha Ratcliff, (BOND) Nov. 7, 1836, (BDMAN) E. Ratcliff, (P) 69

Joshua McKinsey and Susan Rose, (BOND) Dec. 26, 1837, (BDMAN) A. Jones, (P) 88

David McNeill and Eliza Burns, (BOND) Aug. 20, 1836, (BDMAN) Esau S. Bayers, (P) 63

Sandford Meyers and Martha Buskirk, (BOND) Dec. 23, 1833, (BDMAN) Laurens Muskirk, (P) 23

Ebenezer Mildham and Mary Gibson, (BOND) Jan. 30, 1836, (BDMAN) Thomas M. Gibson, (P) 53

Samuel Miller and Mary Jane Armstrong, (BOND) Sep. 21, 1837, (BDMAN) Benjamin K. Merrell, (P) 84

William F. Mitchell and Ann H. Bennett, (BOND) Oct. 29, 1838, (BDMAN) J. L. Robinson, (P) 102

Richard Morris and Winiford Bowling, (BOND) Aug. 16, 1837, (BDMAN) Joel Peak, (P) 82

John Nichols and Mary Ann Lowe, (BOND) Jan. 11, 1836, (BDMAN) Danl. Seward, (P) 52

Solomon Nichols and Martha Glasscock, (BOND) Dec. 6, 1837, (BDMAN) S. S. Donovan, (P) 88

Robert F. Nicholson and Sally Landrum, (BOND) Jan. 27, 1838, (BDMAN) Wm. Smith, (P) 90

James Norton and Sarah Mitts, (BOND) Nov. 21, 1834, (BDMAN) John Mitts, (P) 37

Charles Oder and Caroline Matilda Beverly, (BOND) Aug. 25, 1838, (BDMAN) William Limeback, (P) 99

James H. O'Neal and Arena Webster, (BOND) Feb. 5, 1838, (BDMAN) Samuel Hall, (P) 91

Richardson Osbourne and Margaret Jump, (BOND) Mar. 19, 1836, (BDMAN) William Jump, (P) 56

William H. Parrant and America Johnson, (BOND) Aug. 30, 1836, (BDMAN) Saml. F. Simpson, (P) 62

Hamilton Pernell and Polly Stewart, (BOND) Dec. 9, 1837, (BDMAN) Shelton Stewart, (P) 89

William Plunket and Barbara Jessup, (BOND) Jun. 25, 1832, (BDMAN) Thomas Jessup?, (P) 2

Rawson Plunkett and Ann Ferrell, (BOND) Jun. 2, 1836, (BDMAN) John Lail, (P) 59

Sandford Points and Polly Jump, (BOND) Jun. 24, 1833, (BDMAN) William Jump, (P) 14

William Points and Not Given, (BOND) Oct. 8, 1838, (BDMAN) G. S. Gravit, (P) 100

Jessee Poland and Elizabeth Conover, (BOND) Dec. 17, 1833, (BDMAN) John Conover, (P) 23

Isaac Ramey and Sary Ann Rice, (BOND) May 6, 1837, (BDMAN) Jeremiah Morgan, (P) 79

William Ransom and Fanny P. Clark, (BOND) Mar. 7, 1836, (BDMAN) William T. Clark, (P) 54

John Readnower and Polly Furgerson, (BOND) Jul. 22, 1837, (BDMAN) Harrison Mussleman, (P) 81

Thomas Redman and Catharine Ann Wilson, (BOND) Jan. 21, 1834, (BDMAN) Jesse Wilson, (P) 26

William P. Reed and Sarah Hix, (BOND) Mar. 18, 1837, (BDMAN) Thomas Hix, (P) 77

Hiram G. Richardson and Sarah Ann Williams, (BOND) Feb. 9, 1835, (BDMAN) John Richardson, (P) 40

Wily Richardson and Eliza Jane Lee, (BOND) Dec. 16, 1835, (BDMAN) James Webster, Jr., (P) 49

Richard Robberts and Margaret Gossett, (BOND) Jul. 20, 1836, (BDMAN) Isaac Gossett, (P) 60

Elijah Roberts and Lorinda Tengler, (BOND) Sep. 19, 1836, (BDMAN) Isaac Tinsley, (P) 65

Jesse Robinson and Susan Hix, (BOND) Jul. 22, 1837, (BDMAN) Samuel Hix, (P) 80

John L. Robinson and Luticia O. Mitchell, (BOND) Sep. 10, 1838, (BDMAN) Wm. F. Mitchell, (P) 96

Charles G. Rose and Harriett Peak, (BOND) Apr. 1, 1837, (BDMAN) Joel Peak, (P) 78

James H. Rose and Eliza Jane Cullen, (BOND) Jan. 31, 1838, (BDMAN) James H. O'Neal, (P) 91

Josiah Rosell and Eliza Brasure, (BOND) Jan. 28, 1834, (BDMAN) Levin Brasure, (P) 26

Eden S and ford and Elizabeth M. Sims, (BOND) Feb. 14, 1835, (BDMAN) Saml. P. Sims, (P) 40

Elliott Sewards and Amanda McCarter, (BOND) Dec. 3, 1836, (BDMAN) Samuel Tongate, (P) 71

James Simpson and Polley Ann Jump, (BOND) Feb. 5, 1835, (BDMAN) Anderson Simpson, (P) 39

Lorenzo D. Simpson and Polley Williams, (BOND) Jan. 14, 1833, (BDMAN) Wm. Tongate, (P) 25

Lorenzo Dow Simpson and Polly Williams, (BOND) Jan. 13, 1834, (BDMAN) James McGlasson, (P) 25

Samuel F. Simpson and Mary Ann Gravitt, (BOND) Nov. 5, 1832, (BDMAN) George S. Gravitt, (P) 8

William Simpson and Milly Renaker, (BOND) Apr. 23, 1838, (BDMAN) George Renaker, (P) 96

S. P. Sims and Lucy Mclinn, (BOND) May 2, 1835, (BDMAN) Jno. T. Dickerson, (P) 42

John Sipple and Ann L. Williams, (BOND) Mar. 28, 1833, (BDMAN) Darcas Layton, (P) 13

William H. Sipple and Nancy Ashcraft, (BOND) Jul. 2, 1833, (BDMAN) Alfred Hays, (P) 15

John Skirvin and Polly Ann Bingham, (BOND) Sep. 25, 1833, (BDMAN) Asa Vallandingham, (P) 20

William Skirvin and Sarah Roland, (BOND) Jun. 25, 1832, (BDMAN) Jacob Roland, (P) 2

Joseph Smallwood and Casey Tongate, (BOND) Apr. 6, 1833, (BDMAN) Ephraim Tongate, (P) 13

Joseph Smallwood and Eliza Hopper, (BOND) Oct. 14, 1835, (BDMAN) Lawson Hopper, (P) 47

James Smith and Mary Franks, (BOND) Apr. 6, 1835, (BDMAN) John Franks, (P) 41

Jesse E. Smith and Rosey Ann Beard, (BOND) Oct. 31, 1837, (BDMAN) Jesse S. Beard, (P) 87

Patterson Smith and Mary Simpson, (BOND) Sep. 18, 1837, (BDMAN) Nathaniel Simpson, (P) 84

Thompson Smith and Margaret Hazlewood, (BOND) Jun. 25, 1833, (BDMAN) Wesley Porter, (P) 14

Samuel Speagle and George Ann Webster, (BOND) May 29, 1838, (BDMAN) Thomas Massy, (P) 97

William Spencer and Elizabeth Elliston, (BOND) Oct. 20, 1836, (BDMAN) Robert Elliston, (P) 67

Albert Steele and Emily Hampton, (BOND) Jan. 29, 1838, (BDMAN) John J. Jack, (P) 90

John Steers and Jane Frakes, (BOND) Jan. 9, 1834, (BDMAN) James Pierce, (P) 24

Fielden Stevens and Nancy Stevens, (BOND) Sep. 12, 1833, (BDMAN) Saml. Stevens, (P) 18

Frances Stewart and Manerva Hiler, (BOND) Nov. 2, 1833, (BDMAN) David Hiler, (P) 20

Purnell Stewart and Areana Matilda Masterson, (BOND) Oct. 30, 1832, (BDMAN) John C. Masterson, (P) 8

Samuel Stewart and Elizabeth Hiler, (BOND) Jan. 10, 1834, (BDMAN) David Hiler, (P) 24

James A. Taylor and Sarah M. Westlake, (BOND) Apr. 10, 1838, (BDMAN) Robert J. Dyas, (P) 95

James Theobald and Mary Dickerson, (BOND) Jun. 13, 1837, (BDMAN) Sandford Conrad, (P) 79

Nathaniel J. Theobald and Margaret A. Theobald, (BOND) Aug. 20, 1833, (BDMAN) Samuel T. Durbin, (P) 17

William P. Thomas and Mahala Brown, (BOND) Nov. 3, 1838, (BDMAN) Frances Gaugh, (P) 103

Gibson Tongate and Eliza McCarty, (BOND) Aug. 20, 1834, (BDMAN) John Mccann, (P) 31

John Tongate and Sarah Ann McBee, (BOND) Dec. 21, 1837, (BDMAN) Walter McBee, (P) 89

William Tongate and Nancy Doyal, (BOND) Jul. 8, 1833, (BDMAN) James McGlasson, (P) 16

Alfred Webster and Matilda Burress, (BOND) Dec. 1, 1835, (BDMAN) Emanuel Webster, (P) 48

Henry Webster and Eliza A. Vawter, (BOND) Dec. 26, 1836, (BDMAN) Hiram Vawter, (P) 74

Joseph Webster and Melinda New, (BOND) Jun. 19, 1834, (BDMAN) John Ford, (P) 29

S and ford Webster and Catherine Ann Webster, (BOND) Oct. 30, 1834, (BDMAN) George Roszel, (P) 35

Wiley Webster and Not Listed, (BOND) Jun. 24, 1837, (BDMAN) Martin Webster, (P) 80

William Webster and Salley Webster, (BOND) Oct. 19, 1832, (BDMAN) James Webster, (P) 7

Alfred Williams and Sally Theobald, (BOND) May 6, 1835, (BDMAN) Moses Theobald, (P) 43

William Williams and Mary Jones, (BOND) Oct. 1, 1835, (BDMAN) John Hutchison, (P) 46

Winder Williams and Rebecca Howe, (BOND) Jun. 11, 1838, (BDMAN) Thos. Myers, (P) 98

Austin Willis and Sophia Marksberry, (BOND) Aug. 24, 1836, (BDMAN) Arasha Marksberry, (P) 62

Jameson Wilson and Eleanor Thornhill, (BOND) Oct. 8, 1832, (BDMAN) Louis Myers, (P) 6

Robert E. Wilson and Mary Collins, (BOND) May 4, 1837, (BDMAN) Edward B. Bartlett, (P) 78

Henry Wincle and Mary Ann Ba??h, (BOND) Jun. 28, 1834, (BDMAN) John Wincle, (P) 30

Thomas Wood and Harriet Johnson, (BOND) Dec. 30, 1836, (BDMAN) B. F. Paris, (P) 75

Henry Woodyard and Bridella Block, (BOND) Aug. 31, 1834, (BDMAN) Robt. E. Wilson, (P) 32

Edward Wyatt and Elizabeth Courtney, (BOND) Oct. 17, 1835, (BDMAN) Jesse Coulson, (P) 47

Hiram Zinn and Zerelda Conyers, (BOND) Aug. 2, 1837, (BDMAN) Wm. A. Hazlewood, (P) 82

Union County, Kentucky, Antioch Cemetery, Three Miles West of Morganfield.

| Name | Birth | Death |
|---|---|---|
| Mahalia Blue, consort of Solomon | | |
| Blue (Age: 40Y) | --- | Aug. 3, 1832 |
| Mary Louise Artburn Briscoe, | | |
| wife of Philip Briscoe | Dec. 29, 1824 | Apr. 7, 1859 |
| Alexander Breckinridge (Age: 78Y 10M 3D) | | Oct. 22, 1850 |
| Mary. A. Rowley | Jan. 28, 1821 | Fe. 23, 1875 |
| Robert Rowley | Dec. 10, 1811 | Jan. 22, 1878 |

| Name | Birth | Death |
|------|-------|-------|
| Samuel Blue | May 5, 1830 | Nov. 7, 1836 |
| John Blue | May 12, 1794 | Sep. 22, 1840 |
| Eliza Blue, wife of Soloman Blue | Feb. 28, 1800 | Jan. ??, 1873 |
| Solomon Blue | May 25, 1788 | Jun. 15, 1868 |
| John Connell | Nov. 24, 1804 | Jul. 1, 1860 |
| Nancy Connell, wife of | | |
| John Connell | Nov. 25, 1804 | May 5, 1864 |
| Austin Hughes | Feb. 11, 1823 | Aug. 22, 1850 |
| Catherine Young, wife of | | |
| J. M. Young | Aug. 4, 1816 | Sep. 18, 1881 |
| John M. Young | Nov. 15, 1815 | Aug. 13, 1897 |
| Sanders Sale | Aug. 5, 1837 | Jul. 2, 1873 |
| Joseph H. Hampton | Dec. 10, 1810 | Jan. 7, 1896 |
| S. A. Hampton, wife of | | |
| Joseph H. Hampton | 1813 | Nov. 15, 1885 |
| Mary Sanders Sale | Jan. 22, 1801 | Apr. 20, 1837 |
| Elizabeth Miller, wife of | | |
| E. V. Miller | Mar. 16, 1827 | Jun. 27, 1892 |
| Lucy Floyd Hughes, wife of | | |
| James Thorne Hughes | Jun. 13, 1792 | Aug. 11, 1869 |
| Rebecca G. Day, wife of | | |
| Horatio Day | Aug. 13, 1790 | May 11, 1857 |
| Henry F. Delaney (Age: 47Y) | --- | Mar. 31, 1831 |
| Joseph Delaney | Apr. 15, 1789 | Aug. 31, 1833 |
| Alfred Delaney (Age: 22Y) | --- | Nov. 7, 1831 |
| Jane Duvall, wife of | | |
| Clairborne Duvall | Jul. 30, 1784 | Jan. 10, 1861 |
| Clairborne Duvall | Jan. 4, 1788 | Sep. 13, 1834 |
| Ebenezer Duvall | Mar. 10, 1828 | Sep. 4, 1828 |
| Mary J. Markwell | Nov. 21, 1823 | Jul. 23, 1848 |
| Leverne Moberly, wife of | | |
| Thornton Moberly | Jul. 2, 1806 | Jan. 20, 1859 |
| William T. Taylor | Jul. 20, 1809 | Apr. 21, 1892 |
| Jane W. Taylor, wife of | | |
| W. T. Taylor | Nov. 12, 1814 | Aug. 29, 1897 |
| Oray B. Mattlingly | Jun. 17, 1806 | Oct. 8, 1864 |
| James W. Swope | Sep. 16, 1811 | Jan. 27, 1879 |
| Betty A. Knott, wife of | | |
| George R. Knott | Sep. 13, 1833 | Mar. 3, 1856 |
| Joseph A. Mason (Age: 18Y 4M) | --- | Mar. 4, 1838 |

Kentucky Connections: Obituary of Jehoiada Jeffery, *"Arkansas Gazette,"* December 5, 1846

Died. at his residence in Izard County, Arkansas, on the 19th day of October, A.D. 1846, after an illness of about six weeks, Hon. Jehoiada Jeffery, aged 56 years, 2 months and 9 days. He was born in Rutherford County, North Carolina, August 10, A.D. 1790; and when about ten years of age, his father removed to Knoxville, Tennessee. and soon after, to Christian County, Kentucky. In 1808, he removed to Union County, Illinois. The deceased, during the last war, served his country diligently, as a volunteer, for twelve months, and acquitted himself honorably. In 1816, he removed to White River, where he lived until his death. In 1826, he professed religion, and joined the Cumberland Presbyterian Church, and lived a devoted member, and Elder of that body, until his death. He filled many responsible stations during his long and useful career. He was twenty five years a Justice of the Peace; twelve years a Judge of the Court for the county in which he lived; and four years a member of the Legislature. He was a resolute, energetic pioneer; a man of acute mind, sound judgment and firm integrity. He knew his mortal end was nigh, and told his wife and children not to weep, for he was going home to Paradise, and to met him there.

Kentucky Connections: Fauqier County, Virginia, Deed Book 20, pp. 151-153, 31 Aug 1815.

John Winn formerly of the state of Kentucky to William Tippett of Fauquier for $200 a tract of land in Fauquier viz Beginning at a white oak corner on the west side of Goose Run, running thence N 63 W 112 poles to a whi te oak on the side of a large pond. Thence N 76 E 232 poles by land belonging to ???? O'Rear to a box and red oak. Thence S 3 W by land belonging to John Bredwell to a box oak corner. Thence from said box oak corner S 56 W 140 poles and 23 links to the beginning corner white oak on the west side of Goose Run. The is land bequeathed to said Elizabeth Cox and the children of Thomas Cox, deceased by Abraham Cox deceased. Witnesses: Benj Strother, Walter Oliver, William Bridwell, John Tippet, Bailey George Daniel Winn. Signed: John Winn

22 Jan 1816 on oath of Benjamin Strother, Walter Oliver and John Tippett .

Aug. 1815. John Winn formerly of VA but now of KY made $500 bond that he will obtain the relinquishment of dower from my wife Susan by 25 Dec 1816 to land conveyed to William Tippett it the tract of land and plantation whereon my mother Mary Wynn now lives and conveyed to me by my brother Thomas Wynn. Witnesses: Benjamin Strother, Walter Oliver, John Tippett, Bailey George.

Lawrence County, Kentucky, Marriage Records.

Thomas Auxier and Nancy Larage, (MD) May 23 1822
Hiram Biggs and Patsy Skidmore, (MD) Jul. 21 1822
Thomas Buskirk and Sarah Lower, (MD) Dec. 15 1822
Nathan Adams and Precitta Wilson, (MD) Jul. 25 1823
Ephriam Blevins and Letitha Davidson, (MD) ???. 3 1823
Emanuel Bramer and Polly White, (MD) Mar. 6 1823
Daniel Whitten and Pheby Boggs, (MD) Jun. 15 1823
James Young and Jane White, (MD) Nov. 5 1823
Simeon Auxier and Elizabeth Fugate, (MD) Jul. 30 1824
James Boyd and Abagail Brown, (MD) Dec. 29 1824
Jesse Young and Rachel Adkins, (MD) Apr. 12 1824
David Bartram and Lucy Sperry, (MD) Mar. 27 1825
Jacob Beck and Leaner Selards, (MD) Mar. 21 1825
David Boggs and Sarah Holbrooks, (MD) Jan. 25 1825
Burwell Burchett and Unknown , (MD) Jun. 20 1825
Solomon White and Daces Prichard, (MD) Feb. 10 1825
Aly Adams and Ann Banister, (MD) Dec. 23 1826
John Berry and Elizabeth Thompson, (MD) Jan. 26 1826
Reuben Biggs and Katherine Grubb, (MD) Jul. 6 1826
Christopher Auxier and Pegga Collins, (MD) Aug. 23 1827
John Burchett and Milla Chappin, (MD) May 28 1827
Strother F Burgess and Polly Dyer, (MD) Feb. 10 1827
Jonathan Williams and Polly Cazey, (MD) May 6 1827
Thomas A Wooten and Jane Casel, (MD) Aug. 1 1827
James Blevins and Catherine Tackett, (MD) Dec. 30 1828
William Boggs and Ann Johnson, (MD) Sep. 5 1828
Wm. Brown and Julia Stafford, (MD) Oct. 6 1828
John Bryant and Not Given, (MD) Jan. 2 1828
Evan Burk and E. Loar, (MD) Dec. 23 1828
Elias Williamson and Not Given, (MD) Jun. 28 1828
James Woods and Polly Caius, (MD) Mar. 18 1828
Jesse Workman and Elizabeth Marcum, (MD) May 21 1828
Robert P Biggs and Sally Musgrove, (MD) Oct. 25 1829
John Bradford and Casender Pugh, (MD) May 19 1829
Martin Brumfield and Unknown , (MD) Jul. 5 1829
William Wheeler and Elizabeth Borders, (MD) Sep. 17 1829
Daniel White and Polly Stewart, (MD) Feb. 2 1829
S. Blankenship and Not Given, (MD) Dec. 9 1830
John Bocock and Susan Bryant, (MD) Sep. 3 1830
John Bowen and Elizabeth Chapman, (MD) Feb. 28 1830
James Caloway and Not Given, (MD) Sep. 19 1830
Sol Baisden and Unknown , (MD) Sep. 1 1831

John C Ball and Lulina W Clay, (MD) Aug. 16 1832
Lewis Bench and Nancy Workman, (MD) Feb. 9 1832
C. M. Burgess and Viana Spencer, (MD) Nov. 30 1832
Enock Adkins and Not Given , (MD) Nov. 16 1833
Harvey Barker and Lucinda Wilson, (MD) Apr. 11 1833
James Bartram and Not Given, (MD) Oct. 2 1833
William Bartram and Not Given , (MD) Oct. 3 1833
G. H. Bradley and Not Given, (MD) Aug. 25 1833
Thomas Brown and Nancy Davis, (MD) May 17 1833
M. G. Burres and Not Given, (MD) Jul. 20 1833
Shadrick Williams and Dicy Smith, (MD) Apr. 21 1833
Ald Williamson and Not Given , (MD) Oct. 14 1833
Silas Wooten and Julina Chapman, (MD) Aug. 29 1833
Elias Adams and Not Given, (MD) Sep. 22 1834
John W Blankenship and Eleanor Campbell, (MD) Aug. 7 1834
Benjamin Burchett and Elizabeth Watson, (MD) Nov. 27 1834
Robert Burchett and Polly Roe, (MD) Dec. 12 1834
Harvey Burns and Not Given, (MD) Jul. 14 1834
James Williamson and Not Given, (MD) Jun. 19 1834
James Williamson and Not Given, (MD) Nov. 20 1834
William Williamson and Pamelia Evans, (MD) Aug. 6 1834
Luran Artrip and Newman N. Nichols, (MD) Mar. 16 1835
Hardin Ball and Polly Colwell, (MD) Mar. 4 1835
John Ball and Nancy Berry, (MD) Sep. 1835
Pleasant Bannister and Polly Crum, (MD) Apr. 12 1835
Charles Barber and Pacific Davis, (MD) Mar. 9 1835
John Barber and Massay Wilson, (MD) Sep. 17 1835
William Berry and Elizabeth Burton, (MD) Apr. 1835
Riley Blevins and Sally Barker, (MD) Aug. 12 1835
Andrew Bocock and Sarah Robert, (MD) Dec. 19 1835
James Bowlin and Not Given , (MD) Mar. 22 1835
Thomas Bradley and Mahala Thompson, (MD) Jan. 16 1835
Geany Caldwell and Thaddeus Ramey, (MD) Apr. 2 1835
Massay Wilson and John Barber, (MD) Sep. 17 1835
Samuel Young and Sally Graham, (MD) Nov. 5 1835
James Adair and Catherine Hensley, (MD) Oct. 14 1836
Samuel Adair and Nancy Hensley, (MD) Jul. 7 1836
James Baley and Sarah Davis, (MD) Sep. 29 1836
William Bartram and Lorana Wellman, (MD) Aug. 23 1836
Greenville Bolt and Mary Daves, (MD) Dec. 30 1836
Alfred Bowen and Matilda Cassel, (MD) Feb. 11 1836
James Boyd and Nancy Lemasters, (MD) Jan. 17 1836
John Bryant and Not Given , (MD) Dec. 5 1836

B. Burk and  N. Fulkerson, (MD) Feb. 18 1836
William Wilson and  Rachel Blevins, (MD) Mar. 8 1836
James W Anderson and  Elizabeth Fulkerson, (MD) Feb. 2 1837
John Berry and  Kizziah Lambert, (MD) Jan. 15 1837
Henry Blankenship and  Elizabeth White, (MD) Aug. 22 1837
Madison Bromfield and  Julina Stewart, (MD) Apr. 18 1837
Burrel Williams and  Nancy Ann James, (MD) Oct. 15 1837
John Adams and  Kitty Large, (MD) Oct. 21 1838
James Belcher and  Elizabeth Marcum, (MD) Oct. 18 1838
Wiley Berry and  Martha Miller, (MD) Jul. 8 1838
Johnson Blankenship and  Elizabeth Hoover, (MD) Jan. 19 1838
William Bocock and  Sarah Sperry, (MD) Apr. 10 1838
John Borders and  Elizabeth Pack, (MD) May 6 1838
Eba Williamson and  Abraham Perry, (MD) Jun. 10 1838
Andrew Woods and  Keziah Lambert, (MD) Dec. 19 1838
John Adair and  Swendy Kirk, (MD) Mar. 19 1839
David Bryan and  Mary White, (MD) Jul. 14 1839
Thomas Cains and  Deresa Chaffin, (MD) Dec. 25 1839
Fene Whitley and  James P Kendall, (MD) Aug. 8 1839
Jefferson Williams and  Mary Griffuth, (MD) Mar. 28 1839
Berry Adkins and  Sally Defoe, (MD) Mar. 14 18??
John Adkins and  Nancy Evans, (MD) Dec. 25 18??

Kentucky Connections: 1850 Census, Jackson Township, Buchanan County, Missouri.

| Name | Age | Apx Birth | Page |
| --- | --- | --- | --- |
| Pleasant Yates | 45 | 1805 ca | 261 |
| Mary Story | 28 | 1822 ca | 261 |
| Robert Mclean | 63 | 1787 ca | 261 |
| Sarah Mclean | 63 | 1787 ca | 261 |
| Thomas Brintew | 48 | 1802 ca | 261 |
| Drusilla Brintew | 48 | 1802 ca | 261 |
| Susan Capps | 16 | 1834 ca | 261 |
| Bryant Brintew | 26 | 1824 ca | 262 |
| Elisha Powel | 35 | 1815 ca | 262 |
| Mary Powel | 34 | 1816 ca | 262 |
| James Powel | 15 | 1835 ca | 262 |
| Charles Powel | 13 | 1837 ca | 262 |
| John Powel | 46 | 1804 ca | 262 |
| Mary Powel | 34 | 1816 ca | 262 |
| John G. Powel | 18 | 1832 ca | 262 |
| Elizabeth Powel | 16 | 1834 ca | 262 |
| Henry Powel | 14 | 1836 ca | 262 |

| Name | Age | Apx Birth | Page |
|------|-----|-----------|------|
| Richard Brintew | 28 | 1822 ca | 263 |
| Martha Brintew | 26 | 1824 ca | 263 |
| Mary Carlile | 32 | 1818 ca | 263 |
| Isaac Norman | 43 | 1807 ca | 263 |
| Jemima Norman | 38 | 1812 ca | 263 |
| Margaret Norman | 15 | 1835 ca | 263 |
| Enos Norman | 30 | 1820 ca | 263 |
| Burnice McCarty | 40 | 1810 ca | 263 |
| Clarissa Laplant | 25 | 1825 ca | 264 |
| Elizabeth Reynolds | 30 | 1820 ca | 264 |
| Mary Jackson | 35 | 1815 ca | 264 |
| James Jackson | 14 | 1836 ca | 264 |
| Eli Rucker | 25 | 1825 ca | 264 |
| Elizabeth Rucker | 23 | 1827 ca | 264 |
| James Coil | 25 | 1825 ca | 264 |
| James Ferril | 22 | 1828 ca | 265 |
| Mary Jane Ferril | 17 | 1833 ca | 265 |
| Joh Belcher | 51 | 1799 ca | 265 |
| Elijah (female) Belcher | 47 | 1803 ca | 265 |
| Delila Martin | 40 | 1810 ca | 265 |
| James Robinson | 53 | 1797 ca | 265 |
| Elizabeth Robinson | 45 | 1805 ca | 265 |
| Margaret E. Robinson | 16 | 1834 ca | 265 |
| Frances M. Robinson | 12 | 1838 ca | 265 |
| Harry Robinson | 29 | 1821 ca | 265 |
| Ann Robinson | 25 | 1825 ca | 265 |
| Thomas S. Hill | 21 | 1829 ca | 265 |
| Joseph Rice | 46 | 1804 ca | 265 |
| Eliza Rice | 18 | 1832 ca | 265 |
| George Rice | 17 | 1833 ca | 265 |
| Isaac N. Rice | 41 | 1809 ca | 266 |
| Hannah Rice | 31 | 1819 ca | 266 |
| Rufus Rice | 12 | 1838 ca | 266 |
| Isaac Stanley | 38 | 1812 ca | 266 |
| Wills Harless | 25 | 1825 ca | 266 |
| Frances Watkins | 23 | 1827 ca | 266 |
| Benjamin Riddle | 31 | 1819 ca | 266 |
| Mariam Riddle | 24 | 1826 ca | 266 |
| Frances Reynolds | 31 | 1819 ca | 266 |
| Frances Dowdle | 48 | 1802 ca | 267 |
| William T. Dowdle | 19 | 1831 ca | 267 |
| George W. Dowdle | 13 | 1837 ca | 267 |

| Name | Age | Apx Birth | Page |
|---|---|---|---|
| Lucy Dowdle | 11 | 1839 ca | 267 |
| Thomas Coller | 45 | 1805 ca | 267 |
| Nancy Coller | 36 | 1814 ca | 267 |
| Mary A. Coller | 15 | 1835 ca | 267 |
| Philip Walker | 48 | 1802 ca | 268 |
| Amand Walker | 16 | 1834 ca | 268 |
| Dorinda Walker | 13 | 1837 ca | 268 |
| John Walker | 37 | 1813 ca | 268 |
| Aron Horn | 44 | 1806 ca | 268 |
| Nancy Horn | 44 | 1806 ca | 268 |
| Celia Horn | 17 | 1833 ca | 268 |
| Samuel Cardwell | 24 | 1826 ca | 268 |
| Mary Jane Cardwell | 24 | 1826 ca | 268 |
| John Coriner | 36 | 1814 ca | 269 |
| Garrett Cosine | 23 | 1827 ca | 269 |
| Oliver Browning | 26 | 1824 ca | 269 |
| Arthusa Browning | 20 | 1830 ca | 269 |
| Martha J. Prather | 24 | 1826 ca | 270 |
| Susan H. Prather | 14 | 1836 ca | 270 |
| Milliam M. Prather | 12 | 1838 ca | 270 |
| Elizabeth Cline | 25 | 1825 ca | 270 |
| Reuben Horn | 25 | 1825 ca | 270 |
| Margaret Detts | 18 | 1832 ca | 270 |
| Simeon Coil | 39 | 1811 ca | 271 |
| Silas Barker | 34 | 1816 ca | 271 |
| Mary Barker | 33 | 1817 ca | 271 |
| Alexander Barker | 12 | 1838 ca | 271 |
| Frances McCrary | 33 | 1817 ca | 271 |
| Isaac Farish | 50 | 1800 ca | 272 |
| Caroline Gata | 46 | 1804 ca | 273 |
| Jane E. Gata | 21 | 1829 ca | 273 |
| Mariah Gata | 20 | 1830 ca | 273 |
| Putnam Gata | 18 | 1832 ca | 273 |
| Samuel McGinniss | 40 | 1810 ca | 273 |
| America McGinniss | 34 | 1816 ca | 273 |
| Eliza McGinniss | 16 | 1834 ca | 273 |
| Sarah McGinniss | 12 | 1838 ca | 273 |
| Elvina McGinniss | 11 | 1839 ca | 273 |
| Jeremiah Haynline | 48 | 1802 ca | 273 |
| Patsy Haynline | 48 | 1802 ca | 273 |
| Abner Haynline | 22 | 1828 ca | 273 |
| Nathn Haynline | 21 | 1829 ca | 273 |

| Name | Age | Apx Birth | Page |
|------|-----|-----------|------|
| Arsilla (female) Haynline | 17 | 1833 ca | 273 |
| Sylvester Haynline | 15 | 1835 ca | 273 |
| Margaret Haynline | 13 | 1837 ca | 274 |
| Sydney Haynlinc | 29 | 1821 ca | 274 |
| Dinah Haynline | 25 | 1825 ca | 274 |
| Calvin Haynline | 26 | 1824 ca | 274 |
| Letitia Haynline | 24 | 1826 ca | 274 |

David, Father J. David, St. Thomas Seminary, Bardstown, Kentucky to Father Bruté, Mount St. Mary's Seminary, Emmitsburg, Maryland, Apr. 21, 1814.
Mentioned: Father Shaeffer; Robert Abell, John Mitchell; Ignatius Reynolds; Vincent Badin; Father Chabrat; Fater Dubois; Sister Kitty; Father Tessier.

Virginia Land Grants
Matthews, George: June 8, 1787; Ky. Military District; 1500 acres on the waters of Beaver Dam and Trade Water to the line of William P. Quarles survey No. 194
Matthews, Sarah: June 1, 1787; Jefferson Co., KY; 1500 acres.
Matthews, Sarah McClanahan: Mar. 17, 1786, Jefferson Co., KY, 1000 acres.
Russell, Albert: April 16, 1788, KY Military District,1,000 acres on the waters of the Ohio.
Russell, James: May 24, 1786, Fayette Co., KY, 1856 acres on Licking Creek, Johnson's Fork
Russell, William: Aug. 20, 1786, Jefferson Co., KY, 3851 acres on Indian Camp Creek.
Russell, William: Mar. 1, 1781, KY Military District, 2000 acres on the Kentucky River, 95 miles south of the Ohio River.

Campbell County, Kentucky, Town of Newport Trustees, 1795.
Thomas Kennedy, Washington Berry, Henry Brasher, Thomas Lindfey, Nathan Kelly, James M'Clure, Daniel Duggan.

Kentucky Connections: 1850 Census, Atchison County, Missouri
| Name | Age | Apx Birth | Page |
|------|-----|-----------|------|
| Nancy A. Allen | 19 | 1831 ca | 281 |
| Thomas M. Aull | 44 | 1806 ca | 302 |
| Jeremiah Barlow | 60 | 1790 ca | 287 |
| Louis Barlow | 37 | 1813 ca | 287 |
| Julia A. Beard | 30 | 1820 ca | 278 |

| Name | Age | Apx Birth | Page |
|------|-----|-----------|------|
| Nathaniel Blevins | 21 | 1829 ca | 298 |
| Lucy Blevins | 23 | 1827 ca | 298 |
| Daniel Blevins | 55 | 1795 ca | 299 |
| Wardeman Blevins | 24 | 1826 ca | 299 |
| Dalcina Bony | 17 | 1833 ca | 277 |
| Joseph Bony | 15 | 1835 ca | 277 |
| Nancy Buckham | 30 | 1820 ca | 280 |
| Robert Buckham | 35 | 1815 ca | 300 |
| Susan Bush | 27 | 1823 ca | 296 |
| Elizabeth Campbell | 46 | 1804 ca | 268 |
| Elisa J. Candle | 16 | 1834 ca | 295 |
| Hugh Caudle | 38 | 1812 ca | 295 |
| Harry J. Cer | 38 | 1812 ca | 292 |
| Simon H. Clayton | 29 | 1821 ca | 302 |
| Martin W. Cocine | 28 | 1822 ca | 281 |
| Elizabeth Cocine | 22 | 1828 ca | 281 |
| Jesse Cole | 46 | 1804 ca | 297 |
| Angelina Cole | 40 | 1810 ca | 297 |
| Burcilla Cole | 17 | 1833 ca | 297 |
| Angelina Cole | 16 | 1834 ca | 297 |
| William Combs | 46 | 1804 ca | 298 |
| Margaret Combs | 43 | 1807 ca | 298 |
| Jesse Combs | 16 | 1834 ca | 298 |
| Jackson Combs | 13 | 1837 ca | 298 |
| James K. Cook | 31 | 1819 ca | 265 |
| Sarah Cook | 27 | 1823 ca | 265 |
| Daniel Cooley | 24 | 1826 ca | 275 |
| Frances Cosley | 53 | 1797 ca | 294 |
| Allen Cox | 32 | 1818 ca | 292 |
| Maria Cuvert | 40 | 1810 ca | 279 |
| Margaret Daniel | 30 | 1820 ca | 294 |
| Thomas Dickman | 35 | 1815 ca | 270 |
| Margaret Dickman | 30 | 1820 ca | 270 |
| Grimes Dryden | 54 | 1796 ca | 296 |
| Nancy Farmer | 64 | 1786 ca | 273 |
| Scynta Farmer | 40 | 1810 ca | 273 |
| William Farmer | 24 | 1826 ca | 273 |
| James W. Fowler | 14 | 1836 ca | 278 |
| Dicy Gray | 38 | 1812 ca | 283 |
| John Handley | 63 | 1787 ca | 266 |
| John Handley | 25 | 1825 ca | 267 |
| Archibald Handley | 30 | 1820 ca | 267 |

| Name | Age | Apx Birth | Page |
|------|-----|-----------|------|
| James Handley | 35 | 1815 ca | 267 |
| John Harrington | 35 | 1815 ca | 273 |
| Merida Harrington | 26 | 1824 ca | 273 |
| Elizabeth Hays | 24 | 1826 ca | 302 |
| Henry Hill | 37 | 1813 ca | 266 |
| Elizabeth Hilvey | 36 | 1814 ca | 265 |
| Pacha A. Hollen | 33 | 1817 ca | 272 |
| John Honk | 26 | 1824 ca | 270 |
| Catharine Hopkins | 26 | 1824 ca | 288 |
| William Houck | 24 | 1826 ca | 270 |
| Sarah Hughs | 43 | 1807 ca | 278 |
| Melinda Hughs | 40 | 1810 ca | 302 |
| Asa Jackson | 35 | 1815 ca | 276 |
| Mary A. Jackson | 32 | 1818 ca | 276 |
| Joeph Jameson | 24 | 1826 ca | 276 |
| Elenore Jameson | 26 | 1824 ca | 276 |
| Maria Jameson | 58 | 1792 ca | 276 |
| Melinda J. Jameson | 21 | 1829 ca | 276 |
| Nancy J. Johnson | 20 | 1830 ca | 274 |
| Melvina Johnson | 37 | 1813 ca | 278 |
| Marvel Jones | 45 | 1805 ca | 297 |
| Hannah Keeny | 20 | 1830 ca | 293 |
| Carolina Keim | 21 | 1829 ca | 294 |
| William King | 29 | 1821 ca | 267 |
| Lurelda J. King | 26 | 1824 ca | 267 |
| Elizabeth King | 56 | 1794 ca | 277 |
| Berryman King | 27 | 1823 ca | 277 |
| Samuel King | 25 | 1825 ca | 277 |
| D. Lamb | 38 | 1812 ca | 294 |
| Elizabeth Lamb | 35 | 1815 ca | 294 |
| James M. Lamb | 15 | 1835 ca | 294 |
| Isaack Law | 43 | 1807 ca | 293 |
| Elizabeth Livingston | 32 | 1818 ca | 297 |
| Ellen Lowber | 49 | 1801 ca | 303 |
| Sarah Millsaps | 34 | 1816 ca | 277 |
| Mary J. Mullis | 21 | 1829 ca | 295 |
| John Mullis | 20 | 1830 ca | 295 |
| Ennis Mullis | 29 | 1821 ca | 295 |
| Frances Mullis | 28 | 1822 ca | 295 |
| Henry Mullis | 26 | 1824 ca | 296 |
| Elizabeth Parker | 30 | 1820 ca | 273 |
| Wesley G. Perman | 28 | 1822 ca | 291 |

| Name | Age | Apx Birth | Page |
|------|-----|-----------|------|
| William Perman | 40 | 1810 ca | 292 |
| Hely Perman | 37 | 1813 ca | 292 |
| Amanda J. Perman | 19 | 1831 ca | 292 |
| Giles Perman | 17 | 1833 ca | 292 |
| Rachael Porter | 30 | 1820 ca | 299 |
| William S. Price | 24 | 1826 ca | 281 |
| Mary L. Price | 14 | 1836 ca | 281 |
| Jane Purdam | 34 | 1816 ca | 282 |
| Samuel B. Rafferty | 31 | 1819 ca | 300 |
| Thomas Rash | 32 | 1818 ca | 280 |
| Ann Rash | 29 | 1821 ca | 280 |
| Elizabeth Reed | 59 | 1791 ca | 267 |
| Strother Roberts | 32 | 1818 ca | 267 |
| William Roberts | 44 | 1806 ca | 268 |
| Henry B. Roberts | 39 | 1811 ca | 277 |
| Mary Roberts | 19 | 1831 ca | 277 |
| Spencer Roberts | 30 | 1820 ca | 295 |
| S. F. Roberts | 24 | 1826 ca | 296 |
| Newton Roberts | 22 | 1828 ca | 296 |
| Jane Roberts | 22 | 1828 ca | 296 |
| James Roberts | 35 | 1815 ca | 296 |
| Samuel Roundtree | 29 | 1821 ca | 274 |
| Lucinda Roundtree | 30 | 1820 ca | 274 |
| Elizabeth Roundtree | 15 | 1835 ca | 274 |
| Mary E. Roundtree | 14 | 1836 ca | 274 |
| Irene Roundtree | 25 | 1825 ca | 274 |
| Mary J. Rupe | 36 | 1814 ca | 298 |
| Nancy Scammon | 21 | 1829 ca | 276 |
| Nancy Schield | 55 | 1795 ca | 289 |
| David Schield | 21 | 1829 ca | 289 |
| Angelina Schield | 14 | 1836 ca | 289 |
| Mary Skeen | 30 | 1820 ca | 298 |
| Jacob Slausher | 38 | 1812 ca | 290 |
| William G. Stevens | 36 | 1814 ca | 289 |
| Elizabeth Stintzen | 60 | 1790 ca | 285 |
| Augustin Stone | 18 | 1832 ca | 274 |
| Terry Taylor | 36 | 1814 ca | 267 |
| Nancy Teague | 32 | 1818 ca | 294 |
| Elenore Thompson | 50 | 1800 ca | 274 |
| John A. Thompson | 47 | 1803 ca | 279 |
| Martha Thompson | 36 | 1814 ca | 300 |
| John M. Townsend | 29 | 1821 ca | 283 |

| Name | Age | Apx Birth | Page |
|------|-----|-----------|------|
| Robert Townsend | 22 | 1828 ca | 283 |
| William Townsend | 17 | 1833 ca | 284 |
| Burril Vaughn | 41 | 1809 ca | 283 |
| Merilda Vaughn | 36 | 1814 ca | 283 |
| James Waits | 56 | 1794 ca | 297 |
| Elizabeth Waits | 19 | 1831 ca | 298 |
| Robert Ware | 32 | 1818 ca | 282 |
| Archilles Ware | 35 | 1815 ca | 283 |
| Mary Ware | 25 | 1825 ca | 283 |
| Samuel Wilyard | 24 | 1826 ca | 302 |
| Abner Wolff | 21 | 1829 ca | 286 |
| Beatruly Works | 34 | 1816 ca | 292 |
| Robert Worl | 60 | 1790 ca | 284 |
| Scynta Wright | 23 | 1827 ca | 275 |

Barren County, Kentucky, Resident Heads of Household , 1810
George Akers, Isaac Akers, Thomas Akers, Abner Akins, John Akins, Aaron Alderson, Elisha Allen, John Allen, William Allen, William Allen, Buford Ally, David Ally, John Ally, Merral Ally, William Ally, Joseph Allin, William Ames, Charles Amos, Francis Amos, James Amos, Mordecai Amos, David Anderson, James Anderson, John Anderson, John H. Anderson, Joseph Anderson, Nathan Anderson, Samuel Anderson, Samuel Anderson, William Anderson, William B. Anderson, John Argree, William Asque, Andrew Ash, Mitter Ashworth, Charles Austin, John Ayo, Samuel Azates, Stephen Babb, Benjamin Baily, Callum Baily, Charles Baily, Jesse Baily, John Baily, John Baily, Richard Bailey, John Bailis, John Baker, Patrick Balscaw, Edward Barber, Elizabaeth Barcham, Ambrose Barlow, Absolom Barnett, Absolom Barnet, William Barnet, William Barnet, Solomon Bartlet, Thomas Bartlet, Abner Barton, Jacob Barton, James Baraton, Nathaniel Bass, James Bates, Philip Baugh, William Baugh, Phismon Bays, Andrew Beard, Jacob Bearn, Stephen Beauchamp, Thomas Beauchamp, Daniel Beck, Jacob Beck, William Beco, Samuel Berlinger, Henry Bell, Samuel Bell, William Bell, Zaphaniah Bell, Benjamin Benedick, Fisher Bennet, Stephen Bennet, William Bennet, Austin Berry, Joseph Berry, Biram Bib, Sherod Bib, James Bibb, Stephen Bigs, William Billinger, Thomas Billingsley, Graham Bird, James Bird, John Bird, Jonathan Bird, Mathew Bird, William Bird, William Bird, James Birdell, George Birny, Edmund Bishop, Lowry Bishop, William Bishop Sr., Charles Blacard, Eli Blacard, John Black, Robert Black, Alex Blair, George Blair, Field Blakey, James Blank, John Blinson, Elijah Bloid, John Bloid, Clodias Bogly, John Boilston, James Bonhoney, Abner Bourd, Cliburn Bowls, Elija Bowles,

Jesse Bowls, Andrew Boyd, Susana Boyd, Beverly Bradly, Michael Brancutter, James Brander, James Brander, Edward Bray, Nathan Breed, Jacob Breedlin, Philip Bricknor, Davis Bridges, Jeremiah Bridges, Jonathan Bridges, Zacheus Bushenberry, Martha Bridges, Joseph Britton, parks Britton, Dabny Brooks, George Brooks, James Brooks, John Brooks, John Brooks, Major Brooks, Miles Brooks, John Brothers, William Brothers, Alex. Brown, Alex. Brown, Charles Brown, Hugh Brown, John Brown, Jonas Brown, William Brown, William Brown, William Brown, Daniel Browning, John Brumford, John Brumford, Simeon Buford, John Buller, William Bullingston, Jeremiah Bunnel, Robert S. Burgan, John Birks, Jr., John Birks, Sr., William Burk, James Burnet, Benjamin Burton, George Bush, William Bush, Henry Bushong, George Bushking, Jaacob Bushking, John Bust, John Butler, Joseph Butler, John Butram, Jacob Button, John Button, Jesse Byar, Cann Biby, John Biby, Joseph Biby, Lee Biby, Pleasant Biby, Sharod Biby, Lewis Byrum, Abraham Campbell, James Campbell, Mathew Campbell, Moses Campbell, William Cane, James Canebaugh, Danl Card, Robt Cardin, Andrew Carpenter, Saml. Carpenter, Wade Carson, William Carson, Arnal Carter, Daniel Carter, George Carter, Henry Carter, James Carter, Travan Carter, William Carter, Cornelius Carver, Kelepy Carver, John Carvin, William Casby, William Cates, William Chamberland, William Chandler, George Chapman, William Chapman, William Cheatham, William Cheese, Jaob Chirin, George Chism, Michael Chism, William Chism, Benj. W. Clark, Everet Clark, Jacob Clark, John Clark, John Clark, Jonathan Clark, Ruben Clark, William Clark, William Clark, John Clasby, Auston Clayton, James Clayton, William Clayton, James Clem, Isaac Clendeman, George Coats, John Coats, Thomas Coats, Walter Coats, William Coats, Andrew Cochran, Philip Cochran, Reuben Cochran, Wm. Cockran, Anderson Cockril, William Cockrit, John Colbert, Saml Colbert, Richard Cole, Stephen Cole, Field Coleman, John Coleman, Jos. Coleman, Jos. Coleman, Philip Colman, Thomas Coleman, Levi Collins, John Comanan, Thos Combs, James Condra, John Condra, William Condra, Isaac Connelly, William Conly, David Conyers, David Cook, Henry Cook, Sion Cook, Benj Corena, John Cosby, David Cosly, Robert Cossa, Thos. Cossa, Sr., Moses B. Cox, Moses L. Cox, Archer Craddock, Richard Craddock, David Crawford, James Crawford, Phoebe Crawford, Thompson Creastan, John Crenshaw, John Crock, James Cruss, Redman Cruise, Joshua Crump, Emry Crutcher, Daniel Culp, Saml Cummins, Michael Cup, Jas. V. Curtis, Isaac Dale, Rubin Dale, Wm. Dale, William Dale, Robt. Daugherty, Saml Doughty, Alex. Davidson, Alexander Davidson, Elijah Davidson, Hezekiah Davidson, John Davidson, John Davidson, John Davidson, Thos Davidson, William Davidson, Hardin Davis, Henry Davis, Jacob Davis, Jesse Davis, John Davis, Jonathan Davis, William Davis, Alza Dean, Jane

Dean, John Dean, John Defevers, Michael Denham, Daniel Dennington, Joshua Dennington, Benj. Dennison, Robt. Dennison, Zachariah Dennison, Ellenor Denny, Jonathan Denton, William Depp, Elijah Diceers, Abraham Dick, Henry Dickel, Benj. Dickinson, Henry Dickinson, John Dickinson, Solomon Dickinson, Thos. Dickinson, John Dicket, John Dicus, Joshua Dicus, Wm. Dicus, John Dinkly, Saml. Doney, James Dodd, Levi Dodge, Thomas Dopson, George Dossing, George Douglas, Samuel Douglas, William Douglas, Sary Downing, Ezekial Downs, Thomas Downs, Zachariah Downs, Antony Drain, Allen Drake, Carter Drake, Sary Drake, John Draper, Dempsey Driver, Jesse Driver, David Ducase, Elijah Ducasse, Joshua Duff, David Duggar, Thos Dugly, George Duke, Mony Duke, John Dule, Eliza Duncan, Nancy Duncan, Thomas Dunngim, William Dunwoody, John Durbin, Thomas Durbin, John Dutton, Benj. Earner, Philip Earner, John Easter, Patsy Easter, James Edgar, John Edgar, Alex. Edwards, Cador Edwards, Isaac Edwards, James Edwards, Robt Edwards, James Elbird, Jos. Ellerson, Thos. Elliott, Asa Ellis, Isaac Ellis, John Ellis, William Ellis, John Elmore, Pleasant Emberson, William Emberson, John Emberton, Susanna Emberton, William Emberton, William England, John Ennis, Jeremiah Eubert, Jos. Eubeames, Alex. Evans, Thos Evans, Thomas Evans, Thomas Evans, Sr., Jesse Everett, Thomas Ezel, Clay Farlow, George W. Farris, John Farris, Arthur Furguson, Caty Furgason, Nancy Forguson, Thomas Furguson, James Fields, Robt. Field, Robert Field, William Fielding, James Fisher, John Fisher, William Fisher, Jas. Fitzgerald, Susanna Jerrald, Barnet A. Flanagan, Thos Flanry, John Flatt, George W. Fletcher, Stephen Flinn, James Flippin, John Flippen, Thos. Flippin, William Flippin, James Forbis, James Forbis, John Forbs, John Forbis, Robt Forbis, Joshua Ford, Joel Forrest, James Forter, John Foster, James Franklin, Peter Franks, Christian Frayly, Eds. Frayly, James Frazer, John Freeman, John Fulcher, Richard Fulcher, William Fuller, Henry Gains, Richard Gains, John Galloway, Nicholas Garaway, William Gardner, John Garnitt, Sr., Richard Garnett, Stephen Gaarot, Edmund Garrison, George Garrison, David Garavin, Hannah Garvan, Benj. Gassan, Samuel Gassaway, Jacob Gates, Robt. Gates, John Gee, John Gent, Thos. Geat, Geo. Gentree, Saml. Gentree, Jacob Gibson, Edward Gill, William Gill, Wm. Gillihan, James Gilliland, John Gilleland, Jonathan Gilleland, James Gillock, Lawrence Gillock, William Gillock, Jas. Gist, Sr., Thomas Gist, William Gist, Jordan Glassbrock, Jordan Glassbrook, Richard Glasbrook, William Glazebrook, Morton Glascock, Susana Glascock, Job Glover, William Glover, Jr., William Glover, Jr., William Glover Sr., John Goodall, Peter C Goodall, Jos. Goodin, Lewis Goodin, Abraham Goodman, Alexander Goodman, Anderson Goodman, Amos Goodman, Chas Goodman, Flemin Goodman, George Goodman, Harden Goodman, Jacob Goodman, Jesse

Goodman, John Goodman, John Goodman, John Goodman, Wm. Goodman, Wm. Goodman, Thos Goodwin, James Gore, James Gore, Manson Gore, John Gorin, Jos. Goslin, Jesse Got, William Grayson, Solomon Green, Thos Green, Wm. Green, Amos Greer, John Greer, Jacob Grider, Jr., Jacob Grider, Sr., David Grimsby, Henry Grinstead, Jesse Greenstead, John Grinstead, Philip Grinstead, John Grisom, John Grubs, Jesse Gum, Hawky Gunter.Arthur Hagan, Arthur Hagan, Nancy Hagan, Sam'l Hagan, William Hagan, William Hagan, Elijah Haiden, Cornelius Hall, Edmund Hall, James Hall, John Hall, Michael Hall,Palmer Hall, Sylvester Hall, Thomas Hall, William Hall, Winny Hall, Philip Haller, Enock Hambrick, Johnson Hambrick, Enoch Hames, Abner Hamilton, Abner Hamilton, John Hamilton, Robert Hamilton John Hammit, Elijah Hampton, Jas. Handy, Jesse Handy, Cuthebert Hardan, William Hardridge David Hardus, Benjamin Hardy, Isham Hardy, Thos Hardy, Aron Harlin, Elihu Harlan, Jacob Harlin, Jas. Harlin, John Harlin, John Harlan Jr., Saml Harlin, Anderson Harlow, Clebon Harlow, Jesse Harlow, Michael Harlow, Randal Harlow, Wm. Harlow, Absolom Harper, Hance Harper, Joel B. Harper, Marton Harper, Mathew Harper, Benj. Harris, Benj. Harris, Francis Harris, Francis Harris, John Harris, Jos. Harris, Peggy Harris, Robt Harris, Geo. Harrison, James Harrison, Jesse Harrison, James Hart, John Hart, Charles Harvey, Eliza Harvey, John Harvey, Jos. Harvey, Saml. Haston, Wm. Hathe, Jas. Hathorn, Robt Hathorn, Michael Hatler, Nicholas Hauser Isham Hawkins, Jehue Hawkins, Jehue Hawkins, John Hawkins, Allen Hays, Aron Hays, Henry Hays, John Hay, John Hay, Polly Hays, Rich. Hays, William Hays, Jos. Henderson, Peter Henderson, Danl Hendrick, John W Hendrick, Obediah Hendrick, William Hendricks, Henry Hensley, Frances Hester, Wm. Hicklin, Jesse Hickman, Jos. Higdon, Wm. Higgins, Mark High, Jane Hiletock, Clement Hill, Andrew Hilton, Nathaniel Hilton, Wm. Hindman, James Hinds, Saml. Hinds, Saml. Hitch, Peter Hoback, Absolom Hobston, Achiles Hog, Gibson Hog, Obadiah Hog, Obediah Hog, Rubin Hog, Wm. Hog, Wm. Holder, John Holdman, James Holins, Jacob Holins, Henry Holtclaw, Henry Holoclaw, Jas. Holtclaw, John A. Holladay, Britton Holland, Wm. Holland, Wm. Holland, Richard Hollelam, Jas. Holloway, Richard Holloway, Robt Holloway, Wm. Holms, Jas. Hood, Thos Hood, Rudolph How, Christie Howard, John Howard, Stephen Howard, Wm. Howard, Rebecca Howcheler, Jacob Hawdeshal, James Howel, Polly Howel, Saml. Howel, Wm. Howel, Thos. Howser, Greenbury Hox, Thos. Huckaby, Chas. Hudson, Ambros Huffman, Armstead Huffman, Cornelius Huffman, Henry Huffman, Jalena Huffman, Jesse Huffman, Peter Huffman, John Hummel, John Humphries, James Hunt, Jonathan Hunt, John Ingrim, Benjamin Inlow, Saml. Isaacs, Frederick Jackson, Isaac Jackson, Ruben Jackson, Isam James, Garrard Jamison, Geo Jamison, Jas. Jamison, John

Jamison, Robt Jamison, Isam Jarral, John Jay, Patsy Jefferas, Ann Jinkins, David Jinkins, Jacob Jinkins, Jas. Jinkins, Jeremiah Jinkins, Jos. Jinkins, Nancy Jinkins, Philip Jinkins, Jr., Philip Jinkins, Sr., Wm. Jinkins, Jr., Wm. Jinkins, Chas. Jewel, John Jewel, Wm. Jewel, Wm. Jewel, John Jilis, Robt Johnson, Arthur Johnston, Barton Johnston, Henry Johnston, Isaac Johnston, John Johnston, Mathew Johnston, Susana Johnston, Thos. Johnston, Jas. Jollepp, Richard Jolliff, Abraham Jones, Elijah Jones, Elijah Jones, Jacob Jones, Michael Jones, Wm. Jones, Wm. Jones, Wm. Jones, Saml. Jordan, Danl Kelly, James Kelly, Saml. Kelly, Silas Kelly, James Kelsy, John Kelsy, William Kays, Jos. Kincade, Adam Kinchilow, Ambros Kincelow, Coonrod Kinchiloe, Nimrod Kinchelow, Benjamin King, Henry King, Nicholas King, Robt Kirby, Mathew Kirkendal, Richard Kirkendal, Thos. Kirkpatrick, Nicholas Kirt, John Kirtley, John Lacefield, Wm. Lacefield, Samuel Lackey, Mathew Lair, John Lamb, Robt Lamb, Martin Lance, Adran Lane, Moses Lane, Thomas Lane, Tilman Lain, Henry Lanham, Joe Lanning, Jos. Lard, John Lasly, Frances Lathman, David Laurence, James Laurence, John Laurence, John Leach, Chas. Leags, James Lee, Thos. Lee, Anna Leeper, Wm. Leeper, Wm. Leonard, Jas. Level, Andrew Lewis, George Lewis, James Lewis, Jas. Lewis, James Lewis, Jos. Lewis, Simon Little, Wm. Little, David Lock, Jacob Lock, Jas. Lock, Richard Lock, Jr., Richard Lock, Sr., Isaac Logan, Wm. Logan, Wm. B. Logan, John Logsdon, John Logsdon, Thos. Logsdon, Jacob Lough, Edmund Love, Thos. Love, Andrew Lowry , Wm. Lowry, James Loyd, David Lyon, David Lyon, John Lyon, Elijah McCarty, Wm. McCarty, Thos. McClain, John McClelland, Jos. McClelland, Hugh McCombs, John McCombs, Daniel McCoy, James McCrackin, Lidia McCurry, Jennins McDaniel, Alex McEny, Thomas McEny, Daniel McFarlin, John McFerran, Henry McGehee, William McGinnis, Wm. McGinnis, Squire McGuire, Patrick McKannis, Thos. McMullin, Jas. McMurtry, Aron McPherson, John McPherson, Jacob Magot, Jas. Mahany, Josiah Manes, Thos. Mains, Saml. Malone, Winn Malone, Anna Malox, Jesse Malton, Gabriel Manley, John R Manly, Ambros Manning, Ambrose Manning, Jas. Manning, Jas. Mansfield, Wm. Mansfield, Saml. Mars, Hugh Marshal, John Marshal, John Saml. Marshal, Saml. Marshal, Chas. Martin, Jas. Martin, Jas. Martin, John Martin, Jos. Martin, Nathaniel Martin, Saml. Martin, Thos. Martin, Wm. Murtin, Wm. Martin, Wm. Martin, Jas. Mathews, John Mathews, John Mathews, Jr., Wm. Mattox, Georan Mayfield, George Mayfield, John Mayfield, Jr., John Mayfield, Sr., Thos. Mayfield, Ephraim Maxey, Philip Maxey, Isaac Means, Jas. Mantiloe, Howard Mercer, Owen T Merry, Danl Miles, Henry Miller, Henry Miller, Robt Miller, Elijah Mitchel, Moses Mitchel, Moses Mitchell, Thos. Mitchell, John Monroe, Johnston Monroe, Clement Montague, Andrew Moody, Isaac More, James More, Jas. More, Jas.

More, Jeremy More, Joel Morem, John More, John More, Saml. More, Wm. More, Silas Morgan, Jas. Morrison, John Morrison, Richard Morrison, Wm. Morrison, John Morrow, Wm. Morrow, Wm. Mosby, Frederick Moss, Fredrick Moss, Henry Moss, Wm. Mourning, John Mully, Richard Mumford, Ma??? Murk, Gabriel Murphy, John Murphy Jr., Richard Murphy, Wm. Murphy, Wm. Murphy, Jr., Geo Murrell, Saml. Murrel, Isaac Nation, Nicholas Nailor, Thomas Neel, Josia Neferson, John Nelson, Jas. Nevel, Jas. Nevill, Jr., John Nevel, Jos. Nevel, Wm. Nevel, Levy Newberry, Jas. Newel, Wm. Newel, John Newhouse, Ezekiel Newtin, Andrew Nichols Moses Nix, Jos. Obannion, Tapley Oldham, John Oler, Geo Oller, Obadiah Oliphant, Henry Oncel, Henry O'Neel Benj Osburn, Benj Osburn, Henry Osburn, John Osburn, Jos. Osburn, Robt Osburn,Robt Osburn, Soloman Osburn, Wm. Osburn, Jas. Owen, John Owens, Jos. Owen, Thos. Owens, Wm. Owens, Peter Owley, Wm. Pace, John Paigot, Joel Page, John Painter, Saml. Parker, Jos. Parks, Saml. Parkwood, John Patrick, Lucy Patrick, William Pain, John Peak, John Pearce, John Pease, Moses Pedre, Edward Pedigo, Elkin Pedigo, Joseph Pedigo, Leah Pedigo, Thomas Pelham, William Pinnic, Moses Pennington, Stuart Pennington, Rubon Pennington, Simeon Pennington, Timothy Pennington, John Perkins, Danl Pery, Ralph Petty, Jos. Payton, Stephen Philips, Wm. Picket, Benj. Pinkly, William Piper, Winny Piper, Danl Pitchford, Ely Pitchford, Wm. Pitchford, Wm. Pitchford, Benj Poe, Johnston Poe, Wm. Poe, Thos. Pointer, Wm. Pointer, John Pool, Wm. Pope, Jos. Porter, Danl Price, Wm. Proctor, Timothy Puckit, Barnabas Pullam, Hyram Putman, Cornelius Quest, James Quigley, John Raglen, David Ragsdal, Wm. Ragsdale, Jos. Railes, Jos. Ralston, Mathew Rolston, Wm. Rolston, Saml. Ramsey, Thos. Ramsey, Jos. Randol, Moses Randal, Thos. Randal, John Rankin, Wm. Ratliff, Edmund Ray, James Ray, Polly Ray, John Readman, John Rearch, Levi Rearch, Edw Reed, Jas. Reed, Jas. Reed, John Reed, Leonard Reed, Jr., Isaac Rinfrow, Jesse Renfraw, John Renfraw, Sr., John Renfrow, Henry Rennick, James Rennick, James Rennick, Saml. Rennick, David Reynolds, Mathew Reynolds, Richard Reynolds, Wm. Reynolds, Wm. Reynolds, Dudly Richardson, James H Rice, Andrew Richy, Jas. Richy, Sr., Jas. Richy, Sr., Jas. Riche, John Richy, Saml. Richy, Wm. Richy, Abraham Ritter, Abraham Ritter, Boman Ritter, Isaac Ritter, Jas. Ritter, John Ritter, Margaret Ritter, Wm. Roarch, John Robards, Sary Robards, Drury Roberts, Thomas Roberts., Allin Robertson, David Robertson, John Robertson, John Robertson, John Rock, John Rodes, Bird Rogers, Edmund Rogers, Elijah Rogers, James Rogers, Jesse Rogers, John Rogers, John Rogers, Mathew Rogers, Abner Rollins, Benj Rollins, Travice Ross, Dudly Roundtree, Henry Roundtree, Mary Roundtree, Richard Roundtree, Saml. Roundtree, Jane Rowan, Isaac Ruckman, Jos. Ruckman, Benj Rush, James Rush, John Rush, Buckner

Russel, James Russel, Elijah Samack, James Shism, Thomas Samax, Jesse Saunders, John Saunders, John Saunders, Jr., Jos. Saunders, Robert Sapsly, Jesse Satterfield, Wm. Savage, Sary Saw, Adam Scott, Chump Scott, Francis Scott, John Scott, John Scott, Jos. Scott, Saml. Scott, Thos. Scott, Henry Self, Owmsley Selk, Charles Settle, Elizabeth Settle, Eliz Settle, Willis Settle, Joel Shaw, John Shaw, Martin Shelter, Geo Shipley, Robt Shipley, Robt Shipley, Phebe Shipman, Danl Shirly, Nimrod Shirley, Richard Shirley, Robt Shirly, Thos. Shirly, Thos. Shirly, Thomas Sherily, Sr., John Shism, Sr., Peter Shitle, David Shockly, Saml. Shockly, Flemington Short, Josiah Short, Lannum Short, Nedwman Short, Saml. Shother, James Siddens, Wm. Siddens, Chas. Simmons, Elisha Simmons, Isaac Simmons, N Simmons, Saml. Simmons, Stasa Simmons, Wm. Simmons, Henry Simpson. John Simpson, Jas. Sion, John Siry, Carmon Sivel, Heaks Scags, Richard Scags, John Skidmore, Thos. K Slaughter, Dabny Slaton, John Slone, Absolom Smith, Amos Smith, Coleman Smith, Herrard Smith, Hugh Smith, Jacob Smith, Jacob Smith, Jacob Smith, James Smith, John Smith, John Smith, John Smith, Joseph Smith, Michael Smith, Roderick Smith, Rachel Smith, Samuel Smith, Thomas Smith, of Fallen Timber, William Smith, William Smith, Hugh Smother, John Sniter, John Snow, John Sorrel, Jesse Southers, Joseph Southers, Peter Sparrow, Thomas Speakman, Jas. Spencer, John Spencer, Moses Spencer, Alexander Spotswood, Ezekiel Springer, John Springer, Jesse Stalsworth, Robert Starret, Mehaley Staton, John Steel, John Stephenson, Jas. Stergins, Alexander Stuart, Alex Stuart, Alex Stuart, Chas. Stewart, Chas. Stuart, Lazarus Stuart, Richard Stuart, William Stuart, William Stuart, Saml. Still, Birdis Stinson, Birdis Stinson, James Stinron, James Stinson, James Stinson, James Stinson, Levi Stinson, Jesse Stockton, Robt Stockton, Susanna Stockton, Thos. Stockton, Thos. Stickton, Archibald Stone, Elijah Stone, Jesse Storat, James Stringfield, Wm. Stringfield, Wm. Studz, Thos. Sullavan, Edw Summers, John Summers, Van Swearingin, ???? Swinney, David Swift, Thos. Swift, Thos. Swift Edward Tadlock , Frederick Tanner, John Taylor, Samuel Taylor, Jesse Temple, Lord Temple, Thos. Terry, Jas. Thomas, Jesse Thomas, Umphrey Thompkin, Woody Thompson, Wm. Thompson Zachariah Thorne, Peter Therkill, Joah Tibbudge, John Tilford, Elijah Tinalh, Stailin Tinsley, William Tinsley, Alex. Toney, Duvel Toney, Jesse Toney, Wm. Tooly, John Tox, Erasmus Tracy, Isaac Tracy, John Tracy, Michael Tracy, Harris Jerem. Treble, Alexander Trent, Susanna Trent, Wm. Trent, Haiden Trigg, Wm. Trigg, Marcus Tucker, Henry Tudor, Henry Tuder, Henry Tuder Sr., John Tuder, John Tunnel, John Tunstall, Jos. Tunstil, Leonard Tunstall, Temple Tunstall, Nathan Turpin, Wm. Turpin, John Twilby, Abraham Twyman, Saml. Vaile, Chas. Vandawaugh, Thos. Vatetees, Benj Vaughn, Obadiah Vaughn, Wm. Vaughn Jr., Jos. Venable, Rachel Venable, Garrarad

Vinzant, Obadiah Wade, Stephen Wade, Tignal Wade, William Wade, Jas. Waggoner, Richard Waggoner, Wm. Wakefield, Wm. Walden, David Waldrop, Younger Waldrop, John Walker, John Wallace, Wm. Wallace, Barnabas Walters, Coonrad Walters, Geo. Walters, Jacob Walters, Jas. Walters, Claibourn Walton, Mabon Watson, Andrew Wats, David Watts, John Wats, Chas. Weathers, Richard Weather, Wm. Weatheroe, Wm. Wetheroe, Merry Webb, Moses Webb, Richard Webb, Wm. Webb, Jesse Wells, John Wells, Saml. Wells, Wm. Wells, Eliz. Welsh, Jas. Welsh, John Welsh, Jos. Welsh, Thos. Welsh, John West, Francis Wheeler, John Wheeler, Archibald White, Edmund White, Eliza White, Jas. White, Jas. White, John White, Pleasant White, Thos. White, Wm. White, Thos. Whitledge, Granville Whitlow, Pleasant Whitlow, Sally Whitlow, Jeremiah Whitney, John Whitney, Thos. Whitwell, Gideon Wilbourn, Isaac Wilburns, Jas. Wilbourn, Joshua Wilbourn, Saml. Wilbourn, Saml. Wilbourn, Thomas Wiley, George Willhelms, John Wilkerson, Martin Wilkerson, William Willkerson, Benj Williams, George Williams, Jas. Williams, Jas. Williams, John Williams, John Williams, John Williams, Jonas Williams, Thomas Williams, John Williamson, Thos. Williamson, Thos. Williamson, Jr., Wm. Willis, Isara Wilson, Jacob Wilson, Jas. Wilson, John Wilson, John Wilson, John Wilson, Joshua Wilson, Thos. Wilson, Thos. L. Wilson, Wm. Wilson, Wm. Wilson, Joshua Winfred, Joshua Winn, Joshua Winn Jr., Tho Winn, John Wolf, Anderson Wood, Bartholomew Wood, Jas. Wood, Jesse Wood, Martin Wood, Peter Wood, Saml. Wood, Wm. Wood, Wm. S. Wood, Hannah Woodard, Saml. Woodson, Thos. Woodson, Levy Wooly, Danl Wray, John Wray, Isaac Wren, Christo. Wright, Jacob Wright, John Wright, John Wright, Jos. Wright, Thos. Wright, Henry Yaky, Joel Yancy, John Yancy, John Yates, Sr., John Yates, Edw. Young, Garrard Young, Jas. Young, Phillip Young, Ruben Young

# SURNAME INDEX

AARON, 85
ABBAY, 79
ABBET, 79
ABBETT, 50
ABBOT, 1
ABBOTT, 64 130 154
ABEL, 49 109
ABELL, 109 172
ABERNATHY, 130 154
ABLE, 111
ABNER, 56
ABNEY, 56
ABSHIRE, 33
ACKERS, 111
ACKMAN, 130
ADAIR, 168-169
ADAMS, 1 27 33 50 56 68 70 76 78-79 111 142 150-151 167-169
ADDAMS, 1 79
ADIANO, 1
ADKIN, 72
ADKINS, 27 33 50 68 74-75 77-78 111 151 167-169
ADMIRE, 27
ADMIRES, 1
AEGNOUR, 70
AGEE, 136
AKERS, 27 33 176
AKINS, 176
ALBURT, 92
ALCORN, 64
ALDERSON, 176
ALDRIDGE, 33
ALEXANDER, 1 27 40-41 50 56-57 79 93 130
ALISON, 1 27

ALLEN, 1 27 33 50 55 64-65 72 79 85 92 96 172 176
ALLEY, 33
ALLIN, 27 79 176
ALLINGTON, 33
ALLISON, 27 72 78-79 93 111 154
ALLOWAY, 79
ALLPHIN, 130 155
ALLY, 176
ALPHIN, 130
ALREY, 64
ALVEY, 96
AMES, 33 176
AMIOTE, 149
AMMERMAN, 132 156
AMMONS, 27
AMOS, 176
AMYX, 33
ANDERSON, 1 27 33 48 64 71 76 78-79 83 85 93 108 111 130 134 150 155 169 176
ANGEL, 77
ANGLETON, 50
ANGLIN, 93
ANNESS, 140 155
ANNIS, 63
ANNOLD, 79
ANTLE, 138
APPLEGATE, 50
ARCHER, 1 50 72 74
ARGREE, 176
ARINGTON, 1
ARMES, 103
ARMSTRONG, 1 27 79 140 150 160
ARNETT, 27 33
ARNOLD, 27 79 130 134 137 146 150 158-159

184

ARTMAN, 102 106 109
ARTNETT, 33
ARTRIP, 168
ARYES, 27
ASBELL, 50 57
ASBERRY, 93
ASBURY, 111
ASBY, 130
ASH, 106 176
ASHBY, 1 129
ASHCRAFT, 57 109 130 133 135-136 141
   143-144 156-158 162
ASHER, 1 64 111-112
ASHFORD, 79
ASHHURST, 27
ASHLEY, 79
ASHLOCK, 84
ASHWORTH, 176
ASKEY, 95
ASKIN, 105
ASKINS, 64
ASQUE, 176
ASTERBURN, 1
ATERTON, 105
ATHERSTONE, 130
ATKINS, 50
ATKINSON, 79
ATTERBERRY, 104 107-109
ATWOOD, 79
AUFORD, 50
AULL, 172
AUSTIN, 1 56 71 176
AUSTON, 1
AUTLE, 85
AUXER, 33
AUXIER, 167
AVERALL, 33
AYAGER, 1
AYER, 129
AYNES, 79
AYO, 176
AYRES, 79
AZATES, 176
BA----H, 164
BABB, 79 176
BABBET, 1
BACKSTER, 57
BACON, 27 50 93
BACOR, 27
BADIN, 149 172
BAGBY, 150
BAGS, 27
BAILER, 33
BAILEY, 33 90 112 130 155 176
BAILIS, 176
BAILY, 176

BAIN, 1-2 79
BAINFIELD, 93
BAIRD, 50 130 139
BAISDEN, 167
BAITES, 27
BAKER, 2 27-28 33 50 112 138 148 159 176
BALCH, 49
BALDIN, 28
BALDING, 50
BALES, 112
BALEY, 71-72 168
BALFOUR, 149
BALL, 28 33 93 168
BALLANCE, 64
BALLARD, 2 50 79 102
BALLENGER, 71 112
BALLINGER, 69-70 76
BALLK, 93
BALSCAW, 176
BAMBGARDNER, 144
BANISTER, 167
BANKS, 2 33 130 147 155
BANNISTER, 33 168
BAR, 93
BARATON, 176
BARBEE, 2
BARBER, 168 176
BARBOUR, 2
BARCHAM, 176
BARCLAY, 50 130
BARDUNE, 79
BARETT, 2
BARGER, 2
BARKER, 28 57 130-131 136 155 168 171
BARKLOW, 93
BARLEY, 93
BARLOW, 50 172 176
BARNARD, 67 70 112
BARNES, 57 93 130
BARNET, 176
BARNETT, 28 33 57 131 155 176
BARNHILL, 2 50
BARNS, 79 102
BARR, 33
BARRACHMAN, 2
BARRETT, 28
BARRICK, 2
BARRON, 109 154
BARROW, 64
BARTLET, 28 176
BARTLETT, 2 79 99 131 155 164
BARTLEY, 28 93
BARTON, 28 102 112 134 176
BARTRAM, 167-168
BARZO, 2
BASET, 93

BASHEERS, 50
BASKET, 28
BASS, 103 176
BATE, 2
BATES, 2 79 146 176
BATTLETON, 79
BATTS, 50
BATY, 2
BAUGH, 2 176
BAULDEN, 50
BAULT, 85
BAXTER, 28 50 131 155
BAYERS, 68 74 160
BAYS, 176
BAZE, 2
BAZIL, 33
BEABOUT, 2
BEACH, 2 131 138 142 148 155
BEAK, 28
BEAL, 129
BEALMEAR, 96
BEALY, 75
BEAMS, 77
BEAN, 93
BEARD, 131 144 155 163 172 176
BEARN, 176
BEASLY, 2
BEATES, 50
BEATEY, 50
BEATTY, 57 79 109
BEATY, 33 50 66 107
BEAUCHAMP, 50 152 176
BEAVERS, 33
BEAVIS, 79
BEAZLEY, 79
BECK, 167 176
BECO, 176
BEECH, 131 146 155
BEECHEAM, 112
BEEKERS, 155
BELCHER, 33 169-170
BELEW, 131
BELL, 2-3 28 41 49-50 57 79 85 93 176
BELLEE, 50
BELLETTER, 131
BELLOW, 50
BELSHE, 33
BELSHEY, 67
BENCH, 168
BENEDICK, 176
BENGE, 112
BENNET, 3 68 76 176
BENNETT, 3 131 140 154-155 160
BENNIT, 28
BENOUGH, 93
BENSON, 3

BENTLEY, 33
BENTLY, 79
BENTON, 50
BERLINGER, 176
BERNARD, 48
BERQUIN, 149
BERRY, 3 28 33 50 66 68-71 76 79 154 167-169 172 176
BERTLET, 50
BESHEARS, 33
BEST, 95
BETHUREM, 112
BETNER, 50
BEVERLY, 96 131 138 141 145 159 161
BIB, 176
BIBB, 176
BIBY, 177
BIGGS, 93 167
BIGHAM, 49
BIGS, 176
BILL, 3
BILLETTER, 155
BILLINGER, 176
BILLINGSLEY, 176
BINBRIDGE, 79
BINGHAM, 131 144 155 162
BIRD, 50 57 73 77-79 176
BIRDELL, 176
BIRKS, 177
BIRNY, 176
BISHON, 28
BISHOP, 28 68-70 74 96 151 176
BIVEN, 33
BIVENS, 33
BLACARD, 176
BLACK, 3 28 79 148 176
BLACKBURN, 28 33 41 50 79 93
BLACKBUSH, 3
BLACKFORD, 41 79
BLACKWELL, 57
BLACKWOOD, 3
BLADES, 79 85
BLAIR, 28 33 48 85 176
BLAKE, 3 69 93 112
BLAKELY, 73-74 76
BLAKEMON, 3
BLAKEMORE, 79
BLAKEY, 176
BLAKLEY, 96
BLAKLY, 76
BLANK, 176
BLANKENSHIP, 3 33 79 167-169
BLANTEN, 103
BLANTON, 28 79
BLEDSO, 66
BLEDSOE, 28 67

BLEVINS, 3 72 76 167-169 173
BLINSON, 176
BLOCK, 164
BLOID, 176
BLUE, 96-97 164-165
BLYTHE, 49
BOARD, 137
BOAZ, 50
BOCOCK, 167-169
BODKIN, 77
BOGGS, 28 57 167
BOGLY, 176
BOHAN, 41
BOHANAN, 79
BOHANON, 79
BOILSTON, 176
BOLEN, 75 112
BOLIN, 33 74-75 77-78
BOLING, 50
BOLT, 168
BOMER, 85
BOND, 33 50
BONDERANT, 79
BONDS, 50
BONHONEY, 176
BONY, 173
BOOK, 101
BOOKER, 3 101
BOON, 28
BOONE, 79 93 154
BOOTS, 50
BOOYER, 50
BORDERS, 33 167 169
BORRAS, 148
BOSTON, 28 79 101
BOSWELL, 50
BOTKIN, 69
BOTT, 108
BOTTS, 131
BOULTEN, 138 159
BOULWARE, 3
BOUNEY, 33
BOURD, 176
BOURN, 50 112
BOURNE, 28
BOWDERY, 79
BOWEN, 3 33 70 167-168
BOWLAND, 79
BOWLES, 41 79 176
BOWLIN, 168
BOWLING, 3 161
BOWLS, 50 176-177
BOWMAN, 28 33 49 57 64
BOWMAR, 79
BOYD, 3 28 50 68-70 144 167-168 177
BOYER, 74

BOYERS, 72-73
BOYLES, 28
BOZARTH, 102 104 106
BRACHER, 104-106 108
BRACKET, 3
BRADDON, 33
BRADFORD, 28 50 167
BRADLEY, 28 33 50 168
BRADLY, 50 177
BRADSHAW, 27 85 93
BRADY, 28 50 107 149
BRAFFORD, 33
BRAGG, 93
BRAMER, 167
BRANBARGER, 96
BRANCH, 3
BRANCUTTER, 177
BRAND, 131
BRANDENBURGH, 57
BRANDER, 177
BRANHAM, 3 33 50 72 112
BRANSON, 129
BRASFIELD, 66
BRASHER, 172
BRASIER, 112
BRASURE, 143 162
BRATTON, 131 155
BRAY, 177
BRAZZEL, 95
BRECKINRIDGE, 164
BREDWELL, 166
BREED, 177
BREEDING, 85-86
BREEDLIN, 177
BREES, 112
BREVARD, 40
BREWER, 3 50 112
BRIAN, 50
BRIANT, 33 72 106
BRICKNOR, 177
BRIDGES, 177
BRIDGEWATER, 86
BRIDGEWAY, 95
BRIDGFORD, 79
BRIDWELL, 166
BRIGGS, 33
BRIGHT, 3-4
BRINDLE, 50
BRINK, 28 57
BRINTEW, 169-170
BRISBY, 79
BRISCO, 79
BRISCOE, 100 164
BRISTOW, 28 79
BRITON, 113
BRITT, 103

BRITTON, 113 177
BROCK, 28 50
BROCKMAN, 50
BRODERICK, 96
BROMFIELD, 169
BROOKE, 28 79
BROOKEN, 50
BROOKEY, 28
BROOKING, 79
BROOKS, 4 50 64 107 131 159 177
BROOKY, 4
BROOMFIELD, 93
BROOWS, 131 146
BROTHERS, 177
BROWN, 4 28 33-34 50 57 66-68 70-71 77
　79 93 104 106 113 129-130 132 135 141
　145 149 154-156 158 163 167 177
BROWNING, 171 177
BRUBAKER, 93
BRUCE, 28 93
BRUMAGON, 50
BRUMBACK, 132-133 147 156
BRUMET, 76
BRUMETT, 76
BRUMFIELD, 167
BRUMFORD, 177
BRUMLY, 79
BRUMMET, 74 76
BRUNDEGE, 28
BRUNK, 103
BRUSH, 34
BRUSTER, 34
BRUTE, 172
BRUTEY, 149
BRYAN, 4 28 93 169
BRYANT, 4 28 34 57 74 79 86 98 113 137
　167-168
BRYSON, 93
BUCHANNON, 79 93
BUCHNUNRY, 28
BUCK, 96
BUCKHAM, 173
BUCKHANAN, 4
BUCKHANNON, 79
BUCKLAND, 132
BUCKLES, 93
BUCKLEY, 50 79
BUCKMAN, 109
BUCKNER, 4 40 64 96 113
BUEKENER, 4
BUFORD, 50 177
BULLER, 177
BULLINGSTON, 177
BULLOCK, 4 28 79
BUNCH, 71 113
BUNNEL, 4 177

BUNNELL, 113
BUNTON, 34
BUNYON, 34
BURBRIDGE, 28 50 64 79 93
BURCH, 50
BURCHETT, 34 167-168
BURCHFIELD, 34
BURGAN, 177
BURGESS, 4 34 167-168
BURGHER, 57
BURK, 28 71 167 169 177
BURKS, 4 34
BURNAM, 57
BURNES, 132 140 156 159
BURNET, 105 177
BURNETT, 4 34 57
BURNHAM, 154
BURNS, 4 64 113 132 134 139 146 156 160
　168
BURRES, 168
BURRESS, 132 163
BURROWS, 132 134
BURRUS, 28 57
BURT, 50
BURTLE, 102 105 109
BURTON, 4 28 34 40 86 113 168 177
BUSH, 4 28 57 173 177
BUSHENBERRY, 177
BUSHKING, 177
BUSHONG, 177
BUSKIRK, 113 132 134 137 141 156-158
　160 167
BUSSELL, 50
BUST, 177
BUTLER, 28 34 50 86 107 177
BUTNER, 156
BUTRAM, 177
BUTTER, 146
BUTTERFIELD, 113
BUTTON, 4 177
BYAR, 177
BYBEE, 28
BYERS, 79 105 113
BYRES, 28
BYRON, 113
BYRUM, 177
CADDELL, 76
CADDLE, 69
CADE, 28
CADWELL, 76
CAHILL, 113
CAIN, 57 93 106 113
CAINS, 34 169
CAIUS, 167
CALAHAN, 111
CALAVAN, 69

189

CHILDERS, 34 132 155-156 160
CHILDRES, 131 133-134 137-139 145 155
160
CHINN, 41 93
CHIPMAN, 133 135 156 158
CHIRIN, 177
CHISM, 177
CHITWOOD, 75 93
CHRISTIAN, 28
CHRISTMAN, 79
CHRISTOPHER, 79
CHRISTY, 51
CHURCH, 28 34
CHURCHWELL, 71
CID, 75
CIDER, 6
CINNAMONA, 5
CIRAN, 5
CIRTLEY, 51
CIVIL, 58
CLAGET, 5
CLAGGETT, 79
CLARK, 5 28 34 51 58 93 114 130 132-133
141 149 156-157 159 161 177
CLARKE, 133-134
CLASBY, 177
CLAXTON, 79
CLAY, 28 34 168
CLAYTON, 5 173 177
CLEAKE, 99
CLEAVER, 104
CLEAVLAND, 28
CLEM, 177
CLEMENT, 5
CLEMENTS, 28 97 100 109
CLEMINGS, 34
CLENDEMAN, 177
CLEVENGER, 34
CLEVO, 51
CLICK, 34
CLIFFORD, 27-28
CLIFORD, 79
CLIFTON, 133 140 159
CLINE, 171
CLINTON, 79
CLOAK, 79
CLORIVIERE, 149
CLOVE, 5-6
CLOYCE, 50
CLOYD, 28
CLUTTER, 51
CO, 67
COATS, 86 177
COB, 93
COBB, 51 58 133 156
COBOURN, 28

COBURN, 34 96
COCHRAN, 41 177
COCHRIL, 51
COCHRON, 79
COCINE, 173
COCKE, 99
COCKRAM, 95
COCKRAN, 177
COCKRELL, 34
COCKRIL, 177
COCKRIT, 177
CODY, 34
COFFEE, 28 34 86
COFFER, 28
COFFEY, 86
COGER, 28
COGWELL, 51
COHLIN, 93
COIL, 58 170-171
COLBERT, 6 51 177
COLE, 6 28 34 55 79 173 177
COLEMAN, 6 28 34 79 133 148 156 177
COLINS, 34
COLINSWORTH, 34
COLLARD, 108
COLLER, 171
COLLETT, 114
COLLEY, 51
COLLIER, 28 34 41 114 133 141
COLLIN, 64
COLLINS, 28 34 51 79-80 92 131 134-136
141-142 146-147 150 153 156-157 159
164 167 177
COLLINSWORTH, 34 65
COLLISON, 86
COLLYER, 114
COLMAN, 177
COLSON, 28
COLTON, 157
COLVIN, 34 93
COLWELL, 168
COMANAN, 177
COMBS, 28 34 51 101 173 177
COMPTON, 28 86 92
COMS, 28
CONDIFF, 86
CONDRA, 177
CONGLETON, 28 34
CONGROVE, 109
CONLEY, 34 51
CONLY, 177
CONNELL, 165
CONNELLY, 28 177
CONNER, 28 51 73 134
CONOVER, 51 134 161
CONRAD, 134 157 163

CONREY, 134
CONSTANCE, 149
CONWAY, 27
CONYERS, 6 51 134 154 164 177
COOK, 6 28 34 40 51 58 80 84 96-97 134
   157 173 177
COOKSEY, 34 86
COOLEY, 173
COOLY, 6
COOMER, 86
COON, 6 109
COONFIELD, 114
COONRAD, 108
COOPER, 28 34 51 58 109 134 141
COOTS, 131
COPE, 34 51
COPELING, 6
COPLEY, 34
COPPAGE, 51 146
CORBIN, 132 134 156
CORDWELL, 68 75
CORE, 6
CORENA, 177
CORINER, 171
CORN, 6 27 105
CORNELIUS, 93
CORNETT, 34
CORNS, 114
CORTNEY, 142
COSBY, 177
COSINE, 171
COSLEY, 173
COSLY, 177
COSSA, 177
COSTIN, 114
COSTON, 6
COTHRON, 28
COTTER, 80
COTTLE, 34
COTTON, 80
COUCHMAN, 28
COULSON, 80 155 164
COUN, 34
COURTNEY, 134 148 158 164
COVENHOVEN, 80
COWAN, 96
COWDEN, 51
COWGILL, 136
COX, 28 34 51 58 66-80 86 102 114 133-134
   139 166 173 177
COYLE, 28
COZHILL, 6
COZIER, 6
CRABTREE, 34
CRACE, 34
CRADDOCK, 177

CRAFT, 34 95
CRAFTON, 6
CRAGMILE, 51
CRAIG, 28 34 51 64-65 67-71 73-76 78 80
   90-91 94-95 109 114 134
CRAIGHEAD, 49
CRAIGMILE, 51
CRAIGMYLE, 51
CRAIN, 150
CRAINSHAW, 6
CRANE, 58
CRANK, 34 94 114
CRATEN, 58
CRAVEN, 28
CRAVIN, 28
CRAWFORD, 28 49 58 177
CRAYCRAFT, 94
CREAMER, 6
CREASTAN, 177
CREATH, 65
CREED, 28
CREEKM, 72
CREEKMO, 68
CREEKMORE, 67
CREEKPAUN, 94
CREEL, 28 92
CREIGHTON, 51
CRENSHAW, 40 177
CRIM, 6
CRIMER, 85
CRISCELLIOU, 72
CRISP, 34
CRISS, 51
CRISTIAN, 51
CRISWELL, 51
CRITCHFIELD, 6
CRITTENDEN, 80
CRITTENDON, 28
CROCK, 177
CROCKET, 28
CROFFERD, 28
CROMWELL, 80
CRONKRIGHT, 28
CROOK, 134 146-147
CROPPER, 51 80
CROSBY, 96
CROSSWAIT, 28
CROSTHWAIT, 28
CROUCH, 51 58
CROW, 6 28
CROWDER, 28 51
CRUCE, 50
CRUISE, 177
CRUM, 34 114 168
CRUMP, 67 177
CRUSS, 177

DEVENPORT, 29
DEVINGS, 27
DEVOLAMBRUN, 149
DEWEES, 135 141
DICEERS, 178
DICK, 7 178
DICKEL, 178
DICKENSON, 115
DICKERSON, 135 145 162-163
DICKET, 178
DICKEY, 29 51 80
DICKINSON, 29 80 178
DICKMAN, 173
DICKSON, 35 157
DICTUM, 80
DICUS, 178
DIDDLE, 87
DIJARNETT, 7
DILLAN, 135
DILLEN, 29
DILLON, 29
DILLS, 35
DILSTER, 7
DINGLE, 51
DINKLY, 178
DINWIDDY, 51
DINWIDIE, 29
DIVINE, 139
DIXON, 35
DOCKINS, 7
DODD, 178
DODGE, 97 154 178
DODSON, 115
DOHERTY, 115
DOHONEY, 87 115
DOHORTY, 29
DOLLARD, 7
DOLLS, 7
DOLMAN, 51
DONALD, 49
DONALDSON, 51 115
DONDON, 29
DONEY, 178
DONNELL, 29 80
DONOVAN, 161
DOOLEY, 87
DOOLY, 29 87
DOPSON, 178
DORAN, 101
DORNAN, 29
DORTON, 35
DOSSING, 178
DOTSON, 7
DOTY, 135-136
DOUGHERTY, 80
DOUGHTY, 177

DOUGLAS, 29 115 178
DOUGLASS, 51 80
DOWDLE, 170-171
DOWEL, 7
DOWNEY, 29 51
DOWNING, 7 51 107 178
DOWNS, 94 102 178
DOYAL, 163
DOYLE, 29 146
DRADLEY, 35
DRAIN, 178
DRAKE, 29 35 51 178
DRAKINS, 115
DRAPER, 133 137 144 156 158 178
DRINKARD, 135 157
DRISKELL, 80
DRIVER, 178
DRUMMOND, 152
DRURY, 94
DRYDEN, 29 66 70 173
DUBOIS, 172
DUCASE, 178
DUCASSE, 178
DUDLEY, 65
DUERSON, 7
DUFF, 35 178
DUFFANT, 149
DUGER, 66
DUGGAN, 172
DUGGAR, 178
DUGGER, 67 69
DUGLAS, 29
DUGLY, 178
DUITT, 51
DUKE, 96 109 129 178
DULE, 178
DULEY, 51
DULIN, 29
DUMFORD, 29
DUMMIT, 94
DUMOULIN, 149
DUN, 29 78
DUNAGAN, 115
DUNAWAY, 58
DUNBAR, 35
DUNCAN, 7 29 66 69-71 74 76 78 84 94 178
DUNIGAN, 7
DUNKIN, 51 67
DUNKING, 7
DUNLAP, 29 80
DUNLEVY, 49
DUNN, 41 108 140
DUNNAGAN, 115
DUNNGIM, 178
DUNNIGAN, 115
DUNWIDDY, 51

DUNWOODY, 178
DUPEY, 29
DUPUY, 7 65 80 94
DURBIN, 94 163 178
DURHAM, 69
DURRETT, 96
DURRIT, 51
DURST, 29
DUTTON, 152 178
DUTY, 51
DUVALL, 51 80 165
DUWIT, 106
DYAS, 135 156-157 163
DYE, 7 151
DYER, 29 35 96 99 167
DYKES, 35
EADEN, 51
EAIRLEY, 67
EAKEN, 7
EALEY, 51
EALY, 8
EARLEY, 66
EARLY, 65-66 71 78
EARNER, 178
EASON, 94
EAST, 29
EASTEP, 35
EASTER, 178
EASTERLING, 35
EASTES, 8
EASTHAM, 115
EASTIN, 29
EASTREAG, 51
EATON, 29 58 66 80
EBROAD, 29
EDDLEMAN, 29
EDGAR, 29 178
EDGE, 58
EDGER, 51
EDLRIDGE, 35
EDMONDSON, 131
EDMONSON, 8 132
EDMUNDSON, 8
EDRINGTON, 80 87
EDWARD, 103
EDWARDS, 8 29 35 71 80 94-95 104 115
    133 135 156 178
EELES, 160
EGBIRD, 29
EGGERS, 115
ELAM, 29
ELBIRD, 178
ELDER, 29 51 64 108 149
ELIMBAUGH, 58
ELISON, 76
ELKIN, 29 80

ELKINS, 56 115
ELLERSON, 51 178
ELLETT, 29
ELLIDGE, 35
ELLINGTON, 94
ELLIOTT, 29 35 51 80 87 115 178
ELLIS, 8 35 51 64-65 80 87 135 138 150-151
    156-157 178
ELLISON, 29 68 72 138
ELLISTON, 80 135 144 163
ELLMORE, 115
ELMORE, 178
ELSBURY, 8
ELSTNER, 158
ELSWICK, 35
ELSY, 8
ELUM, 35
ELY, 51
EMBERSON, 178
EMBERTON, 178
EMBREE, 29
EMISON, 51
EMMERSON, 51
EMMONS, 8
ENGLAND, 35 91 178
ENGLE, 71 151
ENGLISH, 8 106 108
ENNIS, 51 115 178
ENOCHS, 8 40
ENOX, 35
EPLEAR, 80
EPPERSON, 41 87 111
ERVIN, 75
ESKUE, 8
ESLEY, 29
ESTEN, 104
ESTES, 8 87
ETHINGTON, 29
EUBANK, 8 29
EUBEAMES, 178
EUBERT, 178
EUDIS, 8
EVANS, 8 29 35 40 58-59 71 74-75 77 80 94
    132 135-137 157-158 168-169 178
EVE, 51 65-66 68-69 71-74 76
EVENS, 70 77
EVERETT, 178
EVERMAN, 94
EVETT, 59
EVINS, 51 95
EWEL, 71
EWING, 51 102 135
EXLINE, 41
EYCOFF, 51
EZEL, 178
FABLE, 8

FRANCIS, 29 51 153-154
FRANCISCO, 80
FRANKLIN, 29 35 116 178
FRANKS, 29 131 135-136 142 144 146 158
  163 178
FRAYLY, 178
FRAZER, 29 35 48 87 178
FRAZIER, 35
FREE, 88
FREEMAN, 178
FRENCH, 66
FREYHOFF, 9
FRIEND, 94
FRIES, 104
FRILEY, 35
FRISBEY, 35
FRITTS, 59
FROWMAN, 80
FROWNER, 80
FRUND, 29
FRYE, 116
FRYER, 29
FUCHES, 103
FUEL, 59
FUGATE, 135-136 158 167
FUGIT, 35
FULCHER, 178
FULKERSON, 169
FULKS, 35
FULLER, 29 101 137 158 178
FULTON, 29 42 44-47
FULTS, 40
FUQUA, 94
FUR, 80
FURGASON, 178
FURGERSON, 116 142-143 161
FURGUSON, 178
FURQUIN, 88
GAAROT, 178
GAILON, 9
GAINE, 94
GAINES, 51 80
GAINS, 51 178
GALASPIE, 95
GALE, 29 51 136 158
GALEY, 29
GALIMON, 9
GALLIAN, 68 74
GALLING, 103
GALLION, 35
GALLOWAY, 35 51 80 178
GAMILTON, 29
GAMMON, 94
GANOE, 51
GARAVIN, 178
GARAWAY, 178

GARDEN, 94
GARDNER, 178
GAREHART, 35
GARISON, 116
GARLAN, 73
GARMON, 91
GARNER, 80
GARNET, 29
GARNETT, 51 80 178
GARNHART, 148
GARNITT, 178
GARRARD, 64
GARRETT, 29 80 94
GARRISON, 35 51 116 178
GARROTT, 35 80
GARTH, 9
GARTON, 29
GARVAN, 178
GASH, 116
GASNEY, 136
GASSAN, 178
GASSAWAY, 80 178
GATA, 171
GATES, 9 178
GATEWOOD, 9 29 80 135
GATHRIGHT, 9
GATLIFF, 66 68-72 74-76 78
GAUGH, 9 130 132 135-136 155 163
GAVIT, 130
GAY, 29 80
GEARHART, 35
GEAT, 178
GEE, 152 178
GENT, 178
GENTREE, 178
GENTRY, 116
GEORGE, 29 35 80 166
GERRALD, 35
GHOLSON, 94
GHOST, 35
GIBBANY, 80
GIBBENS, 29 98
GIBBS, 10 35 51 80 95 116
GIBSON, 10 29 35 51 88 94 140 160 178
GIDDENS, 35
GIDEON, 10
GILDING, 158
GILHAN, 116
GILKEY, 94
GILL, 49 80 88 178
GILLAM, 10 51
GILLASPY, 116
GILLELAND, 178
GILLEM, 10
GILLIHAN, 178
GILLILAND, 178

GILLIS, 68 70 75
GILLISS, 68
GILLOCK, 178
GILLREATH, 66
GILMER, 88
GILMOOR, 29
GILMORE, 35
GILREATH, 68 76
GINES, 64
GIPSON, 51
GIRDNER, 76
GIRTON, 66 70-71 77
GIST, 178
GIVENS, 10 29 97
GLASBROOK, 178
GLASCO, 116
GLASCOCK, 140-141 178
GLASS, 10 29 51
GLASSBROCK, 178
GLASSCOCK, 111 160-161
GLAZEBROOK, 178
GLENN, 41 51 80
GLOVER, 29 80 178
GOBLE, 94
GODDARD, 51
GODEFROY, 149
GOFORTH, 96
GOGGEN, 106
GOGGIN, 76
GOLDING, 29
GOLDSBERRY, 106
GOLDSMITH, 116
GOLLIHAN, 35
GOLSON, 51
GOOCH, 41 116 136
GOODALL, 178
GOODE, 56
GOODEN, 10
GOODIN, 71 178
GOODLET, 51
GOODLOE, 64 80 151
GOODLOW, 29
GOODMAN, 178-179
GOODNIGHT, 10
GOODPASTER, 116
GOODPASTURE, 116
GOODSON, 90
GOODWIN, 10 179
GOORE, 29
GOOSEY, 59
GORDON, 64
GORE, 107 151 179
GORIN, 179
GORMAN, 94
GORNEY, 10
GORON, 29

GOSAY, 106
GOSE, 116
GOSLIN, 179
GOSNEY, 10 116
GOSSETT, 129 136 140 143 147 158 162
GOSTEE, 10
GOT, 179
GOUGE, 147 158-159
GOUGH, 51 101 155
GOURDIN, 29
GRADY, 10 80
GRAHAM, 10 29 35 41 65 84 97 168
GRANPRE, 149
GRANT, 35 51 88 144 157
GRANVILLE, 27
GRAVES, 29 35 80
GRAVIT, 132 136 156 158 161
GRAVITT, 159 162
GRAY, 29 52 56 80 116 173
GRAYHAM, 52
GRAYSON, 94 179
GRAYUM, 29
GREATHOUSE, 29-30
GREEN, 10 52 59 64 80 97 116 135-136 153
    157-158 179
GREENE, 94
GREENLEE, 136
GREENSLATE, 94
GREENSTEAD, 179
GREENWALT, 84
GREENWELL, 52 101
GREENWOOD, 10
GREER, 30 52 116 179
GREGG, 52 101 136 158
GREGORY, 30 80 86 130 136 158
GRESHAM, 10 52 117
GREY, 27
GRIDER, 88 179
GRIER, 52
GRIFFEN, 30 71 74-75
GRIFFET, 72
GRIFFETS, 73
GRIFFETTS, 72
GRIFFIN, 30 74 76 78
GRIFFITH, 35 52 59 86
GRIFFUTH, 169
GRIGGS, 110
GRIMES, 10 30 80
GRIMSBY, 179
GRIMSLEY, 30 52 140
GRINSTEAD, 30 179
GRISOM, 179
GRISSOM, 88
GROOM, 59 80
GROSS, 117 136
GROVE, 10

GROVES, 155
GRUBB, 35 67-68 73 167
GRUBS, 179
GRUELL, 52
GRUNDY, 97
GUDSHALL, 80
GUILKY, 97
GUITON, 10
GULLETT, 35
GULLIAN, 30
GUM, 117 179
GUNNEL, 52
GUNTER, 179
GURLEY, 146
GUTHERY, 80
GUTHRIE, 80
GUTTREY, 30
GUY, 117
GWIN, 80
HACKLER, 71
HACKWORTH, 35
HADDEN, 30
HADEN, 30 52
HADWAY, 30
HAFF, 30
HAGAN, 136 179
HAGAR, 35
HAGARD, 30
HAGER, 101
HAGGARD, 30
HAGINS, 35
HAGLAND, 10
HAIDEN, 179
HAISLIP, 72-73 75
HALBERT, 30 80
HALE, 35
HALL, 10 30 35 52 59 97 100 107 161 179
HALLADAY, 59
HALLER, 179
HALLOWAY, 30
HALSETT, 30
HAM, 10
HAMBLETON, 30
HAMBLIN, 68-69 73 76 78
HAMBRICK, 52 179
HAMES, 179
HAMILTON, 10 35 52 66 80 88 117 179
HAMM, 94
HAMMACK, 117
HAMMIT, 179
HAMMOCK, 153
HAMMON, 10 35 65
HAMMOND, 30 52 136
HAMMONS, 35
HAMNER, 152
HAMON, 35

HAMOND, 66
HAMPTON, 10-11 30 35 91 97 136 144 158
    163 165 179
HANCOCK, 11 80 89 117
HANDLEY, 173-174
HANDY, 11 179
HANES, 117
HANEY, 35
HANKS, 30 35 80
HANNA, 35 117
HANNAH, 52 80 94
HANSHEW, 35
HARAN, 137
HARBERT, 30
HARBOULT, 11
HARD, 11
HARDAN, 179
HARDEN, 95 117
HARDEST, 106
HARDIN, 11 35 59 80 117
HARDING, 11 152
HARDON, 86
HARDRIDGE, 179
HARDUS, 179
HARDWICK, 94
HARDY, 11 52 117 179
HARE, 88
HARGESTER, 30
HARGET, 30
HARGUS, 94
HARISON, 141
HARISS, 11
HARKNESS, 52
HARLAN, 179
HARLESS, 35 170
HARLIN, 80 105 179
HARLOW, 179
HARMAN, 11 80
HARMON, 30 69 86 133-134 136
HARP, 77-78
HARPER, 30 35 80-81 179
HARRAH, 117
HARREL, 102
HARRINGTON, 174
HARRIS, 30 35 52 59 81 96-97 106 108 110
    137 158 179
HARRISON, 11 30 35 52 81 104 117 137
    147 158 179
HARRO, 53
HART, 64 70-71 84 97 179
HARTMAN, 108
HARVEY, 88 179
HASH, 69
HASTENS, 52
HASTON, 179
HATCH, 94

HATCHER, 35 91
HATFIELD, 35-36 70-71 84
HATHE, 179
HATHMAN, 59
HATHORN, 179
HATHWAY, 30
HATLER, 179
HATTAN, 59
HATTON, 36 94
HAUKS, 106
HAUNERS, 109
HAUSER, 179
HAWDESHAL, 179
HAWK, 117
HAWKINS, 11 30 42 52 59 81 137 141 146
    158 179
HAWS, 11 36 52
HAY, 52 179
HAYDEN, 49 84 117
HAYDON, 30
HAYES, 55
HAYMNES, 27
HAYNLINE, 171-172
HAYS, 11 30 36 75 102 137 158 162 174 179
HAYSLIP, 75
HAYWOOD, 36
HAZARD, 81
HAZELLETT, 117
HAZELRIGG, 30
HAZELWOOD, 52 137 144 158
HAZLE, 36 107
HAZLERIGG, 30
HAZLEWOOD, 137 148 163-164
HAZZARD, 11 30
HEAD, 11 52 81
HEADEN, 30
HEARN, 81
HEAT, 30
HEATH, 52
HEATON, 68 70 72 74 76
HEDDEN, 30
HEDGER, 81
HEDGES, 94
HEFLIN, 148
HELM, 11
HELMS, 52
HELTON, 67 69 117
HENDERSON, 30 40 52 59 66 94 118 135
    137 157-158 179
HENDRICK, 179
HENDRICKS, 11 52 179
HENDRICKSON, 87 89
HENDRIX, 108 158
HENDRON, 118
HENRY, 36 49 52 59 100 130
HENSHAW, 11 97

HENSLEY, 11 30 36 94 118 158 168 179
HENSLY, 137
HENSON, 142
HERNDO, 67
HERNDON, 52
HERONS, 30
HERRAL, 106
HERRELL, 36
HERRINGTON, 12
HERRMAN, 12
HERRON, 158
HESTER, 179
HESTINGS, 30
HEURY, 99
HEWETT, 97
HEWITT, 110
HEYNON, 12
HIBBS, 110
HICHCOCK, 74
HICKERSON, 65 135
HICKEY, 30
HICKLIN, 81 118 179
HICKMAN, 12 30 64 88 154 179
HICKS, 81 118
HIEATT, 81
HIGDON, 103 107 179
HIGENS, 93
HIGGINBOTTOM, 66
HIGGINS, 30 97 118 179
HIGGINSON, 109
HIGH, 179
HIGHTOWER, 59
HILER, 30 145 163
HILETOCK, 179
HILL, 12 30 36 59 71 81 118 137 170 174
    179
HILLIS, 30
HILTON, 36 81 132 179
HILVEY, 174
HIMPENSTALL, 81
HINDMAN, 179
HINDS, 179
HINKLE, 12
HINTON, 52 81
HIS, 30
HISER, 118
HITCH, 179
HITCHCOCK, 36 94
HITE, 97 118 150
HITER, 27 81
HITT, 81
HIX, 59 118 130 132 137 142-143 147 155
    159 161-162
HIXMAN, 137
HOAGLAND, 42
HOBACK, 179

HOBBS, 118
HOBSTON, 179
HOCKADAY, 94
HOCKENSMITH, 12
HOCKINSMITH, 59
HODGE, 49
HODINS, 52
HOFF, 36
HOFFMAN, 36
HOG, 179
HOGAN, 12 30 84 137-138 159
HOGE, 81
HOGG, 36
HOGLAN, 118
HOGLAND, 12
HOGLENN, 12
HOLBROOK, 36 145
HOLBROOKS, 167
HOLDER, 30 179
HOLDMAN, 179
HOLDON, 52
HOLEMAN, 30 59 81
HOLIDAY, 36
HOLINS, 179
HOLLADAY, 88 179
HOLLAND, 52 81 94 179
HOLLELAM, 179
HOLLEN, 174
HOLLIDAY, 88 135
HOLLINGSHEAD, 30
HOLLINGSWORTH, 81
HOLLOWAY, 12 81 179
HOLMAN, 104 118
HOLMES, 81
HOLMS, 179
HOLOCLAW, 179
HOLSCLAW, 118
HOLSTON, 12
HOLT, 36 88 101 129
HOLTCLAW, 179
HON, 30
HONAKER, 36
HONE, 143
HONK, 174
HONORY, 12
HOOD, 12 52 67 71 73 94 179
HOOP, 52
HOOPER, 97
HOOVER, 84 169
HOPKINS, 36 52 81 108 174
HOPPER, 12 92 137 144 155 159 163
HORGAN, 12
HORN, 59 171
HORNACHER, 52
HORNBACK, 101 106
HORNBECK, 30

HORSELEY, 94
HORSLEY, 40 59
HORTON, 137
HOSKINS, 12 107
HOTTON, 81
HOUCK, 174
HOUR, 118
HOUSE, 30
HOUSTON, 30 49 52
HOW, 147 179
HOWARD, 12 27 30 36 52 60 81 118 129
  137 159 179
HOWCHELER, 179
HOWDY, 12
HOWE, 36 49 94 131 148 164
HOWEARD, 30
HOWEL, 12 179
HOWELL, 36 118
HOWERTON, 36 103
HOWSER, 179
HOX, 179
HOYLE, 52
HUBBARD, 52
HUBBLE, 118
HUBBS, 69
HUCKABY, 179
HUCKSTEP, 30
HUDSON, 12 30 81 97 118 179
HUEY, 52
HUFFMAN, 12 30 94 131 133 144 147 179
HUFFORD, 81
HUFFT, 68
HUFMAN, 12
HUGGARD, 88
HUGHES, 12 81 88 118 165
HUGHS, 30 174
HULAN, 60
HULSEY, 12
HUMMEL, 179
HUMMER, 52
HUMPHREY, 30
HUMPHREYS, 91
HUMPHRIES, 27 90 137 179
HUNSINGER, 30
HUNT, 30 36 64 66-67 69 73 76 81 179
HUNTER, 12-13 30 52
HURLEY, 36 118
HURST, 36 52
HURT, 118
HURY, 99
HUSON, 30 94
HUSTEN, 102
HUSTON, 42 52
HUTCHERSON, 81 130
HUTCHESON, 52 81 137
HUTCHINSON, 159

HUTCHISON, 52 136-138 147 164
HUTSON, 30
HUTTON, 30 138 159
HYNES, 30
HYTER, 81
ILIFF, 36
INDECUT, 30
INDICUT, 36
INDICUTT, 27
INGELS, 154
INGLE, 13 36
INGRAM, 13 36 138
INGRIM, 179
INLOW, 179
IRELAND, 30 52 138 159
IRWIN, 81
ISAACS, 36 179
ISLES, 152
ISON, 36
JACK, 30 81 163
JACKMAN, 89
JACKSON, 13 30 52 81 94 170 174 179
JACO, 52
JACOB, 13
JACOBS, 36 154
JACOWAY, 72
JAKSON, 13
JAMASON, 30
JAMES, 13 30 36 52 55 65 81 97 101 118
    138 169 179
JAMESON, 30 36 64 174
JAMISON, 30 106-107 179-180
JANE, 13
JANES, 36 88
JANUARY, 30 81
JARRAL, 180
JAY, 180
JEFFERAS, 180
JEFFERSON, 64 97
JEFFERY, 166
JENKINS, 30 36 52 101 130 155
JENSKINS, 55
JEREMIAH, 105
JERRALD, 178
JERRY, 38
JERVIS, 52
JESSUP, 161
JETT, 13
JEWEL, 180
JEWETT, 138
JILIS, 180
JINKINS, 180
JINNINGS, 13
JOBE, 13
JOHN, 52 138 159
JOHNS, 30 36 153-154

JOHNSON, 13 30 36 52 60 71 75 78 81 88
    94 96-97 99 106-107 119 129 131-132
    138 148 153 159 161 164 167 174 180
JOHNSTON, 30 52 60 81 93 180
JOLLEPP, 180
JOLLIFF, 180
JONAS, 155 157
JONES, 13 27 30 36 42 52 55 60 65 68-69 72
    75-78 81 87-89 94 97 103 108 119 138-
    139 143 145 147 158-160 164 174 180
JONSE, 30
JONSON, 71
JONSONS, 149
JONSTON, 30
JORDAN, 94 119 180
JOSEPH, 13
JOST, 36
JOUITT, 81
JOURDAIN, 149
JOURDAN, 36
JUDD, 86 89
JUDY, 129
JUMP, 132 136-139 141-143 148 156 158-
    162
JUSTICE, 36
KAIN, 52
KASH, 36
KAY, 13 30
KAYS, 107 119 180
KEE, 52
KEEN, 30
KEENE, 52
KEENY, 174
KEER, 72
KEETH, 81
KEETON, 36
KEEZEE, 36
KEIFFER, 30
KEIM, 174
KEIRMAN, 97
KEISER, 49
KEITHLEY, 30
KELDAR, 30
KELL, 30
KELLAM, 30
KELLER, 13 102
KELLEY, 36 52
KELLY, 13 30 106-107 172 180
KELSO, 13
KELSOE, 86
KELSY, 180
KELTER, 89
KEMP, 13 119
KEMPER, 49
KENDALL, 52 156 159 169
KENNARD, 36

KENNEDY, 119 172
KENNY, 30
KENT, 119
KEPHART, 119
KERLEY, 97
KERNEY, 97
KERR, 49 52 70
KERRELL, 78
KERSNER, 30
KESCH, 13
KESNER, 36
KETHLEY, 30
KEY, 52
KIBBEE, 94
KIBBY, 96-97
KIDD, 78
KIDWELL, 138 155
KIGHLLEY, 13
KILGORE, 111
KILGOUR, 94
KILLININCREEK, 30
KIMBLE, 105
KINCADE, 30-31 180
KINCELOW, 180
KINCHELOE, 13
KINCHELOW, 180
KINCHILOE, 180
KINCHILOW, 180
KINCHLOE, 135 146
KINDER, 31
KINDLE, 106
KINDRED, 31
KINELLE, 13
KING, 31 36 42 52 55 60 65 67 70-71 75 81
    89-90 103 119 174 180
KINGSBURY, 110
KINKADE, 31
KINKEAD, 81
KINMAN, 133-134 138 156-157 159
KINNEY, 49
KIPER, 105
KIPPHART, 119
KIRBY, 119 180
KIRK, 36 119 169
KIRKENDAL, 180
KIRKENDOLL, 119
KIRKHAM, 31
KIRKPATRICK, 31 180
KIRT, 180
KIRTLEY, 81 180
KISER, 13 94 119
KITE, 94
KITTY, 172
KIZER, 31
KNAP, 94
KNAVE, 14

KNIGHT, 31
KNOTT, 165
KNOWLES, 100
KNOX, 119
KOONS, 14 119
KOUNS, 94
KOWLES, 14
KRANIGAN, 14
KYES, 158
KYLE, 81
LACEFIELD, 180
LACEY, 36
LACKEY, 36 60 180
LACKY, 31
LACOMBE, 149
LACY, 14 94 130 154
LAFEVER, 119
LAFLIN, 136 148
LAFORCE, 31
LAHUE, 105
LAIL, 31 138 140 161
LAIN, 36 180
LAIR, 42 180
LAISFIELD, 119
LAKE, 14 134
LALLY, 14
LAMB, 31 174 180
LAMBDON, 76
LAMBERT, 52 110 119 138 169
LAMBURT, 52
LAME, 52
LAMKIN, 81
LANCASTER, 14 152
LANCE, 180
LANCER, 97
LANDESS, 131
LANDIS, 152
LANDRUM, 40 52 137-139 141 158 161
LANDS, 14 104
LANDSAW, 36
LANE, 14 81 180
LANGFORD, 81
LANHAM, 180
LANNING, 180
LANNOM, 56
LANSLEY, 105
LAPLANT, 170
LARAGE, 167
LARD, 180
LARGE, 36 169
LASH, 97
LASLEY, 119
LASLY, 180
LATALLAYE, 149
LATHAM, 97
LATTA, 110

LOWRY, 31 53 94 180
LOY, 89
LOYD, 56 139 153 159 180
LOYE, 157
LUCAS, 31 53 139 159-160
LUKERS, 53
LURTON, 81
LUSH, 31
LUSK, 31
LUTIN, 31
LUTTRELL, 15 97
LYCAN, 36-37
LYLE, 49
LYNN, 81
LYON, 15 180
LYONS, 94
M'CLURE, 172
MACHIN, 96
MACINGTIRE, 31
MACK, 15
MACKAY, 130
MACKOY, 94
MACLAIN, 15
MADDEN, 94
MADDOX, 15 37 98
MADDUX, 81
MADISON, 31
MADOX, 15
MAFFET, 49
MAGAFFOCK, 53
MAGARY, 53
MAGEE, 37
MAGOT, 180
MAGRAW, 53
MAGRUDER, 15
MAGUISTY, 15
MAHAM, 81
MAHAN, 15 65-66 69-71 75
MAHANY, 180
MAHON, 49
MAHONEY, 15
MAINOR, 37
MAINS, 180
MAJOR, 81
MALDEN, 104
MALES, 120
MALLEN, 84
MALLETT, 37
MALLORY, 120
MALONE, 81 180
MALOX, 180
MALTON, 180
MANAFFE, 53
MANES, 180
MANGRUM, 56
MANKINS, 37

MANLEY, 15 180
MANLY, 180
MANN, 37 81 120 139 160
MANNAN, 37
MANNING, 53 72 180
MANNON, 78
MANSFIELD, 81 180
MANTILOE, 180
MANTLE, 85
MARCH, 31
MARCUM, 37 167 169
MARCUS, 159
MARGROV, 70
MARKER, 53
MARKESBERRY, 140
MARKHAM, 101 151
MARKS, 140
MARKSBERRY, 131 135 139 141 144-148
   160 164
MARKSBURY, 140 160
MARKWELL, 165
MARLER, 76
MARMADUKE, 15
MARRS, 15
MARS, 180
MARSCHAL, 110
MARSHAL, 31 160 180
MARSHALL, 31 37 49 53 65 81 96 120 138
MARTEN, 31
MARTIN, 15 31 37 53 60 65 79 81 91 95 120
   170 180
MARTINY, 31
MASON, 15 165
MASSEY, 53 139 157
MASSY, 163
MASTEN, 31
MASTERSON, 31 135 139 145 163
MATHEW, 94
MATHEWS, 37 60 180
MATHIS, 104-105
MATTHEWS, 15 81 172
MATTLINGLY, 165
MATTOCK, 53
MATTOX, 53 180
MAULDEN, 95
MAWHINEY, 53
MAXBERRY, 160
MAXEY, 180
MAXWELL, 31 120
MAY, 37
MAYES, 37 42
MAYFIELD, 31 68 71 79 180
MAYHEW, 94
MAYO, 37
MAYS, 15 37 68
MCADOW, 49

MCAFEE, 42
MCALESTER, 94
MCALLESTER, 15
MCBEE, 139-140 146 160 163
MCBRAYER, 37
MCBRIDE, 31 81
MCBROOM, 37
MCCALISTER, 53
MCCALLISTER, 94
MCCAMMON, 81
MCCAMPBELL, 64
MCCANLEY, 31
MCCANN, 163
MCCARTER, 162
MCCARTY, 53 60 139 143 146 160 163 170 180
MCCAUHEY, 120
MCCAULEY, 37
MCCAWLEY, 53
MCCAY, 53
MCCLAIN, 27 53 180
MCCLANE, 81
MCCLARY, 31 81 120
MCCLELAND, 120
MCCLELLAN, 15
MCCLELLAND, 180
MCCLEMURRY, 95
MCCLENNON, 53
MCCLINTICK, 37
MCCLINTOCK, 53
MCCLISTER, 85
MCCLUNG, 53
MCCLURE, 31 37 49 53 81 98 109 132 139 156 160
MCCLUSKEY, 95
MCCOMBS, 180
MCCOMMON, 31
MCCONEL, 53
MCCONNEL, 31
MCCONNELL, 49 81
MCCORKLE, 31
MCCORMACK, 53
MCCORMICK, 53
MCCOUTRY, 98
MCCOWN, 37
MCCOY, 37 53 68 72 81 133 140 156 160 180
MCCRACKEN, 37
MCCRACKIN, 31 81 180
MCCRAKIN, 81
MCCRARY, 81 171
MCCREERY, 60
MCCROSKY, 53
MCCRUREY, 60
MCCRURY, 60
MCCUDDY, 81

MCCULLOCH, 53 131
MCCULLOCK, 138 145
MCCULLOH, 81
MCCULLOUGH, 138 157
MCCUMSEY, 31 81
MCCUNE, 31 150
MCCURDA, 15
MCCURRY, 180
MCCUTCHEN, 53
MCDANIEL, 31 37 42 99 120 180
MCDANUEL, 105
MCDONALD, 81
MCDONNEL, 81
MCDONNOL, 31
MCDOWELL, 31 37 81
MCEARLY, 140
MCELROY, 110
MCENY, 180
MCFADDEN, 15
MCFARLAN, 71
MCFARLAND, 53 60
MCFARLIN, 120 180
MCFERRAN, 180
MCFERSON, 60
MCGANNON, 81
MCGEE, 49 60 70 99 105
MCGEHEE, 180
MCGHEE, 140 160
MCGIBNEY, 140
MCGILL, 31
MCGINIS, 89
MCGINNESS, 140
MCGINNIS, 120 140 160 180
MCGINNISS, 171
MCGLASSON, 89 134 140 160 162-163
MCGLONE, 94
MCGOWAN, 81
MCGREADY, 49
MCGREW, 53
MCGUIER, 81
MCGUINN, 15
MCGUIRE, 31 37 94 180
MCHARNEY, 15
MCHATTON, 53 140
MCHENRY, 37
MCHURG, 66
MCHURON, 31
MCILROY, 81
MCILVAIN, 31 81
MCINTIRE, 154
MCINTOSH, 15
MCINTYRE, 140
MCIVER, 16
MCKANNIS, 180
MCKAY, 16
MCKEE, 81

MCKEHAN, 70
MCKENNY, 31 98
MCKENZIE, 140
MCKINLEY, 121
MCKINNEY, 16 89
MCKINNY, 60 70-71 77-78 81
MCKINSEY, 37 140 160
MCKINSTER, 37
MCKNIGHT, 81
MCLAIN, 92 95
MCLANANE, 31
MCLANE, 31
MCLAUGHLIN, 94
MCLEAN, 169
MCLINN, 143 162
MCLONEY, 31
MCLOUCKLIN, 31
MCMAHAL, 15
MCMAHAN, 16 60
MCMAHON, 31 149
MCMANOMY, 53
MCMILLEN, 140 148
MCMILLIN, 31
MCMIRRON, 134
MCMULLEN, 31
MCMULLIN, 180
MCMUNNINGDALE, 60
MCMURRY, 42
MCMURTRY, 31 180
MCNAB, 121
MCNARY, 31
MCNEAL, 31
MCNEIL, 140
MCNEILL, 155 160
MCNEMAR, 49 53
MCPHERSON, 180
MCQUADE, 81
MCQUADY, 31 81
MCQUINN, 37
MCWHORTER, 86 89
MCWILLIAMS, 31
MEAD, 37
MEADORS, 67 70 72-73
MEADOW, 75 94
MEADOWS, 60 68 73-74 76
MEANS, 180
MEAR, 88
MEASLES, 121
MEDERS, 75
MEDLEY, 110
MEEK, 31 81 94
MEEKS, 37 104
MEFFORD, 53
MEGEE, 31
MELSON, 42 89
MELTON, 53 140 151

MENIX, 37
MERCER, 180
MERIDETH, 107
MERRELL, 160
MERRIL, 16
MERRILL, 60
MERRY, 180
MERSHON, 16
MERYWETHER, 16
MESSAK, 53
MESSER, 40
METCALF, 16
MEYERS, 160
MICKIN, 31
MIDDLETO, 70
MIDDLETON, 31 69 76
MIFFORD, 53
MILAM, 81
MILBURN, 31
MILDHAM, 139-140 143 157 160
MILES, 31 81 106 121 180
MILLAR, 81
MILLER, 16 31 37 40 53 89-91 94 98 102
  106 108 140 160 165 169 180
MILLION, 140
MILLS, 97 121
MILLSAPS, 174
MILTON, 90 130
MINER, 53
MINTER, 81
MIRAN, 149
MITCHEL, 16 31 81 180
MITCHELL, 31 42 53 55-56 81 121 140 143
  160 162 172 180
MITCHIEL, 31
MITCHUM, 65 81 143
MITHCEL, 53
MITTS, 136 141 161
MIZE, 60
MOBERLY, 165
MOFFET, 31
MOFFITT, 81
MOLINA, 148
MONCEY, 89
MONHOLLAN, 68 75
MONRO, 81
MONROE, 16 180
MONTAGUE, 31 53 142 180
MONTGOMERY, 16 31 37 53 140
MOODY, 53 121 180
MOONEY, 31 48
MOOR, 31
MOORE, 16 31 37 53 61 65 81-82 90 95-96
  101 121 140 142 144 154 158
MORAN, 90
MORE, 53 104 136 180-181

MOREHEAD, 37
MORELAND, 16
MOREM, 181
MORFET, 31
MORGAN, 16 31 37 66 71 82 89-90 93 103
   131 134 140 161 181
MORRE, 31
MORRIS, 16 31 37 53 65 82 90 103 107-108
   130 135 137 139-140 160-161
MORRISE, 37
MORRISON, 31 84 88 90 110 121 181
MORROW, 53 181
MORTON, 27 31 44-47 65 82 94
MOSBY, 53 82 181
MOSES, 72 77
MOSLEY, 37 53
MOSS, 16 31 53 82 181
MOSTON, 31
MOTHERSHEAD, 53
MOULTON, 31
MOUNT, 16
MOUNTS, 16 53 82
MOURNING, 181
MUIR, 31
MULBERY, 53
MULDERY, 31
MULDROW, 42
MULKY, 71
MULLETT, 37
MULLIKIN, 82
MULLIN, 66
MULLINS, 37 61 93
MULLIS, 174
MULLY, 181
MUMFORD, 181
MUNCEY, 37
MUNHOLLIN, 66
MUNSEY, 37
MUNSFORD, 36
MUNSON, 31
MURDOCK, 53
MURK, 181
MURPHEY, 37
MURPHY, 37 73 75-76 121 181
MURRAY, 37 90
MURREL, 181
MURRELL, 90 181
MURREY, 16
MURTIN, 180
MUSGROVE, 167
MUSICK, 82
MUSIE, 82
MUSKIRK, 160
MUSSELMAN, 31
MUSSER, 63
MUSSLEMAN, 161

MUTER, 82
MUTRE, 31
MUTTER, 37
MYERS, 82 104 130 133 141-142 164
NAILOR, 131 141 181
NALL, 53
NAPPER, 31 102
NARSLEY, 103
NASH, 31 101
NATHAN, 141
NATIO, 74
NATION, 16 181
NAY, 16
NAYLOR, 87 155
NEAL, 31 53 121 141
NEALE, 32
NEAT, 89
NEEL, 181
NEFERSON, 181
NEIGHBOURS, 16 108
NEIL, 72
NEILLE, 27
NEISBIT, 53
NELL, 90
NELSON, 32 37 53 84 105 181
NESBIT, 153
NESS, 103
NETHERTON, 17
NEVEL, 181
NEVELL, 32
NEVENS, 32
NEVILL, 181
NEVINGHAM, 53
NEW, 82 136 164
NEWBERRY, 181
NEWCUM, 37
NEWEL, 181
NEWHOUSE, 181
NEWKIRK, 61
NEWSOM, 37
NEWTIN, 181
NEWTON, 37 61 70 106 121
NIBLICK, 32
NICHOLLS, 94
NICHOLS, 17 108 121 135 141 159 161 168
   181
NICHOLSON, 32 72 78-79 131 134 141 146
   155 161
NICKEL, 37
NICKELL, 32
NICKLE, 37
NIEVES, 154
NILL, 17
NIPPS, 37
NIX, 37 121 181
NIXON, 32

NOE, 17 140-141 160
NOEL, 17 65
NOLAND, 61
NOLIN, 37
NOLLEY, 64
NOOVIL, 17
NORLEY, 98
NORMAN, 17 94 121 170
NORMAND, 121
NORRIS, 82
NORTON, 17 32 94 136 141 147 161
NOSMAN, 37
NOURSE, 82
NOWL, 17
NOX, 32
NOXE, 17
NOYE, 95
NUCKLES, 53
NUCKOLLS, 66 75
NUTTER, 53 121
NUTTLE, 32
O'BANION, 17
O'BANNON, 82
O'BRIAN, 37
O'KEEFE, 17
O'NEAL, 17 32 141 161-162
O'NEEL, 181
OAARD, 98
OAK, 72-74
OAKLEY, 37 98 121-122
OAKLY, 122
OARD, 98
OATS, 17
OBANNION, 181
ODER, 141 147 161
ODEY, 134
OFFICER, 53
OFFIELD, 65
OGDEN, 17 37 108
OGDON, 53
OGLES, 37 122
OGLESBY, 17
OGLSBY, 17
OLD, 32
OLDER, 32
OLDFIELD, 37
OLDHAM, 17 53 61 104 181
OLDRUM, 130 154
OLER, 181
OLIPHANT, 181
OLIVER, 17 32 61 77-78 166
OLLEMAN, 122
OLLER, 181
OMER, 100 154
ONCEL, 181
ONEAL, 122

ONROIEE, 98
OOSLEY, 65
ORE, 53
ORMAN, 151
ORR, 96
ORROURCK, 149
OSBORN, 37 141
OSBORNE, 94
OSBOURNE, 72 141 161
OSBURN, 53 71 141 181
OSCAR, 94
OTWELL, 53
OVERSTREET, 17
OVERTON, 53
OVERTREET, 17
OWEN, 181
OWENS, 32 37 55 61 90 122 134 141 181
OWINS, 53 61
OWLEY, 181
OZBURN, 82
PABTEAN, 32
PACE, 181
PACK, 37 169
PACKWOOD, 37
PADDOCK, 32
PAGE, 37 82 87 90 95 181
PAIGOT, 181
PAIN, 53 181
PAINS, 141
PAINTER, 181
PALMER, 82
PALSGROVE, 53
PANNEL, 56
PAPLETT, 37
PARAM, 17
PARICK, 38
PARILAND, 32
PARIS, 32 101 164
PARISH, 32 141
PARK, 111 122
PARKE, 53 61
PARKER, 17 32 94 96 122 174 181
PARKHURST, 32 122
PARKINSON, 17
PARKS, 17 61 66-68 73 122 181
PARKWOOD, 181
PARNELL, 145
PARRANT, 142 161
PARRISH, 61 65
PARRY, 94
PARSONS, 38 66-67 72-73
PARSONSTO, 72
PARTON, 74
PASLEY, 32
PASSMORE, 122
PATEN, 87

POWER, 32 38 53
POWERS, 77-79 82 133 156
POWTER, 103
PRAIT, 32
PRATHER, 171
PRATOR, 38
PRATT, 38 53
PRAUL, 82
PRESTON, 38 65 82 105
PREWET, 72
PREWETT, 72 74
PREWIT, 38 75 77
PREWITT, 38
PRICE, 17 32 38 53 64 82 94 154 175 181
PRICHARD, 167
PRICHETT, 38
PRIDEMORE, 38
PRIEST, 17
PRINCE, 38
PRITCHER, 32
PRITCHETT, 38
PROCTER, 38
PROCTOR, 32 181
PROFFIT, 38
PROSSER, 122
PROVENCE, 122
PRUET, 17 76
PRUETT, 122
PRUIT, 32 75
PRUITT, 17 40 122
PRY, 82
PRYER, 82
PRYOR, 17
PUCKETT, 38
PUCKIT, 181
PUCKITT, 32
PUFF, 82
PUGH, 167
PULHAM, 82
PULLAM, 181
PULLUM, 19
PURCELL, 61
PURDAM, 175
PURKINS, 75
PURNELL, 98 155
PURSALL, 122
PURTLE, 102
PUTMAN, 181
PUTT, 104 106
QUARLES, 73 82 172
QUESENBERRY, 32
QUEST, 181
QUICK, 61 101 106
QUIGLEY, 181
QUILLAN, 38
QUINN, 53 100

QUISENBERRY, 32
RADCLIFF, 122
RADCLIFFE, 94 140
RADER, 19
RADFORD, 122
RAFFERTY, 175
RAGIN, 53
RAGLAND, 32
RAGLEN, 181
RAGSDAL, 181
RAGSDALE, 19 181
RAGSDELL, 122
RAILES, 181
RAILEY, 82
RAINES, 155
RAINEY, 53 82
RAINS, 72 130
RAIZEL, 53
RALSTON, 181
RAMA, 19
RAMER, 56 103 108
RAMEY, 38 161 168
RAMLEY, 107
RAMSAY, 82
RAMSEY, 38 53 64 98 122 181
RANDAL, 181
RANDOL, 181
RANDOLPH, 110 122
RANES, 74-75
RANEY, 53
RANKIN, 49 82 96 122 181
RANKINS, 19 32
RANNELS, 49
RANSDELL, 53
RANSFORD, 82
RANSOM, 161
RAPIER, 149
RARDIN, 82
RASH, 175
RATCLIFF, 82 160
RATLIFF, 38 181
RAVENCRAFT, 53
RAWSON, 141
RAY, 61 122 181
RAYBURN, 32
RAYLEY, 19
RAYNEY, 32
READ, 82 91
READEN, 53
READING, 151
READMAN, 181
READNOWER, 142 161
REAGEN, 38
REARCH, 181
REARDEN, 82
REASE, 53

SHACKLEFORD, 20 74
SHAEFFER, 172
SHAIN, 104
SHAKE, 20 124
SHANKS, 20 105 154
SHANNON, 38 49 54 82
SHANON, 54
SHARLEY, 20
SHARP, 20 56 62 65-66 72 76 82 143
SHARPE, 62
SHAVER, 142
SHAW, 20 82 102 154 182
SHAWHAN, 152
SHEETS, 82
SHEFFIELD, 62
SHELTER, 182
SHELTON, 54 94 124
SHEPARD, 54
SHEPHERD, 20 32 38 82 91 124
SHERILY, 182
SHERLEY, 20 54
SHERMAN, 40 153
SHIELDS, 94 102
SHILCERS, 155
SHIP, 54 82
SHIPLEY, 32 182
SHIPMAN, 182
SHIPP, 64 82
SHIREY, 96
SHIRLEY, 54 91 124 182
SHIRLY, 182
SHISM, 182
SHITLE, 182
SHIVELY, 140 143
SHOCKEY, 38
SHOCKLY, 182
SHORES, 32
SHORT, 20 38 54 82 94 182
SHORTRIDGE, 32 54 94
SHOTE, 62
SHOTHER, 182
SHOTWELL, 64
SHOUSE, 82 100
SHROPSHIRE, 38 82
SHROTE, 100
SHROUTT, 82
SHUCK, 40
SIBLEY, 21 96 98
SIDDENS, 182
SILER, 70 73
SIMMONS, 42 182
SIMMS, 143
SIMONIS, 82
SIMPKINS, 38
SIMPSON, 32 91 124 133 136 139-140 143-
144 148 156 161-163 182

SIMS, 82 162
SINCLAIR, 54 91
SINGER, 21
SINGLETON, 65 82
SINOTT, 149
SION, 182
SIPPLE, 131 136 138 144 157 159 162
SIPPS, 27
SIRY, 182
SISK, 82
SIVEL, 182
SKAGGS, 38
SKEAN, 75 77
SKEEN, 175
SKIDMORE, 21 38 94 167 182
SKILLMAN, 150
SKINNER, 62
SKIRVIN, 132 140 144 156 162
SLANING, 108
SLATON, 182
SLAUGHTER, 21 182
SLAUSHER, 175
SLAVE, Aaron 85
SLAVIN, 32
SLAWTER, 94
SLIGAR, 125
SLIGER, 125
SLOAN, 125
SLONE, 38 182
SLOO, 96
SLOWERS, 21
SLUSHER, 38
SMALL, 82
SMALLWOOD, 144 162-163
SMILLIS, 89
SMISER, 21
SMITH, 21 32 38 40 42 54 62 65 67-68 70
72-74 78-79 82 91 94 96 99 101 105 107-
108 125 129 134-135 142 144 150-151
155-158 161 163 168 182
SMITHER, 21
SMITHY, 125
SMOOT, 107
SMOTHERS, 38
SMYTH, 67 69
SMYTHEY, 82
SNADY, 32
SNEED, 21
SNELL, 54
SNELLING, 82
SNIDER, 38 54 67 74 109
SNITER, 182
SNOW, 62 182
SNOWDEN, 21
SNYDER, 21 77
SOLITS, 21

STORY, 54 83 169
STOTT, 27
STOTTS, 39 65 67 92 125
STOUT, 32 83 153
STOUTT, 83
STOVALL, 55
STOW, 66 70
STRADER, 125
STRATTON, 22 39 94
STRIBLING, 54
STRICKLER, 54
STRINGER, 125
STRINGFIELD, 182
STRODE, 145
STROHER, 83
STROTHER, 166
STROUD, 39 145
STRUNK, 75 77
STUART, 65 182
STUBVILLE, 106
STUCKER, 22 54 83
STUDZ, 182
STULIVILLE, 102
STUMP, 94
STURGEON, 125 145
STUTEVILLE, 103
STUTTERLE, 32
STUTWILLE, 106
STYLE, 32
SUBLET, 22
SUBLETT, 83
SUDDITH, 54
SUGG, 98
SUGGATE, 54
SULIVAN, 70 74-76
SULLAVAN, 182
SULLENGER, 22 83
SULLINGER, 104
SULLIVAN, 22 39 73 83
SUMMERS, 125-126 131 182
SUMNER, 39
SUNASTER, 22
SUNNING, 103
SURBER, 126
SURNDELL, 22
SURNNEY, 22
SUTER, 83
SUTFIN, 54
SUTTLE, 22 105
SUTTON, 54 72-73 104
SWANGO, 39
SWANN, 54
SWANSON, 39
SWEARINGIN, 126 182
SWEATMAN, 39
SWEET, 126

SWEIGART, 145
SWENK, 76
SWETNUM, 54
SWIFT, 65 182
SWIGATE, 54
SWIM, 153
SWINDELL, 22
SWINNEY, 22 32 42 182
SWOPE, 165
SWORD, 39
SYCK, 39
TABB, 84
TABOR, 126
TACKET, 74 126
TACKETT, 39 74 167
TADLOCK, 182
TAILOR, 22
TALBOT, 22 54
TALBOTT, 22 128-129
TALIAFERRO, 22
TALTON, 54
TANDY, 22
TANGLER, 54
TANNER, 32 83 182
TANSEL, 54
TAPP, 22 54 150
TARLETON, 126
TARLTON, 54 101 126
TATE, 153
TAURENCE, 83
TAWBERT, 83
TAYLOR, 22-23 27 32 39 42 54 62 79 83-84
    89 92 96 102 126 145 163 165 175 182
TEAGUE, 73 78-79 175
TELL, 145
TEMPLE, 182
TEMPLETON, 145
TEMPLIN, 49
TENGLER, 162
TENNELL, 32
TERRY, 39 84 94 182
TERVEY, 32
TESSIER, 172
THACKER, 39 126
THARP, 54
THEOBALD, 133-134 143 145 147 156-158
    163-164
THEOBALDS, 54
THERKILL, 182
THIDWELL, 159
THOMAS, 32 39 42 54 62 77-78 83 92 96
    126 130 145 159 163 182
THOMASON, 54
THOMASTANT, 32
THOMPKIN, 182
THOMPSEN, 32

VANDAWAUGH, 182
VANDEGRIFF, 126
VANHOOSE, 39 63
VANLANDINGHAM, 145
VANMATRE, 103 108
VANN, 54
VANOY, 69
VANSKIKE, 42
VARIE, 24
VARNEY, 39
VARVEL, 83
VARVIL, 39
VATETEES, 182
VAUGHAN, 27 83 146
VAUGHN, 39 42 83 98 176 182
VAULERS, 24
VAWTER, 24 83 164
VEACH, 76 78 83
VENABLE, 32 157 182
VENTERS, 39
VENTRESS, 84
VERBEL, 24
VERBLE, 24
VERNUM, 54
VERTREES, 104
VERULE, 24
VESS, 39
VICE, 95
VIGERS, 92
VILEY, 54
VINCENT, 24 106
VINCIN, 83
VINEHEUER, 24
VINNES, 137
VINSANT, 54
VINZANT, 183
VIOLA, 92
VIOLET, 83
VIRGIN, 95
VIRSER, 63
VIVIAN, 63
VIVION, 32
VORIS, 49
VOROUS, 54
WADE, 24 183
WADKINS, 39 65
WADLE, 24
WAGAMAN, 127
WAGER, 24
WAGERS, 39
WAGES, 63
WAGGENER, 85
WAGGENOR, 98
WAGGONER, 92 98 183
WAIN, 63
WAINOCK, 54

WAITS, 176
WAKEFIELD, 183
WALBUT, 93
WALDEN, 24 54 83 146 183
WALDROP, 183
WALKER, 24 27 32 39 49 54 63 65 67-74
    76-77 83 104 127 146 171 183
WALKUP, 93
WALL, 127
WALLACE, 42 44-47 49 54 64 83 92 146
    183
WALLER, 24 39 64-65 98 146
WALLICE, 137
WALLS, 54
WALSH, 149
WALTER, 39
WALTERS, 24 39 109 127 183
WALTON, 65 183
WAMPL, 70
WAMPLER, 67 70
WARD, 32-33 39 54 71 95-96 127
WARDEN, 39
WARE, 24 33 65 127 176
WAREFORD, 63
WARING, 95-96
WARMOTH, 127
WARNER, 70 75-76 127
WARNICK, 146
WARNOCK, 55 95
WARREN, 39 54 83
WARSON, 154
WARTERS, 33
WARWICK, 54 83
WASH, 146
WASHBURN, 24
WATERS, 63
WATKINS, 65-75 77-78 83 102-103 107 170
WATS, 183
WATSON, 24 33 39 83 104 108 146 168 183
WATTS, 27 33 39 183
WEADE, 33
WEATHER, 183
WEATHEROE, 183
WEATHERS, 54 183
WEAVER, 54 83
WEBB, 24 39 54 83 183
WEBBER, 63
WEBSTER, 130 138 141-142 146-147 159
    161-164
WEDDINGTON, 39
WEEDEN, 42
WEEDMAN, 109
WEIR, 54 98
WELCH, 24 33 63
WELLMAN, 24 127 168
WELLMON, 39

WELLS, 13 24-25 33 39 63 69 95 183
WELMAN, 25 127
WELMON, 39 83
WELSH, 25 49 183
WELSON, 63
WELTS, 25
WELTY, 33
WENDLING, 83
WERTTEG, 25
WESLEY, 93
WESMOLAND, 127
WEST, 25 33 54 63 83 183
WESTERMAN, 27
WESTFALL, 105
WESTLAKE, 145 163
WETHAM, 147
WETHEROE, 183
WHALEY, 33
WHARTON, 127
WHEAT, 85 90 93
WHEATLEY, 95
WHEELER, 25 33 39 92 111 127 130 134
   147 155 167 183
WHELOR, 25
WHITAKER, 27 39 127
WHITE, 25 39 54 63 67 70-71 78 83-84 95
   102 111 127 167 169 183
WHITEHORN, 106
WHITEIAR, 33
WHITEKER, 83
WHITELER, 25
WHITELY, 39
WHITESIDES, 25
WHITTINGTON, 83
WHITLEDGE, 183
WHITLEY, 169
WHITLOW, 183
WHITNEY, 183
WHITSITT, 33
WHITSON, 25 127
WHITT, 39
WHITTAKER, 25 127
WHITTIKER, 39
WHITTINGTON, 83
WHITTSON, 25
WHITWELL, 183
WIBLE, 127
WICKERSHAM, 83
WICKLIFF, 99
WIGAL, 25
WIGGINS, 54
WIGGINTON, 127
WILBOURN, 183
WILBURNS, 183
WILCOX, 95 110
WILDER, 69 72 78

WILEY, 39 56 127 183
WILHITE, 25 83 127-128
WILHOIT, 147 150
WILHOITE, 25
WILKERSON, 33 93 183
WILKESON, 107
WILKINS, 83
WILKINSON, 25
WILLEBY, 33
WILLENS, 128
WILLETT, 25 110
WILLHELMS, 183
WILLHITE, 128
WILLHOITE, 25-26
WILLIAM, 65
WILLIAMS, 26-27 33 39 55 83 90-91 95 106
   128 135-138 141-142 144 147 157 161-
   162 164 167-169 183
WILLIAMSON, 39 55 132 137 148 159 167-
   169 183
WILLIS, 33 93 101 147 164 183
WILLIT, 95
WILLKERSON, 183
WILLS, 33 39 55
WILLSON, 26 55 104-105
WILSON, 26 33 39 55 65 68-69 73 75 83 93
   95-96 104 106 111 128 131 133 137 139-
   140 142-143 147-148 156 158-161 164
   167-169 183
WILYARD, 176
WINANS, 136 148
WINCHESTER, 128
WINCLE, 164
WINEBRINER, 83
WINER, 26
WINFRED, 183
WINFREY, 89
WININGS, 135
WINKLE, 148
WINKLER, 63
WINKLES, 39
WINKLESS, 39
WINN, 33 166 183
WINTERS, 26 33 55
WINTMERTH, 92
WIREMAN, 39
WISEMAN, 63
WISMERLAND, 93
WITT, 63
WITTEN, 40
WOBY, 106
WOLCOXON, 83
WOLDORD, 85
WOLF, 183
WOLFF, 176
WOMACK, 95

219

Other Heritage Books by Sherida K. Eddlemon:

*Missouri Genealogical Records and Abstracts:*
*Volume 1: 1766-1839*
*Volume 2: 1752-1839*
*Volume 3: 1787-1839*
*Volume 4: 1741-1839*
*Volume 5: 1755-1839*
*Volume 6: 1621-1839*
*Volume 7: 1535-1839*

*Missouri Genealogical Gleanings 1840 and Beyond, Volumes 1-9*

*1890 Genealogical Census Reconstruction: Mississippi, Volumes 1 and 2*

*1890 Genealogical Census Reconstruction: Missouri, Volumes 1-3*

*1890 Genealogical Census Reconstruction: Ohio, Volume 1*
(with Patricia P. Nelson)

*1890 Genealogical Census Reconstruction: Tennessee, Volume 1*

*A Genealogical Collection of Kentucky Birth and Death Records*

*Callaway County, Missouri, Marriage Records: 1821 to 1871*

*Cumberland Presbyterian Church, Volume One: 1836 and Beyond*

*Dickson County, Tennessee Marriage Records, 1817-1879*

*Genealogical Abstracts from Missouri Church Records and*
*Other Religious Sources, Volume 1*

*Genealogical Abstracts from Tennessee Newspapers, 1791-1808*

*Genealogical Abstracts from Tennessee Newspapers, 1803-1812*

*Genealogical Abstracts from Tennessee Newspapers, 1821-1828*

*Tennessee Genealogical Records and Abstracts, Volume 1: 1787-1839*

*Genealogical Gleanings from New York Fraternal Organizations*
*Volumes 1 and 2*

*Index to the Arkansas General Land Office, 1820-1907*
*Volumes 1-10*

*Kentucky Genealogical Records and Abstracts, Volume 1: 1781-1839*

*Kentucky Genealogical Records and Abstracts, Volume 2: 1796-1839*

*Lewis County, Missouri Index to Circuit Court Records, Volume 1, 1833-1841*

*Missouri Birth and Death Records, Volumes 1-4*

*Morgan County, Missouri Marriage Records, 1833-1893*

*Our Ancestors of Albany County, New York, Volumes 1 and 2*

*Our Ancestors of Cuyahoga County, Ohio, Volume 1*
(with Patricia P. Nelson)

*Ralls County, Missouri Settlement Records, 1832-1853*

*Records of Randolph County, Missouri, 1833-1964*

*Ten Thousand Missouri Taxpayers*

*The "Show-Me" Guide to Missouri: Sources for
Genealogical and Historical Research*

*CD: Dickson County, Tennessee Marriage Records, 1817-1879*

*CD: Index To The Arkansas General Land Office, 1820-1907, Volumes 1-10*

*CD: Missouri, Volume 3*

*CD: Tennessee Genealogical Records*

*CD: Tennessee Genealogical Records, Volumes 1-3*

2006481

Made in the USA